A
SWEDENBORG
SAMPLER

Volition : power of using one's will.

A SWEDENBORG SAMPLER

Selections from

HEAVEN AND HELL

DIVINE LOVE AND WISDOM

DIVINE PROVIDENCE

TRUE CHRISTIANITY

SECRETS OF HEAVEN

*E*MANUEL *S*WEDENBORG

translated by

GEORGE F. DOLE, LISA HYATT COOPER, & JONATHAN S. ROSE

**SWEDENBORG
FOUNDATION**
West Chester, Pennsylvania

Reprinted with changes 2016; reprinted without changes 2019, 2022.

All of the selections in this volume were taken from the New Century Edition translations published by the Swedenborg Foundation in West Chester, Pennsylvania.

Divine Love and Wisdom, translated by George F. Dole (2003)
Portable edition: 978-0-87785-404-3 pb

Divine Providence, translated by George F. Dole (2003)
Portable edition: 978-0-87785-405-0 pb

Heaven and Hell, translated by George F. Dole (2000)
Deluxe edition: 978-0-87785-475-3 hc; 978-0-87785-476-0 pb
Portable edition: 978-0-87785-406-7 pb

Secrets of Heaven, volume 1, translated by Lisa Hyatt Cooper (2008)
Deluxe edition: 978-0-87785-486-9 hc; 978-0-87785-504-0 pb
Portable edition: 978-0-87785-408-1 pb

True Christianity, volume 1, translated by Jonathan S. Rose (2006)
Deluxe edition: 978-0-87785-484-5 hc; 978-0-87785-485-2 pb
Portable edition: 978-0-87785-407-4 pb

Library of Congress Cataloging-in-Publication Data

Swedenborg, Emanuel, 1688-1772.
  [Selections. English. 2011]
  A Swedenborg sampler : selections from Heaven and hell, Divine love and wisdom, Divine providence, Secrets of heaven, and True Christianity / Emanuel Swedenborg ; translated by George F. Dole, Lisa Hyatt Cooper, and Jonathan S. Rose ; edited by Morgan Beard, Jonathan S. Rose, and Stuart Shotwell.
     p. cm.
  ISBN 978-0-87785-410-4 (alk. paper)
  1. New Jerusalem Church—Doctrines. I. Beard, Morgan. II. Rose, Jonathan S. III. Shotwell, Stuart, 1953– IV. Dole, George F. V. Cooper, Lisa Hyatt. VI. Title.
  BX8711.A7B43 2011
  230'.94--DC22

                            2010051357

Edited by Morgan Beard, Jonathan S. Rose, and Stuart Shotwell
Design and typesetting by Karen Connor

Manufactured in the United States of America

Swedenborg Foundation
320 North Church Street
West Chester, PA 19380
www.swedenborg.com

CONTENTS

Introduction   IX

✎ HEAVEN AND HELL ✎

About *Heaven and Hell*   3

What the World of Spirits Is   7

Each of Us Is Inwardly a Spirit   12

Our Revival from the Dead and Entry into Eternal Life   18

After Death, We Are in a Complete Human Form   23

After Death, We Enjoy Every Sense, Memory, Thought,
    and Affection We Had in the World: We Leave
    Nothing Behind except Our Earthly Body   31

Our Nature after Death Depends on the Kind of Life
    We Led in the World   44

After Death, the Pleasures of Everyone's Life Are Turned
    into Things That Correspond   61

✎ DIVINE LOVE AND WISDOM ✎

About *Divine Love and Wisdom*   71

[The Lord's Love & Wisdom]   75

✎ DIVINE PROVIDENCE ✎

About *Divine Providence*   115

Evils Are Permitted for a Purpose: Salvation   117

Divine Providence Is for Evil People
    and Good People Alike   136

✑ TRUE CHRISTIANITY ✑

About *True Christianity*   165

Goodwill (or Loving Our Neighbor) and Good Actions   169

There Are Three Universal Categories of Love: Love for
    Heaven; Love for the World; and Love for Ourselves   171

When the Three Universal Categories of Love Are
    Prioritized in the Right Way They Improve Us;
    When They Are Not Prioritized in the Right Way
    They Damage Us and Turn Us Upside Down   189

All Individual Members of Humankind Are the
    Neighbor We Are to Love, but [in Different Ways]
    Depending on the Type of Goodness They Have   194

The Neighbor We Are to Love Is Humankind on a
    Wider Scale in the Form of Smaller and Larger
    Communities and Humankind in the Aggregate
    as a Country of Such Communities   199

On an Even Higher Level, the Neighbor We Are to
    Love Is the Church, and on the Highest Level, Our
    Neighbor Is the Lord's Kingdom   202

Loving Our Neighbor Is Not in Fact Loving the Person
    but Loving the Goodness That Is inside the Person   203

Goodwill and Good Actions Are Two Distinct Things:
    Wishing People Well and Treating Them Well   205

Goodwill Itself Is Acting Justly and Faithfully in Our
    Position and Our Work and with the People with
    Whom We Interact   208

Acts of Kindness Related to Goodwill Consist in Giving
  to the Poor and Helping the Needy, Although with
  Prudence   210

The First Step toward Goodwill Is Removing Evils; the
  Second Step Is Doing Good Things That Are Useful
  to Our Neighbor   213

As Long as We Believe That Everything Good Comes
  from the Lord, We Do Not Take Credit for the Things
  We Do As We Practice Goodwill   217

A Life of Goodwill Is a Moral Life That Is Also Spiritual   222

🖎 SECRETS OF HEAVEN 🖎

About *Secrets of Heaven*   227

[The Essential Nature of the Word]   231

Genesis I   233

Summary of Genesis I   235

Inner Meaning of Genesis I   237

[Content and Mode in the Word]   276

*Appendix: Theological Works Published
  by Emanuel Swedenborg*   279

INTRODUCTION

The life of Emanuel Swedenborg (1688–1772) was steeped simultaneously in the rational world of the physical sciences and a deep Christian faith. He lived during the height of the Enlightenment, a period when intellectuals rejected dogmatic religious teachings in favor of science and reason, and his theology reflects a long struggle to understand the world of spirit through investigation of the physical world. Ultimately, that struggle was resolved when (as he described it) his spiritual senses were opened and he began to interact directly with the denizens of heaven, hell, and the world of spirits between. Although his theological writings are based on experiences and visions that may seem unbelievable to a modern reader—as they did to many of Swedenborg's contemporaries—he writes with full awareness of how difficult his accounts may be to accept. In keeping with his early scholarly training, he presents his ideas in a logical order, drawing examples from everyday life as proof of the truth of his words, inviting readers to judge for themselves.

Born Emanuel Swedberg in Stockholm, Sweden, on January 29, 1688, he was the second son of Jesper Swedberg, a pastor in Sweden's Lutheran state church. At the age of eleven Emanuel entered the University of Uppsala, where his father was a professor. Although Jesper left the university to become bishop of Skara a few years later, Emanuel remained at Uppsala, completing his studies in 1709. As was customary for wealthy young Swedish men of his time, he then journeyed abroad to expand on what he had learned. His first stop was England—a worldwide center of learning and a major maritime power—where he studied the observational techniques of royal astronomer John Flamsteed (1646–1719) and traveled in the same intellectual circles as luminaries like Sir Isaac Newton (1643–1727) and

Edmund Halley (1656–1742). Emanuel also studied geology, botany, zoology, and the mechanical sciences under a number of scholars, inventors, and mechanics, later continuing those studies in Amsterdam and Paris.

When he returned to Sweden more than five years later, he worked as an assistant to Swedish inventor Christopher Polhem (1661–1751). As a result of the association, Emanuel was introduced to Sweden's King Charles XII (1682–1718), who was impressed with Emanuel's intellect, and arranged for him to be given a position at the Board of Mines. The appointment was significant and prestigious because at that time the mines were a vital part of Sweden's economy. The position suited Emanuel, not only because of family connections to the mining industry, but because it gave him ample opportunities for scientific research. After Charles XII's death in 1718, his sister Ulrika Eleonora (1688–1741) ascended to the throne. In 1719, she ennobled the Swedberg family, changing their name to Swedenborg, the name by which Emanuel is known today.

During this early period, most of Swedenborg's intellectual energy was funneled into scientific and technical work. In the years immediately following his return to Sweden, he published a scientific journal titled *Daedalus Hyperboreus*. Although the journal was intended to highlight Polhem's accomplishments, it also included a number of Swedenborg's own ideas and inventions, including plans for a flying machine. The journal was followed by books on chemistry and physics, as well as the first book in Swedish on algebra.

Swedenborg's first major publication was *Opera Philosophica et Mineralia* (Philosophical and Metallurgical Works), a three-volume set printed in 1734. *Philosophical and Metallurgical Works* was written in Latin and published abroad for circulation to an international audience. While the second and third volumes—one on iron and the other on copper and brass—attracted attention for their technical information on metallurgy, it was the first volume, titled *Principia Rerum Naturalium* (Basic Principles of Nature), that laid the philosophical groundwork for Swedenborg's later investigations into the nature of the soul. In it, Swedenborg reasons deductively from "first principles": he postulates a mathematical point that forms the bridge between the infinite world of the spirit and the finite world of physical matter. From this first point, he says, nature begins to form increasingly complex compounds that follow geometrical rules; thus, the smallest divisions of physical matter obey the same laws as the planets and the solar system, and the nature of everything in the physical world can be deduced mathematically.

Philosophical and Metallurgical Works was followed by a series of books on anatomy. The first of these, the two-volume *Oeconomia Regni Animalis* (Dynamics of the Soul's Domain), was published in 1740 and 1741. The first volume addresses the heart and blood; the second, the brain, nervous system, and the soul. Here again, Swedenborg was looking for a connection between the spiritual and physical worlds. Drawing on the works of contemporary scientists and philosophers, he describes a subtle spiritual fluid that permeates and sustains all living creatures, existing in a complicated interaction with the blood and the cerebrospinal fluid. The origin of life is a sustaining energy that pervades all of creation, and the source of that energy is God. Thus nature, in Swedenborg's view, derives life in all its forms from that creative energy and would be dead without divine influence.

Although *Dynamics of the Soul's Domain* sold well and received favorable reviews, Swedenborg himself wasn't satisfied, and almost immediately began work on a series of follow-up volumes that dealt with anatomy in more depth. He published three volumes in this series, titled *Regnum Animale* (The Soul's Domain), and wrote drafts of several more, but that work was interrupted by a time of spiritual crisis that would mark the beginning of his visionary period.

Beginning in 1743 and continuing throughout 1744, Swedenborg experienced intense dreams and visions at night, which he recorded in his personal diary. Many of them revolved around a sense of spiritual unworthiness, a feeling that he had to purify himself of sin. In one dream, a man appeared and asked him if he had a health certificate; Swedenborg interpreted this as Christ asking him if he were prepared to undertake a spiritual vocation. In another case several months later, he was thinking about his work and heard a voice say, "Hold your tongue or I will strike you!" This Swedenborg understood as a warning against immersing himself in worldly tasks on a Sunday.

The opening of his spiritual vision—by day, in a state of full wakefulness—began in April 1745, although the exact circumstances surrounding it remain mysterious and a matter of debate. From this point onward, he began to record experiences of being in contact with the spiritual world.

Swedenborg simultaneously started writing an exploration of the inner meaning of the Bible based on the new understanding he gained from his visions. In the beginning, it appears to have been difficult for him; he left the initial drafts of this exposition unpublished. In 1747, he refused a promotion that had been offered to him, instead petitioning the king to be released from his service on the Board of Mines. He devoted himself full-time to writing what would become his first published theological work, *Arcana Coelestia* (Secrets of Heaven). The first volume was published in London in 1749; the eighth and final was published in 1756.

Secrets of Heaven is a verse-by-verse discussion of the inner meaning of the Bible, beginning with Genesis and then moving through Exodus. Swedenborg writes that the Bible should not be taken literally—in fact, parts of it make no sense if taken at face value—but everything written there has an inner spiritual meaning he calls a "correspondence." For example, Genesis 1:1: "In the beginning, God created heaven and earth." The word "beginning," Swedenborg says, corresponds to the start of a process called regeneration, when a person's inner spiritual self is starting to awaken and receive its true life from the Lord (by which he means both God and Christ, seeing them as one and the same). Heaven in this verse refers to the inner self or soul, while the earth is the outer self or the lower mind most closely connected to the body. Swedenborg then goes on to describe the process of regeneration as reflected in the Creation story. (The excerpt from *Secrets of Heaven* in this volume includes the text of Genesis 1 and Swedenborg's commentary in its entirety.) Interspersed between the chapters of commentary are explanations of principles that would become key parts of Swedenborg's theology: the correspondence between the physical world and the spiritual world, the structure of heaven and hell and the lives of angels and devils, the interaction between the soul and body, and the interconnectedness of faith and charity.

Although it seems that Swedenborg intended to go through the entire Bible in this type of verse-by-verse exegesis, he never did so. Instead, he returned to London in 1758 with five new titles to publish: *Heaven and Hell*, a description of the afterlife and the lives of its inhabitants; *White Horse*, which talks about the inner meaning of the Bible; *Other Planets*, which describes the beings that live on other planets, some within and some outside our solar system; *Last Judgment*; and *New Jerusalem*. These last two refer to a unique aspect of Swedenborg's theology. He writes that the Last Judgment is not a future event that will mark the end of our world, but a spiritual event where evil spirits who had managed to infiltrate heaven were cast down to hell, allowing human beings on earth and in heaven to receive spiritual truths more clearly. Further, he claims to have witnessed this event in 1757, a year that marked the beginning of a new spiritual age for humankind. In *New Jerusalem*, he lays out the general principles for the new church that was to follow the Last Judgment.

With the exception of *Last Judgment,* the content of the five volumes he published in 1758 was taken from *Secrets of Heaven,* sometimes with very little revision. *Secrets of Heaven* had been published anonymously, and its initial sales were very poor. Separating elements of this magnum opus into smaller volumes may have been an attempt to make the content more accessible.

Starting in 1759, however, a series of incidents demonstrating Swedenborg's interactions with the spirit world drew international attention. The first, in July 1759, happened while Swedenborg was attending a dinner party in the Swedish city of Göteborg. During the party, he suddenly became agitated and began describing a fire in Stockholm—more than 250 miles away—that was threatening his home. Two hours later, he reported that the fire had been extinguished three doors down from his house. It was not until two days later that messengers from Stockholm arrived in Göteborg and confirmed the details as Swedenborg had relayed them.

In 1760, the widow of the recently deceased French ambassador to Sweden was presented with a bill for a very expensive silver service her husband had bought. She was sure he had paid, but could not find the receipt. After asking Swedenborg for help, she had a dream in which her husband revealed the location of the receipt, a dream which turned out to be accurate.

In 1761, Swedenborg was presented at the court of Sweden's Queen Louisa Ulrika (1720–1782), and she asked him to relay a particular question to her deceased brother, Prince Augustus Wilhelm of Prussia (1722–1758). Swedenborg returned to court three weeks later and gave her the answer privately, upon which she was heard to exclaim that only her brother would have known what Swedenborg had just told her.

These three well-documented incidents, in conjunction with some others, made Swedenborg the subject of conversation not just in his own country, but in continental Europe as well. The attention prompted Swedenborg to acknowledge that he was the author of the books he had written, although it was not until *Marriage Love* in 1768 that he began including his name on title pages.

In the years that followed the incidents described above, Swedenborg would publish several more key theological works: *Divine Love and Wisdom* (1763), *Divine Providence* (1764), *Revelation Unveiled* (1766), and *Marriage Love* (1768). *Divine Love and Wisdom* and *Divine Providence*, although published separately, could be taken as two parts of the same theme: The first deals with the nature of God, who in his essence is both love and wisdom, and—echoing Swedenborg's earlier works on the origin of the material world—is the source of all life. *Divine Providence* tackles free will and the nature of evil and suffering, and describes the spiritual laws that govern the world.

Revelation Unveiled is a return to Swedenborg's early discourse on the inner meaning of the Bible, this time examining the book of Revelation in much the same verse-by-verse format as *Secrets of Heaven*. *Revelation Unveiled* was the first book in which Swedenborg included what he called *memorabilia* (memorable occurrences): descriptions of encounters with angels, devils, or spirits, usually illustrating a theological point he wanted to make. These memorable occurrences were generally added to the end of a chapter and often had no apparent connection to what he had written immediately before, although in two personal letters he advised people to read the memorable occurrences before moving on to the main text.

Contrary to its title, *Marriage Love* deals with love between the sexes in all its aspects, including sexual relations outside of marriage. Swedenborg considered married love to be the highest form of connection between a man and a woman. He writes that the masculine and feminine aspects of human beings are complementary. In heaven, where our true natures are fully revealed, a man and a woman who share real compatibility will instantly know each other when they meet, and eventually will become joined in spirit as if they were one person. That person is not necessarily an earthly spouse. People who are in unhappy marriages on earth, or who never marry, may still find true love once they move on to heaven—a teaching that may have had personal significance for Swedenborg, who never married.

All of Swedenborg's theological books were written in Latin and published outside of Sweden, most often in London or Amsterdam. This was doubtless a deliberate strategy to avoid running afoul of Sweden's strict censorship laws, which forbade publishing anything that contradicted the teachings of the Lutheran state church. Although Swedenborg was never the direct target of an investigation, two of his followers were charged with heresy in 1769 after publishing books and articles about Swedenborg's ideas in Swedish. During the course of the trial, Swedenborg's published theological works also came under question. When a royal ruling was finally rendered in 1770, it was decreed that Swedenborg's books contained errors of doctrine, but were not heretical. Swedenborg's books were banned, and the two followers were forced out of their teaching positions.

Partly in response to the initial news of these charges, Swedenborg began work on *True Christianity* (1771), a systematic discussion of his theological ideas as they relate to many aspects of Christian (and specifically Lutheran) belief. In the process, he laid out the tenets of the new church that he believed was to come.

Swedenborg himself expresses no desire to be revered as a prophet or to be the founder of a new religious movement; when he talks about the "new church" or the "new Jerusalem," he is referring to a shift in the way that humanity as a whole experiences and practices religion. In various places throughout his theological books, Swedenborg describes five ages in humankind's spiritual history, from the most ancient church, when human beings were in their spiritual infancy and were most in tune with God, to the fourth age, Christianity, when people possessed true teachings in the form of the Word (the Bible), but those teachings had gradually been corrupted by human misinterpretation. In the coming fifth age, a completely new religion would emerge in which people would have a much clearer and more direct understanding of spiritual truth.

True Christianity was the last book Swedenborg published. Although the main text was printed in Amsterdam, Swedenborg traveled to London to publish a supplement. That supplement was not printed during his lifetime. In December 1771, while still in London, Swedenborg suffered a stroke. Though he partially recovered, he seemed to sense that he was not long for this world. In February, in response to a letter suggesting a meeting in six months, he responded that it would be impossible, because he would die on the twenty-ninth of the next month. True to his word, Swedenborg passed away on March 29, 1772, at the age of eighty-four.

After Swedenborg's death, groups of his followers—particularly in England—broke away from their respective denominations to form the Church of the New Jerusalem, often called the New Church. Settlers brought these new teachings to the Americas, Africa, and Australia, and other groups formed throughout continental Europe as people encountered Swedenborg's writings. However, Swedenborg's greatest influence may have been felt on people who never counted themselves as part of the Swedenborgian church: For example, his vivid descriptions of heaven and hell inspired nineteenth-century utopian communitarians to try to create societies patterned after heaven. Around the same time, the emerging Spiritualist movement embraced Swedenborg as an early example of a medium (although Swedenborg himself had warned against attempting to contact the spirits of the dead). Artists and thinkers such as William Blake, Ralph Waldo Emerson, Helen Keller, and Henry James Sr. read Swedenborg and absorbed his insights into their own philosophy.

This volume includes extracts from five of Swedenborg's most popular works: *Heaven and Hell*, *Divine Love and Wisdom*, *Divine Providence*, *True Christianity*, and *Secrets of Heaven*. Each extract covers key concepts from Swedenborg's writings, including descriptions of the afterlife, the nature of God and of evil, the importance of doing good works, and the inner meaning of the Bible. Introductions to each extract provide background on the book and the overall context of the excerpted piece.

Swedenborg numbered each section of his works and often cross-referenced other sections of a particular book or other books he had written using those section numbers. The extracts in this book retain the original section numbers, which are uniform across most editions and translations, as well as Swedenborg's cross-references.

For a more detailed overview of Swedenborg's theology, interested readers are referred to *Swedenborg's Garden of Theology* by Jonathan S. Rose. A full list of Swedenborg's published theological works appears in the back of this volume; for a complete bibliography of Swedenborg's writings on all topics, published and unpublished, see the *Swedenborg Explorer's Guidebook: A Research Manual* by William Ross Woofenden.

A SWEDENBORG SAMPLER

ABOUT *HEAVEN AND HELL*

Heaven and Hell is the best known and most popular of Swedenborg's books. Published in 1758 as *De Coelo et Ejus Mirabilibus, et de Inferno, ex Auditis et Visis* (Heaven and Its Wonders and Hell: Drawn from Things Heard and Seen), the work describes Swedenborg's view of the spiritual realms and their inhabitants.

In Swedenborg's cosmology, the physical world that we live in is surrounded by the world of spirits, an intermediate realm between heaven and hell. When our physical bodies die, angels help our souls transition into the world of spirits, where we undergo a process of instruction and review of our lives. During this time, our true inner natures are gradually revealed. If we have done good works out of a genuine love of service and desire to help others, we are drawn toward heaven; if we are inherently selfish and enjoy causing pain and suffering, we are pulled toward hell. But the Lord does not judge or condemn people, Swedenborg emphasizes; people find their true home based on what they love most. A person who ends up in hell will find it more pleasant and comfortable than heaven. In a departure from the commonly held beliefs of his time, Swedenborg asserts that people of all faiths can be accepted into heaven, and that even unbaptized children will go there after death. Children, he writes, have a special place in heaven, where they grow to adulthood under the care of angels.

One unusual feature of Swedenborg's theology is that spiritual worlds are populated entirely by human beings—from the highest heaven to the deepest hell, there are no angels or demons who were not once living as people in the physical world. These spirits maintain their human form after death, although that form is affected by their inner nature. People who are good will become more beautiful in heaven. The evil will grow ugly and deformed, particularly when seen in the light of heaven, although to other evil spirits they will look normal, even attractive.

Life in heaven may seem remarkably similar to life on earth. Angels wear clothes, have houses and jobs, and fall in love and get married. However, Swedenborg also describes some significant differences between this world and the next. For example, travel between two places is instantaneous, and people can communicate with each other simply by thinking.

Much of the material for *Heaven and Hell* was drawn from the first theological work Swedenborg published, *Secrets of Heaven*. Issued in eight quarto volumes between 1749 and 1756, *Secrets of Heaven* was Swedenborg's first published attempt to put the information gleaned from his visions into writing. Though the work is primarily an exposition on the inner meaning of Genesis and Exodus, interspersed with the commentary are descriptions of Swedenborg's experiences in the spiritual realms and the things he learned there. However, the length of *Secrets of Heaven*, combined with the heavy biblical exegesis, daunted many readers in his day. *Heaven and Hell* was an attempt to reach a broader audience by producing a short work focused specifically on the spiritual realms. This approach found more success: *Heaven and Hell* attracted an audience of both skeptics and admirers, and, as Swedenborg's fame spread, was translated into German (1775), English (1778), and French (1782). The English edition had a particularly fateful impact when it found its way into the hands of a young man named Robert Hindmarsh, who became one of the key early organizers of the Church of the New Jerusalem, a denomination founded on the teachings of Emanuel Swedenborg.

In the following extract, Swedenborg describes how he was allowed to experience the process of dying firsthand and discusses the world of spirits, where souls first arrive after leaving their bodies. The footnotes in this translation are Swedenborg's own annotations of the original Latin edition, and the numbers in them refer to sections in *Secrets of Heaven*.

What the World of Spirits Is

THE world of spirits is neither heaven nor hell but a place or state between the two. It is where we first arrive after death, being in due time either raised into heaven or cast into hell from it depending on our life in this world.

The world of spirits is a place halfway between heaven and hell, and it is also our own halfway state after death. I have been shown that it is a halfway place by seeing that the hells were underneath it and the heavens above it, and that it is a halfway state by learning that as long as we are in it, we are not yet in either heaven or hell.

A state of heaven for us is the union of what is good and true within us, and a state of hell is a union of what is evil and false within us. When the good in a spirit-person is united to the true, then that individual arrives in heaven, because as already stated that union is heaven within us. On the other hand, when the evil is united to the false within us, then we arrive in hell, because that union is hell within us. The process of union takes place in the world of spirits because then we are in a halfway state. It amounts to the same thing whether you say the union of intellect and will or the union of the true and the good.

First I need to say something about the union of intellect and will and its resemblance to the union of the good and the true, because this union does take place in the world of spirits. Each of us has an intellect and a will, the intellect being open to truths and formed from them and the will being open to things that are good and formed from them. So whatever we understand and therefore think, we call true; and whatever we intend and therefore think, we call good. We are capable of thinking from our intellect and thus observing what is true and also what is good, but we still do not think from our will unless we intend and do it. When we intend it and do it intentionally, then it is in both our intellect and our will and therefore in us. This is because the intellect alone is not what makes a person, nor the will alone, but the intellect and the will together. This means that anything that is in both intellect and will is in us and is therefore attributed to us. Whatever is only in the intellect is associated with us but is not in us. It is only a matter of our memory, an item of information in our memory that we can think about when we are not in private but are with other people. So it is something we can talk and argue about and even something we can imitate with our affections and behavior.

424   Our ability to think from our intellect and not at the same time from our will is provided us so that we can be reformed, for we are reformed by means of truths; and truths, as already noted, are matters of intellect. We are actually born into total evil as far as our wills are concerned, wishing well to no one but ourselves; if we wish well to ourselves alone, we are delighted when harm comes to others, especially when it is to our advantage. We actually want to channel everyone else's assets to ourselves, whether those assets are high rank or wealth, and are happy to the extent that we succeed. To correct and reform this kind of intent, we are given the ability to understand things that are true and to use them to control the evil urges that well up from our will. This is why we can think true things from our intellect and talk about them and do them even though we cannot think them from our will until we have changed in nature so that on our own, that is from the heart, we intend them and do them. When we have this nature, then the things we think from our intellect are matters of our faith and the things we think from our will are matters of our love. This means that faith and love are now united within us, just as intellect and will are.

425   To the extent that truths of the intellect are united to good things of the will, then, or to the extent that we intend and therefore do truths, we have heaven within us, because as already noted the union of the good and the true is heaven. However, to the extent that false elements of intellect are united to evil elements of will, we have hell within us, because the union of the false and the evil is hell. Still, to the extent that truths of intellect are not united to good elements of will, we are in the halfway state. Almost all of us nowadays are in a state in which we know things that are true and think about them on the basis of our information and also from our intellect. We act on either a lot of them or a few of them or none of them or act contrary to them because of our love of evil and consequent trust in what is false. So in order that we may gain either heaven or hell, after death we are first taken to the world of spirits, where either the union of the good and the true takes place for people who are to be raised into heaven, or the union of the evil and the false for people who are to be cast into hell. This is because no one in heaven or in hell is allowed to have a divided mind, to understand one thing and intend something else. What we intend we understand and what we understand we intend. Consequently, anyone in heaven who intends what is good understands what is true, and anyone in hell who intends what is evil understands what is false. So for good people, the false elements are taken away and they are given truths suited and fitted to their virtue, while for evil people truths are taken away and they are given false elements suited and fitted to their vice. This enables us to see what the world of spirits is.

There is a vast number of people in the world of spirits, because that is where everyone is first gathered, where everyone is examined and prepared. There is no fixed limit to our stay there. Some people barely enter it and are promptly either taken up into heaven or cast down into hell. Some stay there for a few weeks, some for a number of years, though not more than thirty. The variations in length of stay occur because of the correspondence or lack of correspondence between our deeper and our more outward natures.

In the following pages I will be explaining just how we are led from one state into another and prepared.

426

427   After we die, just as soon as we arrive in the world of spirits, we are carefully sorted out by the Lord. Evil people are immediately connected with the hellish community their ruling love had affiliated them with in the world, and good people are immediately connected with the heavenly community their love and thoughtfulness and faith had affiliated them with in the world.

Even though we are sorted out in this way, we are still together in that world and can talk to anyone when we want to, to friends and acquaintances from our physical life, especially husbands and wives, and also brothers and sisters. I have seen a father talking with his six sons and recognizing them. I have seen many other people with their relatives and friends. However, since they were of different character because of their life in the world, they parted company after a little while.

However, people who are coming into heaven from the world of spirits and people who are coming into hell do not see each other any more. They do not even recognize each other unless they are of like character because of a likeness in love. The reason they see each other in the world of spirits but not in heaven or hell is that while they are in the world of spirits they are brought into states like the ones they were in during their physical lives, one after another. After a while, though, they settle into a constant state that accords with their ruling love. In this state, mutual recognition comes only from similarity of love, for as we explained above (§§41–50), likeness unites and difference separates.

428   Just as the world of spirits is a state halfway between heaven and hell within us, it is a halfway place. The hells are underneath it and the heavens above it.

All the hells are closed on the side that faces that world, accessible only through holes and crevices like those in rocks and through broad gaps that are guarded to prevent anyone from coming out without permission, which happens in cases of real need, as will be discussed later. Heaven too is bounded on all sides, and the only access to any heavenly community is by a narrow way whose entry is also guarded. These exits and entrances are what are called the doors and gates of hell and heaven in the Word.

The world of spirits looks like a valley surrounded by mountains and cliffs, with dips and rises here and there. The doors and gates to heavenly communities are visible only to people who are being readied for heaven. No one else finds them. There is one entrance to each community from the world of spirits with a single path beyond it; but as the path climbs, it divides into several.

429

The doors and gates to the hells are visible only to the people who are going to enter them. They open for them, and once they are opened you can see dark, sooty caves slanting downward into the depths, where there are still more gates. Rank, foul stenches breathe out from them, stenches that good spirits flee because they are repelled by them, while evil spirits are drawn toward them because they find them delightful. In fact, just as we find delight in our own evil in this world we find delight after death in the stench that corresponds to our evil. We might compare this with the delight of carrion birds and beasts like crows and wolves and pigs who fly or run toward rotting corpses as soon as they get wind of them. I heard one man who screamed aloud in utter torment at a breath of air from heaven, but was calm and happy when a breath from hell reached him.

There are two doors in each of us as well, one facing hell and open to evil and false things from hell, the other facing heaven and open to good and true things from heaven. The door of hell is opened for people who are involved in what is evil and its consequent falsity, though just a little light from heaven flows in through the cracks, which enables us to think, reason, and talk. On the other hand, the door of heaven is opened for

430

people who are focused on what is good and therefore on what is true. There are actually two paths that lead to our rational mind, one from above or within, through which the good and the true enter from the Lord, and one from below or outside through which the evil and the false infiltrate from hell. The rational mind itself is at the intersection of these two paths, so to the extent that light from heaven is let in, we are rational; but to the extent that it is not let in, we are not rational even though we seem so to ourselves.

I have mentioned these things so that our correspondence with heaven and with hell may be known. While our rational mind is in the process of being formed, it is responsive to the world of spirits. What is above it belongs to heaven, and what is beneath it belongs to hell. The higher things open, and the lower close against the inflow of evil and falsity, for people who are being readied for heaven; while the lower things open, and the higher close against the inflow of goodness and truth, for people who are being readied for hell. As a result, these latter can only look downward, toward hell, and the former can only look upward, toward heaven. Looking upward is looking toward the Lord, because he is the common center that everything in heaven faces. Looking downward, though, is looking away from the Lord toward the opposite center, the center toward which everything in hell faces and gravitates (see above, §§123 and 124).

431 In the preceding pages, where it said "spirits," it meant people in the world of spirits; while "angels" meant people in heaven.

Each of Us Is Inwardly a Spirit

432 ANYONE who thinks things through carefully can see that it is not the body that thinks, because the body is material. Rather, it is the soul, because the soul is spiritual. The human soul, whose immortality has been the topic of many authors, is our spirit; it is in fact immortal in all respects, and it is also what does the thinking in our bodies. This is because it is spiritual and the spiritual is open to the spiritual and lives spiritually, through thought and intention. So all the rational life we can observe in our bodies belongs to the soul and none of it to the body. Actually, the body is material, as just noted, and the matter that is proper to the body is an addendum and almost an attachment to the spirit. Its purpose is to enable our spirit to lead its life and perform its services in a natural world that is material in all respects and essentially lifeless. Since matter is not alive—only spirit—we may conclude that whatever is alive in us is our spirit and that the body only serves it exactly the way a tool serves a live and activating force. We may of course say that a tool works or moves or strikes, but it is a mistake to believe that this is a property of the tool and not of the person who is wielding it.

Since everything that is alive in the body—everything that acts and feels because of life—belongs to the spirit alone and none of it belongs to the body, it follows that the spirit is the actual person. In other words, we are essentially spirits and have much the same form as well. You see, everything that is alive and sensitive within us belongs to our spirit, and there is nothing in us, from head to toe, that is not alive and sensitive. This is why when our bodies are separated from our spirits, which is called dying, we still continue to be human and to be alive.

433

I have heard from heaven that some people who die, while they are lying on the slab, before they have been revived, are still thinking in their cold bodies, and cannot help but feel that they are alive, but with the difference that they cannot move a single part of the matter that makes up their bodies.

We could not think or intend if there were no agent, no substance as the source and focal point of thought and intent. Anything we may imagine happening apart from a substantial

434

agent is nothing. We can tell this from the fact that we could not see without an organ serving as the agent of our sight or hear without an organ as the agent of our hearing. Apart from these, sight and hearing would be nothing, would not exist. The same holds true for thought, which is inner sight, and for attention, which is inner hearing. Unless these happened in and from agents that are organic forms, as subjects, they would not happen at all. We may gather from this that our spirit is also in a form and that it is in human form, that it enjoys sensory organs and senses when it is separated from the body just as it did when it was in it. We may gather that all of the eye's life, all of the ear's life, in fact all of our sensory life belongs not to the body but to the spirit that is in these functions and even in their least details. This is why spirits see and hear and feel just as much as we do, though after we have left the body this does not happen in the natural world but in the spiritual one. The reason the spirit was sensitive on the natural level when it was in the body is that it worked through the material part that was appended to it. However, it was still spiritually sensitive in its thinking and intending.

435   I have presented this to convince rational people that, seen in our own right, we are spirits, and that the physical nature appended to us so that we can function in the natural and material world is not the real person but only the tool of our spirit.

But some supporting instances from experience would be better, because rational arguments are beyond many people, and the ones who have convinced themselves of opposite opinions make these arguments grounds for their skepticism by arguing on the basis of sensory illusions.

People who have convinced themselves of an opposite opinion tend to think that animals live and sense just the way we do, so that they too have a spiritual nature like ours; yet this dies along with their bodies. However, the spiritual nature of animals is not the same as ours. We have an inmost nature that animals do not, a nature into which the Divine flows and which it raises toward itself, in this way uniting us to itself. So we, unlike animals, can think about God and about divine matters of heaven and the church. We can love God because of these matters and by engaging with them; and can so be united to him; and anything that can be united to the Divine cannot be destroyed. Anything that cannot be united to the Divine, though, does disintegrate. In §39 above, I discussed this inmost that we have and animals do not. The reason for mentioning it again here is that it is important to dispel the illusions many people get from [believing that animals are just like humans], people who cannot draw rational conclusions about these subjects because they lack information or because their intellect is not open. What I said there was as follows:

> I should like to disclose a particular secret about the angels of the three heavens that people have not been aware of until now because they have not understood the levels discussed in §38. It is this, that within every angel—and within every one of us here—there is a central or highest level, or a central and highest something, where the Lord's divine life flows in first and most intimately. It is from this center that the Lord arranges the other, relatively internal aspects within us that follow in sequence according to the levels of the overall design. This central or highest level can be called the Lord's gateway to angels or to us, his essential dwelling within us.
>
> It is this central or highest level that makes us human and distinguishes us from the lower animals, since they do not have it. This is why we, unlike animals, can be raised up by the Lord toward himself, as far as all the deeper levels of our mind and character are concerned. This is why we can believe in him, be

moved by love for him, and therefore see him. It is why we can receive intelligence and wisdom, and talk rationally. It is also why we live forever.

However, what is arranged and provided by the Lord at this center does not flow into the open perception of any angel, because it is higher than angelic thought, and surpasses angelic wisdom.

436 A great deal of experience has taught me that we are spirits inwardly, experience that would fill whole volumes, as they say, if I were to include it all. I have talked with spirits as a spirit and I have talked with them as a person in a body. When I have talked with them as a spirit, they could not tell that I was not a spirit myself, in just as human a form as theirs. That is how my inner nature looked to them, because when I talked with them as a spirit, they could not see my material body.

437 We may gather that inwardly we are spirits from the fact that after we depart from our bodies, which happens when we die, we are still alive and just as human as ever. To convince me of this, [the Lord] has allowed me to talk with almost all the people I had ever met during their physical lives, with some for a few hours, with some for weeks and months, and with some for years. This was primarily so that I could be convinced and could bear witness.

438 I may add here that even while we are living in our bodies, each one of us is in a community with spirits as to our own spirits even though we are unaware of it. Good people are in angelic communities by means of [their spirits] and evil people are in hellish communities. Further, we come into those same communities when we die. People who are coming into the company of spirits after death are often told and shown this.

Actually, we are not visible as spirits in our [spiritual] communities while we are living in the world because we are thinking on the natural level. However, if our thinking is withdrawn from the body we are sometimes visible in our communities because we are then in the spirit. When we are visible, it is easy to tell us from the spirits who live there because we walk along deep in thought, silent, without looking at others, as though we did not see them; and the moment any spirit addresses us, we disappear.

To illustrate the fact that we are spirits inwardly, I should like to explain from experience what happens when we are *taken out of the body* and how we are *led by the spirit into another place.*

The first experience, being taken out of the body, is like this. We are brought into a particular state that is halfway between sleep and waking. When we are in this state, it seems exactly as though we were awake; all our senses are as alert as they are when we are fully awake physically—sight, hearing, and strange to say, touch. These senses are more perfect than they can ever be during physical wakefulness. This is the state in which people have seen spirits and angels most vividly, even hearing them and, strange to say, touching them, with hardly anything physical interfering. It is the state described as *being taken out of the body* and *not knowing whether one is in the body or outside it.*

I have been admitted to this state three or four times, simply to let me know what it was like, and also to teach me that spirits and angels enjoy all the senses and that we do too, as to our spirits, when we are taken out of the body.

As for the second kind of experience, being led by the spirit into another place, I have been shown by firsthand experience what happens and how it happens, but only two or three times. I should like to cite just one experience. While I was walking through city streets and through the countryside, absorbed in conversation with spirits, it seemed exactly as though I were just as awake and observant as ever, walking without straying, though all the while I was in visions. I was seeing groves, rivers, mansions, houses, people, and more. After I had been walking for some hours, though, I suddenly found myself back in

439

440

441

consciousness of my physical sight and realized that I was some-where else. I was utterly stunned by this, and realized that I had been in the state of people described as *being led by the spirit into another place;* for as long as it lasted I was not thinking about my route, even though it might have been many miles, or about the time, though it might have been many hours or even days. I was not conscious of any fatigue, either. This is how we can be led by ways we know nothing of all the way to some predetermined place, without straying.

442   These two states, though, which are states we have when we are awake to our deeper nature or (which is the same thing) our spirit, are out of the ordinary. They were shown me simply to teach me what they were like because they are known in the church. But talking with spirits, being with them as one of them—this is something I have been granted when I was fully awake physically, and it has been going on now for years.

443   There is further support of our being spirits inwardly in the material presented in §§311–317 above, where I discussed the fact that heaven and hell are from the human race.

444   Our being spirits inwardly has reference to our capacities for thinking and intending because these are our actual inner natures. They are what make us human, and the quality of our humanity depends on their quality.

Our Revival from the Dead and Entry into Eternal Life

445   WHEN someone's body can no longer perform its functions in the natural world in response to the thoughts and affections of its spirit (which it derives from the spiritual world), then we say that the individual has died. This happens when the lungs' breathing and the heart's systolic motion have ceased. The person, though, has not died at all. We are only separated from the physical nature that was useful to us in the world. The essential person is actually still alive. I say that the essential person is still alive because we are not people because of our bodies but

because of our spirits. After all, it is the spirit within us that thinks, and thought and affection together make us the people we are.

We can see, then, that when we die we simply move from one world into another. This is why in the inner meaning of the Word, "death" means resurrection and a continuation of life.[a]

The deepest communication of our spirit is with our breathing and our heartbeat; thought connects with our breathing, and affection, an attribute of love, with our heart.[b] Consequently, when these two motions in the body cease, there is an immediate separation. It is these two motions, the respiratory motion of the lungs and the systolic motion of the heart, that are essential ties. Once they are severed, the spirit is left to itself; and the body, being now without the life of its spirit, cools and decays.

The reason the deepest communication of our spirit is with our breathing and our heart is that all our vital processes depend on these, not only in a general way, but in every specific.[c]

After this separation, our spirit stays in the body briefly, but not after the complete stoppage of the heart, which varies depending on the cause of death. In some cases the motion of the heart continues for quite a while, and in others it does not. The moment it does stop, we are awakened, but this is done by the Lord alone. "Being awakened" means having our spirit

446

447

a. Death in the Word means resurrection because when we die, our life still goes on: *Secrets of Heaven* 3498, 3505, 4618, 4621, 6036, 6222 *[6221]*.

b. The heart corresponds to our volition and therefore to affection of love as well, while the breathing of the lungs corresponds to our intellect and therefore to thought: 3888. In the Word, then, the heart means volition and love: 7542, 9050, 10336; and the soul means intellect, faith, and truth, so that "from the soul and from the heart" means what comes from intellect, faith, and truth, and what comes from intent, love, and good: 2930, 9050. On the correspondence of the heart and lungs [Latin *anima*, "soul," also means "breath"] with the universal human or heaven: 3883–3896.

c. The heartbeat and the breathing of the lungs are regulative throughout the body and flow in together everywhere: 3887, 3889, 3890.

led out of our body and into the spiritual world, which is commonly called "resurrection."

The reason our spirit is not separated from our body until the motion of the heart has stopped is that the heart answers to affection, an attribute of love, which is our essential life, since all of us derive our vital warmth from love.[d] Consequently, as long as this union lasts there is a responsiveness, and therefore the life of the spirit is [still] in the body.

448 I have not only been told how the awakening happens, I have been shown by firsthand experience. The actual experience happened to me so that I could have a full knowledge of how it occurs.

449 I was brought into a state in which my physical senses were inoperative—very much, then, like the state of people who are dying. However, my deeper life and thought remained intact so that I could perceive and retain what was happening to me and what does happen to people who are being awakened from death. I noticed that my physical breathing was almost suspended, with a deeper breathing, a breathing of the spirit, continuing along with a very slight and silent physical one.

At first then a connection was established between my heartbeat and the heavenly kingdom, because that kingdom corresponds to the human heart.[e] I also saw angels from that kingdom, some at a distance, but two sitting close to my head. The effect was to take away all my own affection but to leave me in possession of thought and perception. [2] I remained in this state for several hours.

Then the spirits who were around me gradually drew away, thinking that I was dead. I sensed a sweet odor like that of an

---

d. Love is the very being of human life: 5002. Love is spiritual warmth and is therefore our own vital essence: 1589, 2146, 3338, 4906, 7081–7086, 9954, 10740. Affection is a corollary of love: 3938.

e. The heart corresponds to the Lord's heavenly kingdom and the lungs to his spiritual kingdom: 3635, 3886, 3887.

embalmed body, for when heavenly angels are present anything having to do with a corpse smells sweet. When spirits sense this, they cannot come near. This is also how evil spirits are kept away from our spirit when we are being admitted into eternal life.

The angels who were sitting beside my head were silent, simply sharing their thoughts with mine (when these are accepted [by the deceased], the angels know that the person's spirit is ready to be led out of the body). They accomplished this sharing of thoughts by looking into my face. This is actually how thoughts are shared in heaven.

[3] Since I had been left in possession of thought and perception so that I could learn and remember how awakening happens, I noticed that at first the angels were checking to see whether my thoughts were like those of dying individuals, who are normally thinking about eternal life. They wanted to keep my mind in these thoughts. I was later told that as the body is breathing its last, our spirit is kept in its final thought until eventually it comes back to the thoughts that flowed from our basic or ruling affection in the world.

Especially, I was enabled to perceive and even to feel that there was a pull, a kind of drawing out of the deeper levels of my mind and therefore of my spirit from my body; and I was told that this was being done by the Lord and is what brings about our resurrection.

When heavenly angels are with people who have been awakened they do not leave them, because they love everyone. But some spirits are simply unable to be in the company of heavenly angels very long, and want them to leave. When this happens, angels from the Lord's spiritual kingdom arrive, through whom we are granted the use of light, since before this we could not see anything but could only think.

450

I was also shown how this is done. It seemed as though the angels rolled back a covering from my left eye toward the center of my nose so that my eye was opened and able to see. To the spirit, it seems as though this were actually happening, but it is only apparently so. As this covering seemed to be rolled back, I could see a kind of clear but dim light like the light we see through our eyelids when we are first waking up. It seemed to me as though this clear, dim light had a heavenly color to it, but I was later told that this varies. After that, it felt as though something were being rolled gently off my face, and once this was done I had access to spiritual thought. This rolling something off the face is an appearance, for it represents the fact that we are moving from natural thinking to spiritual thinking. Angels take the greatest care to shield the awakening person from any concept that does not taste of love. Then they tell the individual that he or she is a spirit.

After the spiritual angels have given us the use of light, they do everything for us as newly arrived spirits that we could ever wish in that state. They tell us—at least to the extent that we can grasp it—about the realities of the other life. However, if our nature is such that we do not want to be taught, then once we are awakened we want to get out of the company of angels. Still, the angels do not leave us, but we do leave them. Angels really do love everyone. They want nothing more than to help people, to teach them, to lead them into heaven. This is their highest joy.

When spirits leave the company of angels, they are welcomed by the good spirits who are accompanying them and who also do all they can for them. However, if they had led the kind of life in the world that makes it impossible for them to be in the company of good people, then they want to get away from these as well. This happens as long and as many times as necessary, until they find the company of people their earthly life has fitted them for. Here they find their life; and remarkable as it may sound, they then lead the same kind of life they had led in the world.

This first stage of our life after death does not last more than a few days, though. In the following pages I will be

451

describing how we are then brought from one state into another until finally we arrive either in heaven or in hell. This too is something I have been allowed to learn from a great deal of experience.

I have talked with some people on the third day after their death, when the events described in §§449 and 450 have been completed. I talked with three whom I had known in the world and told them that their funeral services were now being planned so that their bodies could be buried. When they heard me say it was so that *they* could be buried, they were struck with a kind of bewilderment. They said that they were alive, and that people were burying what had been useful to them in the world. Later on, they were utterly amazed at the fact that while they had been living in their bodies they had not believed in this kind of life after death, and particularly that this was the case for almost everyone in the church.

Some people during their earthly lives have not believed in any life of the soul after the life of the body. When they discover that they are alive, they are profoundly embarrassed. However, people who have convinced themselves of this join up with others of like mind and move away from people who had lived in faith. Most of them link up with some hellish community because such people reject the Divine and have no use for the truths of the church. In fact, to the extent that we convince ourselves in our opposition to the ideal of the eternal life of the soul, we also convince ourselves in opposition to the realities of heaven and the church.

452

After Death, We Are in a Complete Human Form

THE fact that the form of a spirit-person is the human form or that a spirit is a person as far as form is concerned follows from what has been presented in a number of the earlier chapters, especially where I explained that every angel is in a perfect human form (§§73–77), that everyone is a spirit inwardly

453

(§§432–444), and that the angels in heaven are from the human race (§§311–317).

[2] This may be grasped even more clearly from the fact that we are human because of our spirit, not because of our body, and because our physical form is appended to the spirit in keeping with its form, not the other way around, since a spirit is clothed with a body that suits its form. As a result, the human spirit acts upon the individual parts of the body, even the smallest ones, even to the point that any part that is not activated by the spirit, any part in which there is no spirit acting, is not alive. Anyone may realize this by considering that thought and intent activate absolutely everything in the body and are so completely in control that nothing dissents, and that if anything does not consent it is not part of the body. It is actually expelled as something with no life in it. Thought and intent are attributes of our spirit, not of the body.

[3] The reason we cannot see the human form of spirits who have left the body and spirits still within the people we meet is that our physical organ of sight, the eye, is material to the extent that it can see in this world, and what is material sees only what is material. What is spiritual, though, does see what is spiritual; so when the material eye is covered over and loses its coordination with the spirit, then spirit is visible in its own form. This is a human form not only for spirits who are in the spiritual world but also for spirits in people we meet while they are still in their bodies.

454   The reason the form of a spirit is a human one is that in regard to our spirits we have been created in the form of heaven, since all the elements of heaven and its design are summed up in the elements of the human mind.[a]

a. In us all the elements of the divine design are gathered together, and by virtue of creation we are the divine design in form: 4219, 4220, 4223, 4523, 4524, 5114, 5368, 6013, 6057, 6605, 6626, 9706, 10156, 10472. To the extent that we

This is the source of our ability to accept intelligence and wisdom. It makes no difference whether you talk about our ability to accept intelligence and wisdom or our ability to accept heaven, as you may gather from what has been presented concerning heaven's light and warmth (§§126–140), heaven's form (§§200–212), angels' wisdom (§§265–275), and from the chapter titled "The Whole Heaven, Grasped as a Single Entity, Reflects a Single Individual" (§§59–77). This is caused by the Lord's divine human nature, which is the source of heaven and its form (§§78–86).

Rational individuals can understand what has been said so far because they can see this from the chain of causes and from truths in their pattern. However, people who are not rational do not understand these things. There are several reasons why they do not understand. The primary one is that they do not want to understand because these things contradict the false opinions that they have made their truths. People who do not want to understand for this reason close off the path of heaven into their rational ability. Even so, it can still be opened if only their will does not offer resistance (see above, §424). A great deal of experience has shown me that people can understand what is true and be rational if only they are willing. Quite often, evil spirits who have become irrational by denying the Divine and the truths of the church in this world (and convincing themselves in their denial) have by divine compulsion been faced toward people who were in the light of truth. Then they understood everything like angels and admitted that they were true and that they understood everything. However, the moment they turned back toward the love proper to their own intentions, they did not understand anything and said just the opposite. [2] I have

455

---

live according to the divine design, in the other life we look like complete and lovely people: 4839, 6605, 6626.

even heard some hellish people saying that they knew and recognized that what they were doing was evil and what they were thinking was false, but that they could not resist the gratification of their love and therefore of their will. This moved their thoughts to see evil as good and falsity as true. I could see from this that people who are immersed in false notions because of their malice could understand and could therefore be rational, but that they did not want to. The reason they did not want to was that they loved false notions more than true ones because the former supported the evil pursuits they were engaged in. Loving and intending are the same thing because we love what we intend and intend what we love.

[3] Since we are by nature able to understand what is true if we are willing to, I have been granted the privilege of supporting spiritual truths, truths of the church and heaven, by rational considerations. This is to the end that the false notions that have obscured the rational functioning of many people may be dispelled by rational considerations and their eyes perhaps opened a little. If people are focused on truths, it is granted them to support spiritual truths by rational ones. Who would possibly understand the Word simply from its literal meaning unless they saw some truths in it by enlightened reason? What else is the cause of the many heresies drawn from the same Word?[b]

---

b. A starting point should be derived from the truths of church doctrine drawn from the Word, and these should be acknowledged first; then it is all right to take factual knowledge into account: 6047. So if people have an affirmative attitude toward truths of faith, it is all right for them to support them rationally with factual knowledge; but this is not appropriate for people who have a negative attitude: 2568, 2588, 4760, 6047. It is in accord with the divine design to work rationally from spiritual truths into factual knowledge, natural truths, but not from the latter into the former, because there is an inflow of spiritual things into natural ones but not from natural or physical things into spiritual ones: 3219, 5119, 5259, 5427, 5428, 5478, 6322, 9110, 9111.

Years and years of daily experience have witnessed to me
that after separation from the body the human spirit is a person
and is in a similar form. I have seen this thousands of times, I
have heard such spirits, and I have talked with them even about
the fact that people in the world do not believe that they are
what they are, and that scholars think people who do believe
are simpletons. Spirits are heartsick over the fact that this kind
of ignorance is still common in the world and especially in the
church. [2] They say, however, that this belief stems especially
from academics who have thought about the soul on the basis
of physical sensory reality. The only concept this can yield is
one of pure thought, and when this lacks any medium in which
and on the basis of which it is examined, it is like some volatile
form of pure ether that can only dissipate when the body dies.
Since the church believes in the immortality of the soul on the
basis of the Word, though, they cannot help but attribute something vital to it, something thoughtlike. However, they do not
attribute to it any sensory capacity like ours until it is reunited
with its body. Their doctrine of the resurrection is based on this
notion, as is their belief that there will be a reunion [of soul
and body] when the Last Judgment comes. The result is that
when people think about the soul on the basis of both doctrine
and speculation, they do not at all grasp the fact that it is the
spirit and that it is in human form. There is also the fact that
hardly anyone nowadays knows what the spiritual is, let alone
that people who are spiritual, as all spirits and angels are, have
a human form.

[3] This is why almost all the people who arrive from this
world are as astonished as they can be to find that they are alive
and that they are just as human as ever, that they are seeing and
hearing and talking, that their bodies are still endowed with
the sense of touch, and that nothing at all has changed (see §74
above). Once they get over their amazement, though, then they
are amazed that the church does not know anything about this

456

state of ours after death and therefore does not know anything about heaven or hell, even though all the people who have lived in this world are in the other life and are living people. Since they do keep wondering why this has not been made plain to people on earth through visions, inasmuch as it is essential to the faith of the church, they have been told from heaven that such visions could happen whenever it pleased the Lord—nothing could be easier. However, people would not believe even if they were to see, because they have convinced themselves of the opposing false notions. Further, it is dangerous to use visions to convince people of anything if they are immersed in false opinions, because they will believe at first and then deny. In this way they will desecrate the truth itself, since desecration is believing and then denying. People who desecrate truths are forced down into the lowest and direst hell of all.[c]

[4] This is the danger meant by the Lord's words, "He has blinded their eyes and hardened their hearts lest they see with their eyes and understand with their heart and turn themselves

---

c. Desecration is the mingling of the good and the evil and of the true and the false within us: 6348. The only people who can desecrate what is true and good, or the holy things of the Word and the church, are people who have first acknowledged them, all the more if they have lived by them, and later fall away from their faith, deny them, and live for themselves and the world: 593, 1008, 1010, 1059, 3398, 3399, 3898, 4289, 4601, 10284, 10287. If we fall back into prior evils after heartfelt repentance, we commit desecration; and then our later state is worse than our former one: 8394. People cannot desecrate holy things if they have not acknowledged them, and still less if they have not even known about them: 1008, 1010, 1059, 9188, 10284. Non-Christians who are outside the church and do not have the Word are incapable of desecration: 1327, 1328, 2051, 2081. This is why deeper truths were not disclosed to the Jews, because if they had been disclosed and acknowledged, they would have desecrated them: 3398, 3489 [3479], 6963. The fate of desecrators in the other life is the worst of all because the good and truth they acknowledged is still there and so is what is evil and false; and since these coexist, there is a wrenching of their very life: 571, 582, 6348. So the Lord takes the greatest care to prevent desecration: 2426, 10384.

and I might heal them" (John 12:40); and the fact that people
immersed in false opinions still would not believe is meant
when it says, "Abraham said to the rich man in hell, They have
Moses and the prophets, let them heed them. But he said, No,
Father Abraham, but if someone from the dead were to come
to them, they would change. But Abraham said, If they do not
heed Moses and the prophets, then even if someone were raised
from the dead, they would not believe" (Luke 16:29–31).

When we first enter the world of spirits (which happens
shortly after the reawakening just described), our spirit has a
similar face and tone of voice as it did in the world. This is
because at that point we are in the state of our external concerns, with our deeper concerns not yet uncovered. This is our
initial state after decease. Later, though, our face changes and
becomes quite different. It comes to look like the ruling affection in which the deeper reaches of our minds were engaged
in the world, the kind of affection characteristic of the spirit
within our body, because the face of our spirit is very different from the face of our body. We get our physical face from
our parents and our spiritual face from our affection, which it
images. Our spirit takes on this face after our physical life is
over, when the outer coverings have been removed. This is our
third state.

I have seen some newcomers from the world and have recognized them by their faces and voices; but when I saw them later,
I did not recognize them. People who were engaged in good
affections had lovely faces, while people who were engaged in
evil affections had ugly ones. Seen in its own right, our spirit
is nothing but our affections, whose outward form is our face.

The reason our faces change is that in the other life no one
is allowed to pretend to affections they do not really have, so we
cannot put on a face that is contrary to the love we are engaged
in. We are all refined down to a state in which we say what we
think and manifest in expression and act what we intend. This

457

is why our faces all become forms and images of our affections; and this is why all the people who have known each other in the world still recognize each other in the world of spirits, but not in heaven or hell, as already noted (§427).[d]

458   The faces of hypocrites change more slowly than those of other people, because by constant practice they have formed the habit of arranging their inner minds into a counterfeit of good affections. So for a long time they look fairly attractive. However, since this false front is gradually stripped off and the deeper elements of their minds are arranged in the form of their affections, eventually they are uglier than other people.

Hypocrites are people who talk like angels but who inwardly respect only nature, not the Divine Being, and who therefore deny the realities of the church and of heaven.

459   It does need to be known that our human form is lovelier after death to the extent that we have more deeply loved divine truths and have lived by them, since our deeper levels are opened and formed according to both our love of these truths and our life. So the deeper the affection and the more it accords with heaven, the lovelier the face. This is why the angels who are in the inmost heaven are the loveliest—because they are forms of heavenly love. On the other hand, people who have loved divine truths more outwardly and have therefore lived by them more outwardly are less lovely, since only the more outward aspects radiate from their faces, and the deeper heavenly love—which means the form of heaven as it is in its own

---

d. Our faces are formed to be responsive to our inner natures: 4791–4805, 5695. On the correspondence of our faces and their expressions with the affections of our minds: 1568, 2988, 2989, 3631, 4796, 4797, 4800, 5165, 5168, 5695, 9306. For heaven's angels, the face forms a single whole with the deeper levels of the mind: 4796, 4797, 4798, 4799, 5695, 8250. So in the Word, "the face" means the deeper levels of the mind, or of affection and thought: 1999, 2434, 3527, 4066, 4796, 5102, 9306, 9546. How the inflow from the brains into the face changed in the course of time, and with it the face itself in regard to its responsiveness to our deeper natures: 4326, 8250.

right—does not shine through these more outward forms. You can see something relatively dim in their faces, not enlivened by a light of their inner life shining through. In short, all perfection increases as you move inward and lessens as you move outward. As the perfection increases or lessens, so does the beauty.

I have seen faces of angels of the third heaven so beautiful that no painters, with all their skill, could render a fraction of their light with their pigments or rival a thousandth part of the light and life that show in their faces. The faces of angels of the outmost heaven, though, can be mirrored to some extent.

Finally, I should like to offer a secret no one has ever known before, namely that everything good and true that comes from the Lord and makes heaven is in the human form. This is true not only of the greatest whole but also of every least part. This form influences everyone who accepts what is good and true from the Lord, and causes everyone in heaven to be in a human form according to that acceptance. This is why heaven is consistent with itself in general and in particular, why the human form is the form of the whole, of each community, and of each angel, as explained in the four chapters from §59 to §80. I need to add here that this is also the form of the details of thought that come from heavenly love in angels.

This secret may not fit well into the understanding of anyone on earth, but it is clear to the understanding of angels because they are in heaven's light.

460

After Death, We Enjoy Every Sense, Memory, Thought, and Affection We Had in the World: We Leave Nothing Behind except Our Earthly Body

REPEATED experience has witnessed to me that when we move from the natural world into the spiritual, which happens when we die, we take with us everything that pertains to our character except our earthly body. In fact, when we enter the

461

spiritual world or our life after death, we are in a body as we were in this world. There seems to be no difference, since we do not feel or see any difference. This body is spiritual, though, so it has been separated or purified from earthly matter. Further, when anything spiritual touches and sees something spiritual, it is just like something natural touching and seeing something natural. So when we have become a spirit, we have no sense that we are not in the body we inhabited in the world, and therefore do not realize that we have died.

[2] As "spirit-people," we enjoy every outer and inner sense we enjoyed in the world. We see the way we used to, we hear and talk the way we used to; we smell and taste and feel things when we touch them the way we used to; we want, wish, crave, think, ponder, are moved, love, and intend the way we used to. Studious types still read and write as before. In a word, when we move from the one life into the other, or from the one world into the other, it is like moving from one [physical] place to another; and we take with us everything we owned as persons to the point that it would be unfair to say that we have lost anything of our own after death, which is only a death of the earthly body. [3] We even take with us our natural memory, since we retain everything we have heard, seen, read, learned, or thought in the world from earliest infancy to the very end of life. However, since the natural objects that reside in our memory cannot be reproduced in a spiritual world, they become dormant the way they do when we are not thinking about them. Even so, they can be reproduced when it so pleases the Lord. I will have more to say soon, though, about this memory and its condition after death.

Sense-centered people are quite incapable of believing that our state after death is like this because they do not grasp it. Sense-centered people can think only on the natural level, even about spiritual matters. This means that anything they do not sense—that is, see with their physical eyes and touch with their hands—they say does not exist, as we read of Thomas in John

20:25, 27, 29. The quality of sense-centered people has been described above in §267, and in note c there.

Nevertheless, the difference between our life in the spiritual world and our life in the natural world is considerable, in regard both to our outer senses and the way they affect us and to our inner senses and the way they affect us. People who are in heaven have far more delicate senses. That is, they see and hear and also think more discerningly than when they were in this world. This is because they are seeing in heaven's light, which vastly surpasses the world's light (see above, §126), and they hear by way of a spiritual atmosphere that vastly surpasses the atmosphere of the earth (see §235). The difference in their outer senses is like that between something clear and something hidden by a cloud, or like noonday light and the dimness of evening. Because it is divine truth, heaven's light enables angels' sight to notice and differentiate the slightest things. [2] Further, their outer sight is responsive to their inner sight or discernment, since for angels the one sight flows into the other and they act as a single faculty. This is why they are so keen. Their hearing is similarly responsive to their perception, which is a function of both discernment and volition. So they pick up in the tone and words of speakers the slightest shadings of their affection and thought—shadings of affection in the tone, and shadings of thought in the words (see above, §§234–245).

However, the other senses are not as delicate for angels as their senses of sight and hearing, because sight and hearing serve their intelligence and wisdom, while the others do not. If the other senses were as sensitive, they would take away the light and pleasure of angels' wisdom and interject a pleasure of motivations centering in various physical appetites, appetites that obscure and weaken the intellect to the extent that they flourish. This happens to people in the world as well, who become dull and mindless in regard to spiritual truths to the extent that they pander to their taste and to the sensual allurements of the body.

462a

[3] What was presented in the chapter on the wisdom of heaven's angels (§§265–275) may suffice to indicate that the deeper senses of heaven's angels, the senses of their thought and affection, are more delicate and perfect than the ones they had in the world.

As for the difference in state of people who are in hell from their state in the world, this too is substantial. The perfection and wonder of the outer and inner senses of angels in heaven is paralleled by their imperfection for people in hell. However, we need to deal with their state later.

462b As for our keeping our whole memory when we leave the world, I have been shown this by many examples and have seen and heard a great deal worth talking about. I should like to cite a few examples in a sequence. There have been people who denied the crimes and transgressions they had committed in the world. To prevent them from believing they were blameless, everything was disclosed and drawn out of their own memory in sequence from the beginning of their life to the end. Most of these transgressions were acts of adultery and promiscuity.

[2] There were people who had deceived others with malicious skill and had stolen from them. Their deceptions and thefts were also recounted one after the other, many of them known to practically no one in the world other than themselves. They even admitted them because they were made plain as day, along with every thought, intention, pleasure, and fear that mingled in their minds at the time.

[3] There were people who had taken bribes and made money from judicial decisions. They were similarly examined from their own memories, and everything was recounted from their first taking office to the end. The details of amount and value, of the time, and of their state of mind and intention, all consigned to their remembrance together, were brought to view, a hundred or more instances. In some cases, remarkably

enough, the very diaries in which they had recorded these deeds were opened and read to them, page by page.

[4] There were men who had lured virgins to dishonor and violated their chastity. They were summoned to a similar judgment, and the details were drawn out of their memory and listed. The actual faces of the virgins and other women were presented as though they were there in person, along with the places, the words, and the thoughts. It was done as instantaneously as when something is actually being witnessed firsthand. Sometimes these presentations lasted for hours.

[5] There was one man who thought nothing of slandering others. I heard his slanders recounted in sequence as well as his blasphemies, along with the actual words, the people they were about, and the people they were addressed to. All these were presented together as lifelike as could be even though he had very carefully kept them hidden from his victims while he was living in the world.

[6] There was one man who had defrauded a relative of his legacy by some devious pretext. He was exposed and judged in the same way. Remarkably, the letters and documents they exchanged were read aloud to me, and he said that not a word was missing. [7] This same man had also secretly killed a neighbor by poison just before his own death, which was disclosed in the following way. A trench seemed to open under his feet, and as it was opened, a man came out as though from a tomb and screamed at him, "What have you done to me?" Then everything was disclosed—how the poisoner had talked amicably with him and offered him a drink, what he had thought beforehand, and what happened afterward. Once this was uncovered, the murderer was condemned to hell.

[8] In a word, all their evils, crimes, thefts, wiles, and deceptions are made clear to every evil spirit. They are drawn from their own memories and exposed. There is no room for denial because all the circumstances are presented together.

I also heard that angels have seen and displayed from the memory of one individual everything he had thought one day after another over the course of a month, with never an error, recalled as though he himself were back in those very days.

[9] We may gather from these instances that we take our whole memory with us, and that nothing is so concealed in this world that it will not be made known after death, made known in public, according to the Lord's words, "Nothing is hidden that will not be uncovered, and nothing concealed that will not be known. So what you have said in darkness will be heard in the light, and what you have spoken in the ear will be proclaimed from the rooftops" (Luke 12:2–3).

463 When we are being faced with our deeds after death, angels who have been given the task of examining look searchingly into the face and continue their examination through the whole body, beginning with the fingers first of one hand and then of the other and continuing through the whole. When I wondered why this was so, it was explained to me. The reason is that just as the details of our thought and intention are inscribed on our brains because that is where their beginnings are, so they are inscribed on the whole body as well, since all the elements of our thought and intention move out into the body from their beginnings and take definition there in their outmost forms. This is why the things that are inscribed on our memory from our intention and consequent thought are inscribed not only on the brain but also on the whole person, where they take form in a pattern that follows the pattern of the parts of the body. I could therefore see that our overall nature depends on the nature of our intention and consequent thought, so that evil people are their own evil and good people are their own good.[a]

---

a. Good people, spirits, and angels are their own good and their own truth: that is, the nature of the whole person depends on the nature of that good and truth: 10298, 10367. This is because the good constitutes our volition and the true constitutes our intellect, and volition and intellect constitute the entire

We may also gather from this what is meant by our book of
life, mentioned in the Word. It is the fact that all our deeds and
all our thoughts are written on our whole person and seem as
though they are read from a book when they are called out of
our memory. They appear in a kind of image when our spirit is
looked at in heaven's light.

I should like to add to this something noteworthy about the
memory that we keep after death, something that convinced me
that not just the general contents but even the smallest details
that have entered our memory do last and are never erased. I
saw some books with writing in them like earthly writing, and
was told that they had come from the memories of the people
who had written them, that not a single word was missing that
had been in the book they had written in the world. I was also
told that all the least details could be retrieved from the memory of someone else, even things the person had forgotten in the
world. The reason for this was explained as well; namely, that
we have an outer and an inner memory, the outer proper to
our natural person and the inner proper to our spiritual person.
The details of what we have thought, intended, said, and done,
even what we have heard and seen, are inscribed on our inner
or spiritual memory.[b] There is no way to erase anything there,

---

life for a person here, for a spirit, and for an angel: 3332, 3623, 6065. This is the
same as saying that people here, spirits, and angels are their love: 6872, 10177,
10284.

b. We have two memories, an outer and an inner, or a natural one and a spiritual one: 2469–2494. We are not aware that we have this inner memory: 2470,
2471. How much better the inner memory is than the outer one: 2473.
The contents of our outer memory are in the world's light, while the contents
of our inner memory are in heaven's light: 5212. It is because of our inner
memory that we can think and talk intelligently and rationally: 9394. Absolutely everything we have thought, said, done, seen, and heard is inscribed on
our inner memory: 2474, 7398. That memory is our book of life: 2474, 9386,
9841, 10505. In our inner memory are the true things that have become matters of our faith and the good things that have become matters of our love:

since everything is written at once on our spirit itself and on the members of our body, as noted above. This means that our spirit is formed in accord with what we have thought and what we have done intentionally. I know these things seem paradoxical and hard to believe, but they are true nevertheless.

Let no one believe, then, that there is anything we have thought or done in secret that will remain hidden after death. Believe rather that absolutely everything will come out into broad daylight.

464 While our outer or natural memory is still part of us after death, still the merely natural things that are in it are not recreated in the other life, only spiritual things that are connected to the natural ones by correspondence. Still, when they are presented visually, they look just the same as they did in the natural world. This is because everything we see in the heavens looks as it did in the world, even though in essence it is not natural but spiritual, as has been explained in the chapter on representations and appearances in heaven (§§170–176).

[2] As for our outer or natural memory, though, to the extent that its contents are derived from matter, time, space, and everything else proper to nature, it does not fulfill the same function for the spirit that it fulfilled in the world. This is because in the world, when we thought on the basis of our outer sensitivity and not at the same time on the basis of our inner or intellectual sensitivity, we were thinking on the natural level and not on the spiritual one. However, in the other life, when our spirit is in the spiritual world, we do not think on the

---

5212, 8067. Things that have become second nature to us and part of our life and therefore have been erased from our outer memory are in our inner memory: 9394, 9723, 9841. Spirits and angels talk from their inner memory, which is why they have a universal language: 2472, 2476, 2490, 2493. Languages in the world are matters of the outer memory: 2472, 2476.

natural level but on the spiritual one. Thinking on the spiritual level is thinking intelligently or rationally. This is why our outer or natural memory then goes dormant as far as material things are concerned. The only things that come into play are what we have gained in the world through those material things and have made rational. The reason our outer memory goes dormant as far as material things are concerned is that they cannot be recreated. Spirits and angels actually talk from the affections and consequent thoughts of their minds, so they cannot utter anything that does not square with these, as you may gather from what was said about the language of angels in heaven and their communication with us (§§234–257). [3] This is why we are rational after death to the extent that we have become rational by means of languages and the arts and sciences in this world, and emphatically not to the extent that we have become skilled in them.

I have talked with any number of people who were regarded as learned in the world because of their knowledge of such ancient languages as Hebrew and Greek and Latin, but who had not developed their rational functioning by means of the things that were written in those languages. Some of them seemed as simple as people who did not know anything about those languages; some of them seemed dense, though there still remained a pride, as though they were wiser than other people.

[4] I have talked with some people who had believed in the world that wisdom depends on how much we have in our memory and who had therefore filled their memories to bursting. They talked almost exclusively from these items, which meant that they were not talking for themselves but for others; and they had not developed any rational function by means of these matters of memory. Some of them were dense, some silly, with no grasp of truth whatever, no sense of whether anything was true or not. They seized on every false notion sold as true by people who called themselves scholars. They were actually

incapable of seeing anything as it actually was, whether it was true or not, so they could not see anything rationally when they listened to others.

[5] I have talked with some people who had written a great deal in the world, some of them in all kinds of academic fields, people who had therefore gained an international reputation for learning. Some of them could quibble about whether truths were true or not. Some of them understood what was true when they turned toward people who were in the light of truth; but since they still did not want to understand what was true, they denied it when they focused on their own false opinions and were therefore really being themselves. Some of them did not know any more than the illiterate masses. So they varied depending on the way they had developed their rational ability through the treatises they had written or copied. Still, if people had opposed the truths of the church, had based their thinking on the arts and sciences, and had used them to convince themselves of false principles, they had not developed their rational ability but only their skill in argumentation—an ability that is confused with rationality in the world, but is in fact a different ability from rationality. It is an ability to prove anything one pleases, to see false things rather than true ones on the basis of preconceptions and illusions. There is no way people like this can be brought to recognize truths because it is impossible to see truths from false principles, though it is possible from true principles to see what is false.

[6] Our rational faculty is like a garden or flower bed, like newly tilled land. Our memory is the soil, information and experiential learning are the seeds, while heaven's light and warmth make them productive. There is no germination without these latter. So there is no germination in us unless heaven's light, which is divine truth, and heaven's warmth, which is divine love, are let in. They are the only source of rationality.

Angels are profoundly grieved that scholars for the most part keep attributing everything to nature and therefore close the deeper levels of their minds so that they can see no trace of truth from the light of truth, the light of heaven. As a result, in the other life they are deprived of their ability to reason so that they will not use reason to spread false notions among simple people and mislead them. They are dismissed to desert areas.

One particular spirit resented the fact that he could not remember much of what he had known during his physical life. He was grieving over the pleasure he had lost because it had been his chief delight. He was told, though, that he had not lost anything at all and that he knew absolutely everything. In the world where he was now living he was not allowed to retrieve things like that. It should satisfy him that he could now think and talk much better and more perfectly without immersing his rational functioning in dense clouds, in material and physical concerns, the way he had before, in concerns that were useless in the kingdom he had now reached. Now he had whatever he needed for his functioning in eternal life, and there was no other way he could become blessed and happy. So it was the counsel of ignorance to believe that the removal and dormancy of material concerns in the memory led to the disappearance of intelligence, when in fact the more the mind can be led out of the sensory concerns that are proper to the outer person or the body, the more it is raised up to spiritual and heavenly concerns.

465

In the other life, people are sometimes shown what memories are like by having them presented visually in forms that are merely appearances (many things are presented visually there that for us here are strictly conceptual). The outer memory there looks like a callus, while the inner looks like the medullary substance found in the human brain. This also enables us to recognize their quality.

466

For people who have focused solely on memorization during their physical lives, without developing their rational ability, their memory has a callused quality that looks hard and streaked with tendons inside. For people who have filled their memories with false notions it looks shaggy because of the random mass of disorganized stuff. For people who have focused on memorization with themselves and the world first in mind, it looks stuck together and bony. For people who have tried to probe divine secrets through acquired information, especially philosophical information, without believing anything before they are convinced by the information, their memory looks dark, with a quality that actually absorbs rays of light and turns them into darkness. For people who have been guileful and hypocrites it looks bony and hard as ebony that reflects light rays.

However, for people who have focused on the good of love and truths of faith, no such callus is visible. This is because their inner memory is transmitting rays of light into their outer memory, and those rays find definition in its objects or concepts as though it were their foundation or their soil, and find congenial vessels there. This is because the outer memory is the outmost element of the design, where spiritual and heavenly matters come gently to rest and dwell when there are good and true contents in it.

467 While we are living in the world, if we are engaged in a love for the Lord and in thoughtfulness toward our neighbor, we have with and within us an angelic intelligence and wisdom, but it is hidden away in the depths of our inner memory. There is no way this intelligence and wisdom can become visible before we leave our bodies. Then our natural memory is put to sleep and we are awakened into consciousness of our inner memory and eventually of our actual angelic memory.

468 I do need to explain briefly how our rational ability is developed. A genuine rational ability is made up of true elements and not of false ones. Anything made up of false elements is not rational. There are three kinds of true elements: civic, moral, and spiritual. Civic truths have to do with judicial matters and the governmental affairs of nations—in general, with what is fair and equitable. Moral truths have to do with matters of personal life in its societal and social contexts, in general with what is honest and upright, and in particular with all kinds of virtues.

Spiritual truths, however, have to do with matters of heaven and the church, in general with what is good in respect to love and what is true in respect to faith.

[2] There are three levels of life in every individual (see above, §267). Our rational ability is opened at the first level by means of civic truths, at the second level by moral truths, and at the third level by spiritual truths.

We need to realize, though, that our rational ability is not formed and opened simply by virtue of our knowing these truths, but by virtue of our living by them. Living by them means loving them out of a spiritual affection; and loving them out of a spiritual affection means loving what is fair and equitable because it is fair and equitable, what is honest and upright because it is honest and upright, what is good and true because it is good and true. On the other hand, living according to them and loving them out of a physical affection is loving them for the sake of oneself, one's repute, prestige, or profit. Consequently, to the extent that we love these truths out of a carnal affection, we do not become rational because we do not love them; we love ourselves, with the truths serving us the way slaves serve their master. When truths become slaves, they do not become part of us or open any level of our life, not even the first. Rather, they stay in our memory like information in material form and unite with love for ourselves there, which is a physical love.

[3] We may gather from this how we become rational, namely that at the third level it is through a spiritual love of what is good and true in regard to heaven and the church; at the second level it is through a love of what is honest and upright; and on the first level it is through a love of what is fair and equitable. The latter two loves also become spiritual from a spiritual love of what is good and true that flows into them and unites itself to them and forms its own face in them, so to speak.

Spirits and angels have memory just as we do. What they hear and see and think and intend and do stays with them;

469

and through their memory they are constantly developing their rational ability forever. This is why spirits and angels are being perfected in intelligence and wisdom through experiences of what is true and good just the way we are.

I have been shown that spirits and angels have memory by a great deal of experience as well. I have seen everything they had thought and done called up from their memory both in public and in private, when they were with other spirits. I have also seen people who had been focused on some truth from simple virtue become steeped in insights and in a consequent intelligence and then taken up into heaven.

It should be realized, though, that they are not steeped in insights and a consequent intelligence beyond the level of the affection for what is good and true that engaged them in the world. In fact, each spirit and angel retains the amount and kind of affection she or he had in the world, and this is afterward perfected by being filled in. This too goes on forever, since everything is capable of infinite variation and enrichment by different means, so it can be multiplied and can bear fruit. There is no end to any instance of goodness, since its source is the Infinite.

The fact that spirits and angels are constantly being perfected in intelligence and wisdom by means of insights into what is true and good has been presented in the chapters on the wisdom of heaven's angels (§§265–275); on non-Christians or people outside the church in heaven (§§318–328); and on infants in heaven (§§329–345). This happens at the level of the affection for the good and the true that engaged them in the world, and not beyond it (§349).

Our Nature after Death Depends on the Kind of Life We Led in the World

470 ANY Christian knows from the Word that our life is still with us after death, since it says in many places that we will be judged

according to our deeds and works and rewarded accordingly. Further, anyone who thinks on the basis of what is good and from real truth cannot help but see that people who live well enter heaven and people who live evil lives enter hell. However, people who are intent on evil do not want to believe that their state after death depends on their life in the world. They think rather, especially when their health begins to fail, that heaven is granted to all on the basis of mercy alone no matter how people have lived, and that this depends on a faith that they keep separate from life.

It does say in many places in the Word that we will be judged and requited according to our deeds and works. I should like to cite a few passages here.

471

> The Human-born One is to come in the glory of the Father with his angels, and then he will render to everyone according to his or her works. (Matthew 16:17 [*16:27*])

> Blessed are the dead who die in the Lord. Truly, says the spirit, so that they may rest from their labors, their works follow them. (Revelation 14:11 [*14:13*])

> I will give to all according to their works. (Revelation 2:23)

> I saw the dead, small and great, standing in the presence of God, and books were opened, and the dead were judged according to what was written in the books, according to their works; the sea gave up those who had died in it, and death and hell gave up the people who were in them, and they were all judged according to their works. (Revelation 20:13, 15 [*20:12, 13*])

> See, I am coming; and my reward is with me, and I will give to all according to their works. (Revelation 22:12)

Everyone who hears my words and does them I will compare to a prudent person, but everyone who hears my words and does not do them is like a foolish person. (Matthew 7:24, 26)

Not everyone who says to me, "Lord, Lord," will enter into the kingdom of the heavens, but the one who does the will of my Father who is in the heavens. Many people will say to me on that day, "Lord, Lord, have we not prophesied through your name, and through your name cast out demons, and in your name done many powerful deeds?" But then I will confess to them, "I do not recognize you. Get away from me, workers of iniquity." (Matthew 7:22, 23)

Then you will begin to say, "We have eaten in your presence and drunk, and you have taught in our streets." But he will say, "I tell you, I do not recognize you, workers of iniquity." (Luke 13:25–27)

I will repay them according to their work, and according to the deeds of their hands. (Jeremiah 25:14)

Jehovah, whose eyes are open upon all our paths, to give to us all according to our ways and according to the fruit of our works. (Jeremiah 32:19)

I will visit upon their ways and repay them their works. (Hosea 4:9)

Jehovah deals with us according to our ways and according to our works. (Zechariah 1:6)

Where the Lord is predicting the Last Judgment, he recounts only deeds, and [says] that the people who have done good works will enter eternal life, and that the people who have done

evil works will enter damnation (Matthew 25:32–46). There are
many other passages as well that deal with our salvation and
damnation.

We can see that our outward life consists of our works
and deeds, and that the quality of our inner life is manifested
through them.

"Works and deeds," though, does not mean works and deeds
solely the way they look in outward form. It also includes their
deeper nature. Everyone knows, really, that all our deeds and
works come from our intention and thought, for if they did
not come from there they would be no more than motions like
those of machines or robots. So a deed or work in its own right
is simply an effect that derives its soul and life from our volition
and thought, even to the point that it is volition and thought
in effect, volition and thought in an outward form. It follows,
then, that the quality of the volition and thought that cause
the deed or work determines the quality of the deed or work.
If the thought and intent are good, then the deeds and works
are good; but if the thought and intent are evil, then the deeds
and works are evil, even though they may look alike in outward form. A thousand people can behave alike—that is, can
do the same thing, so much alike that in outward form one
can hardly tell the difference. Yet each deed in its own right is
unique because it comes from a different intent.

[2] Take for example behaving honestly and fairly with
an associate. One person can behave honestly and fairly with
someone else in order to seem honest and fair for the sake of
self and to gain respect; another person can do the same for the
sake of worldly profit; a third for reward and credit; a fourth to
curry friendship; a fifth out of fear of the law and loss of reputation and office; a sixth to enlist people in his or her cause, even
if it is an evil one; a seventh in order to mislead; and others for
still other reasons. But even though all of their deeds look good
(for behaving honestly and fairly toward a colleague is good),

472

still they are evil because they are not done for the sake of honesty and fairness, not because these qualities are loved, but for the sake of oneself and the world, because these are loved. The honesty and fairness are servants of this love, like the servants of a household whom their lord demeans and dismisses when they do not serve.

[3] People behave honestly and fairly toward their colleagues in a similar outward form when they are acting from a love of what is honest and fair. Some of them do it because of the truth of faith, or obedience, because it is enjoined in the Word. Some of them do it for the sake of the goodness of faith or conscience, because they are moved by religious feeling. Some of them do it out of the good of thoughtfulness toward their neighbor, because one's neighbor's welfare is to be valued. Some of them do it out of the goodness of love for the Lord, because what is good should be done for its own sake; so too what is honest and fair should be done for the sake of honesty and fairness. They love these qualities because they come from the Lord, and because the divine nature that emanates from the Lord is within them. So if we see them in their true essence, they are divine. The deeds or works of these people are inwardly good, so they are outwardly good as well; for as already noted, the nature of deeds and works is entirely determined by the nature of the thought and intent from which they stem, and apart from such thought and intent they are not deeds and works but only lifeless motions.

We may gather from this what is meant by works and deeds in the Word.

473 Since deeds and works are matters of intention and thought, they are also matters of love and faith to the point that their quality is the quality of their love and faith. That is, it amounts to the same thing whether you talk about our love or about our intentions, whether you talk about our established faith or about our thought, since what we love we also intend, and what we believe we also think. If we love what we believe, we intend it as well and do it to the extent that we can. Anyone can realize that love and faith dwell within our intentions and thought and not outside them, since intent is what is kindled by love and thought is what is enlightened in matters of faith. This means that only people who can think wisely are enlightened; and depending on their enlightenment they think what is true and intend what is true, they believe what is true and love what is true.[a]

We do need to recognize, though, that volition makes us who we are. Thought does so only to the extent that it arises from our volition, while deeds and works come from both. Or in other words, love is what makes us who we are; faith does so only to the extent that it arises from love, and deeds and works come from both. It follows from this that love or intent is the actual person, for the things that come forth belong to the person they come forth from. To come forth is to be produced and presented in a form suited to observation and sight.[b]

474

a. Just as everything in the universe that occurs in an orderly fashion goes back to what is good and true, so everything in us goes back to volition and intellect: 803, 10122. This is because it is our volition that receives what is good and our intellect that receives what is true: 3332, 3623, 5332, 6065, 6125, 7503, 9300, 9930. It amounts to the same thing whether you talk about what is true or faith, since faith is a matter of truth and truth is a matter of faith; and it also amounts to the same thing whether you talk about what is good or love, since love is a matter of what is good, and what is good is a matter of love: 4353, 4997, 7178, 10122, 10367. So it follows that intellect is the recipient of faith and volition the recipient of love: 7178, 10122, 10367; and since our intellect can accept faith in God and our volition love for God, we can be united to God by faith and love; and anyone who can be united to God by faith and love cannot die forever: 4525, 6323, 9231.

b. Our volition is the essential reality of our life, since it is the vessel of love or what is good; and our intellect is the consequent manifestation of life because it is the vessel of faith or what is true: 3619, 5002, 9282; so our voluntary life is our primary life and our intellectual life is secondary to it: 585, 590, 3619, 7342, 8885, 9282, 10076, 10109, 10110. It is like light from a fire or flame: 6032,

We may gather from this what faith is apart from love—no faith at all, only information with no spiritual life in it. The same holds true for deeds apart from love. They are not deeds or works of life at all, only deeds or works of death containing some semblance of life derived from a love of evil and a faith in what is false. This semblance of life is what we call spiritual death.

475 We should realize as well that we present our whole person in our works and deeds and that our volition and thought, or the love and faith that are our inner constituents, are not complete until they are [embodied] in the deeds and works that are our outer constituents. These latter are in fact the outmost forms in which the former find definition; and without such definitions they are like undifferentiated things that do not yet have any real presence, things that are therefore not yet in us. To think and intend without acting when we can is like a flame sealed in a jar and stifled, or it is like seed sown in the sand that does not grow but dies along with its power to reproduce. Thinking and intending and doing, though, is like a flame that sheds its light and warmth all around, or like seed sown in the soil, that grows into a tree or a flower and becomes something. Anyone can see that intending and not acting when we can is not really intending, and loving and not doing good when we can is not really loving. It is only thinking that we intend and love; so it is a matter of isolated thought that disintegrates and

---

6314. It follows from this that we are human because of our volition and our consequent intellect: 8911, 9069, 9071, 10076, 10109, 10110. Every individual is loved and valued by others in proportion to the virtue of her or his intentions and the consequent thought. We are loved and valued if we intend well and understand well, rejected and demeaned if we understand well but do not intend well: 8911, 10076. After death we retain the quality of our intentions and our consequent understanding: 9069, 9071, 9386, 10153. This means that after death we retain the quality of our love and faith. Any elements that are matters of faith but not at the same time of love vanish then because they are not within us and therefore are not part of us: 553, 2364, 10153.

vanishes. Love and intent are the very soul of the deed or work. It forms its own body in the honest and fair things that we do. This is the sole source of our spiritual body, the body of our spirit; that is, our spiritual body is formed entirely from what we have done out of love or intent (see above, §463). In a word, everything of our character and our spirit is [embodied] in our works or deeds.[c]

We may gather from this what is meant by the life that stays with us after death. It is actually our love and our consequent faith, not only in theory but in act as well. So it is our deeds or works because these contain within themselves our whole love and faith.

476

There is a dominant love that remains with each of us after death and never changes to eternity. We all have many loves, but they all go back to our dominant love and form a single whole with it, or compose it in the aggregate. All the elements of our volition that agree with our dominant love are called loves because they are loved. There are deeper and more superficial loves, loves that are directly united and loves that are indirectly united; there are closer and more distant ones; there are loves that serve in various ways. Taken all together they make a kind of kingdom. They are actually arranged in this way within us even though we are utterly unaware of their arrangement. However, the arrangement becomes visible to some extent in the other life because the outreach of our thoughts and affections

477

c. Deeper things flow sequentially into more outward ones and ultimately into what is outmost or final, which is where they find presence and permanence: 634, 6239, 6465, 9216, 9217. They not only flow in, they form a simultaneous whole on that outmost level, in a particular design: 5897, 6451, 8603, 10099. This is why all our deeper elements are held in connection and are stable: 9828. Deeds or works are the final forms in which our deeper elements exist: 10331; so being repaid and judged according to our works is [being repaid and judged] according to everything that pertains to our love and faith or our intentions and thought, since these are the deeper realities within our works: 3147, 3934, 6073, 8911, 10331, 10333.

there depends on it. The outreach is into heavenly communities if our dominant love is made up of loves of heaven, but it is into hellish communities if our dominant love is made up of loves of hell.

On the outreach into communities of all the thought and affection of spirits and angels, see the previous chapters on the wisdom of heaven's angels and on heaven's form, which determines its gatherings and communications [§§265–275, 200–212].

478
What I have said so far, though, is addressed only to our rational thought. In order to present the matter to sensory observation, I should like to add some experiences that may serve to illustrate and support the claims that *first,* we are our love or intention after death; *second,* we remain the same forever in regard to our volition or dominant love; *third,* we come into heaven if our love is heavenly and spiritual, and into hell if our love is carnal and worldly without any heavenly and spiritual dimension; *fourth,* our faith does not stay with us unless it comes from a heavenly love; and *fifth,* love in action, and therefore our life, is what remains.

479
A great deal of my experience has testified to the fact that *we are our love or intention after death.* All heaven is differentiated into communities on the basis of differences in the quality of love, and every spirit who is raised up into heaven and becomes an angel is taken to the community where her or his love is. When we arrive there we feel as though we are in our own element, at home, back to our birthplace, so to speak. Angels sense this and associate there with kindred spirits. When they leave and go somewhere else, they feel a constant pull, a longing to go back to their kindred and therefore to their dominant love. This is how people gather together in heaven. The same applies in hell. There too, people associate according to loves that oppose heavenly ones. On the fact that both heaven and hell are made up of communities and that they are all differentiated according to differences of love, see §§41–50 and 200–212 above.

[2] We may also gather that we are our love after death from the fact that anything that does not agree with our dominant love is then removed and apparently taken away from us. For good people, what is removed and apparently taken away is everything that disagrees and conflicts, with the result that they are admitted to their love. It is much the same for evil people, except that what is taken away from them is everything true, while for good people everything false is taken away. Either way, the result is that ultimately everyone becomes his or her own love. This happens when we are brought into our third state, which will be discussed below.

Once this has happened, we constantly turn our faces toward our love and have it constantly before our eyes no matter which way we face (see above, §§123–124).

[3] All spirits can be led wherever you want as long as they are kept in their dominant love. They cannot resist even though they know what is happening and think that they will refuse. Spirits have often tried to do something in opposition, but without success. Their love is like a chain or rope tied around them, with which they can be pulled and which they cannot escape. It is the same for people in this world. Our love leads us as well, and it is through our love that we are led by others. It is even more so when we become spirits, though, because then we are not allowed to present a different love or pretend to a love that is not ours.

[4] It is obvious in every gathering in the other life that our spirit is our dominant love. To the extent that we act and talk in keeping with someone else's love, that individual looks whole, with a face that is whole, cheerful, and lively. To the extent that we act and talk against someone else's dominant love, though, that individual's face begins to change, to dim, and to be hard to see. Eventually it disappears as though it were not even there. I have often been amazed at this because this kind of thing cannot happen in the world. However, I have been told that the same thing happens to the spirit within us, in that when we

turn our attention away from someone, that individual is no longer in our sight.

[5] I have also seen that our spirit is our dominant love from the fact that every spirit seizes and claims whatever suits his or her love and rejects and repels whatever does not suit it. Our love is like a spongy, porous wood that absorbs whatever liquids prompt its growth, and repels others. It is like animals of various kinds. They recognize their proper foods, seek out the ones that suit their natures, and avoid the ones that disagree. Every love actually wants to be nourished by what is appropriate to it—an evil love by falsities and a good love by truths. I have occasionally been allowed to see that some particular simple and good people wanted to teach evil people things that were true and good. Faced with this teaching, though, the evil people fled far away; and when they reached their own kind, they seized on whatever falsities suited their love with great delight. I have also been allowed to see good spirits talking with each other about truths, which other good spirits in attendance listened to eagerly, while some evil ones who were there paid no attention, as though they did not hear anything.

In the world of spirits you can see paths, some leading to heaven and some leading to hell, each one leading to some specific community. Good spirits travel only the paths that lead to heaven, and to the community engaged in their own quality of love. They do not see paths that lead anywhere else. On the other hand, evil spirits travel only the paths that lead to hell and to that community there which is engaged in the evil of their own love. They do not see paths that lead anywhere else; and if they do see them, they still do not want to follow them.

Paths like this in the spiritual world are "real appearances" that correspond to true and false [understandings]; so this is what "paths" in the Word mean.[d]

---

d. A way, road, track, lane, or street means things that are true and that lead to something good, as well as false things that lead to something evil: 627, 2333,

These proofs from experience support what was said above on rational grounds, namely that after death we are our own love and our own intent. I say "intent" because for each of us, our intent is our love.

A great deal of experience has also convinced me that *after death we remain the same forever in regard to our volition or dominant love.* I have been allowed to talk with some people who lived more than two thousand years ago, people whose lives are described in history books and are therefore familiar. I discovered that they were still the same, just as described, including the love that was the source and determinant of their lives.

480

There were others who had lived seventeen centuries ago, also known from history books, and some who had lived four centuries ago, some three, and so on, with whom I was also allowed to talk and to learn that the same affection still governed within them. The only difference was that the pleasures of their love had been changed into corresponding ones.

Angels have told me that the life of our dominant love never changes for anyone to all eternity because we are our love, so to change it in any spirit would be to take away and snuff out his or her life.

They have also told me that this is because after death we can no longer be reformed by being taught the way we could in this world, since the outmost level, made up of natural insights and affections, is then dormant and cannot be opened because it is not spiritual (see above, §464). The deeper functions of our mind or spirit rest on this level the way a house rests on its foundation, which is why we do stay forever like the life of our love in the world. Angels are utterly amazed that people do not realize that our nature is determined by the nature of

---

10422. To sweep a path is to prepare to accept what is true: 3142. To make a path known, when it is said of the Lord, is to teach people about the truths that lead to what is good: 10564.

our dominant love and that many people actually believe they can be saved by instantaneous mercy, simply on the basis of their faith alone, regardless of the kind of life they have led, not realizing that divine mercy operates through means. The means involve being led by the Lord in the world as well as afterward in heaven, and the people who are led by mercy are the ones who do not live in evil. People do not even know that faith is an affection for what is true, an affection that comes from a heavenly love that comes from the Lord.

481 *We come into heaven if our love is heavenly and spiritual and into hell if our love is carnal and worldly without any heavenly and spiritual dimension.* My evidence for this conclusion is all the people I have seen raised into heaven and cast into hell. The ones who were raised into heaven had lives of heavenly and spiritual love, while the ones who were cast into hell had lives of carnal and worldly love. Heavenly love is loving what is good, honest, and fair because it is good, honest, and fair, and doing it because of that love. This is why they have a life of goodness, honesty, and fairness, which is a heavenly life. If we love these things for their own sakes and do or live them, we are also loving the Lord above all because they come from him. We are also loving our neighbor, because these things are our neighbor who is to be loved.[e] Carnal love, though, is loving what is good and

---

e. In the highest sense, the Lord is our neighbor because he is to be loved above all; however, loving the Lord is loving what comes from him because he is in everything that comes from him, so [our neighbor is] whatever is good and true: 2425, 3419, 6706, 6711, 6819, 6823, 8123. Loving what is good and true, which come from him, is living by them, and this is loving the Lord: 10143, 10153, 10310, 10336, 10578, 10648. Every individual and community, our country and church, and in the broadest sense the Lord's kingdom, is our neighbor; and loving our neighbor is helping them from a love for their good in keeping with their state. This means that their welfare, which we are to value, is the neighbor: 6818–6824, 8123. Moral good, or what is honest, and civic good, or what is fair, are our neighbor as well; and acting honestly and fairly out of a love for what is honest and fair is loving the neighbor: 2915, 4730, 8120, 8121, 8122, 8123. Consequently, thoughtfulness toward our

honest and fair not for their own sakes but for our own sake, because we can use them to gain prestige, position, and profit. In this case we are not focusing on the Lord and our neighbor within what is good and honest and fair but on ourselves and the world, and we enjoy deceit. When the motive is deceit, then whatever is good and honest and fair is actually evil and dishonest and unfair. This is what we love within [the outward appearance].

[2] Since these loves define our lives, we are all examined as to our quality immediately after death, when we arrive in the world of spirits, and we are put in touch with people of like love. If we are focused on heavenly love, we are put in touch with people in heaven; and if we are focused on carnal love, we are put in touch with people in hell. Further, once the first and second states have been completed the two kinds of people are separated so that they no longer see or recognize each other. We actually become our own love not only as to the deeper levels of our minds but outwardly as well, in face, body, and speech, since we become images of our love even in outward things. People who are carnal loves look coarse, dim, dark, and misshapen; while people who are heavenly loves look lively, clear, bright, and lovely. They are completely different in spirit and in thought as well. People who are heavenly loves are intelligent and wise, while people who are carnal loves are dense and rather silly.

[3] When leave is given to examine the inner and outer aspects of the thoughts and affections of people engaged in heavenly love, the inner reaches look as though they were made of light, in some cases like the light of a flame; and their outer

---

neighbor includes all aspects of our lives, and doing what is good and fair, and acting honestly from the heart in every position we hold and in everything we do, is loving our neighbor: 2417, 8121, 8124. The doctrine of the early church was a doctrine of charity, and this was the source of their wisdom: 2417, 2385, 3419, 3420, 4844, 6628.

manifestations are of various lovely colors, like a rainbow. In contrast, the inner reaches of people who are engaged in carnal love look gloomy because they are closed in, in some cases like a smoky fire for people who were inwardly maliciously deceptive. Their outer manifestations have an ugly color, depressing to look at (both the inner and outer aspects of the mind and spirit are presented visually in the spiritual world whenever it so pleases the Lord).

[4] People who are engaged in carnal love do not see anything in heaven's light. Heaven's light is darkness to them, while hell's light, which is like the light of glowing embers, is like daylight to them. In fact, in heaven's light their inner sight is deprived of light to the point that they become insane. As a result, they run away from it and hide in caves and caverns of a depth that corresponds to the false convictions that stem from their evil intentions. Exactly the reverse is true for people who are engaged in heavenly love, though. The deeper or higher they enter into heavenly light, the more clearly they see everything and the lovelier it all looks, and the more intelligently and wisely they grasp what is true.

[5] There is no way that people who are engaged in carnal love can live in heaven's warmth, because heaven's warmth is heavenly love. They can live in hell's warmth, though, which is a love of cruelty toward people who do not support them. The pleasures of this love are contempt for others, hostility, hatred, and vengefulness. When they are absorbed in these they are in their very life, with no knowledge whatever of what it means to do good for others out of sheer goodness and for the sake of the good itself. All they know is how to do good out of malice and for the sake of malice.

[6] People who are engaged in carnal love cannot breathe in heaven either. When evil spirits are taken there, they draw breath like someone who is struggling painfully. On the other hand, people who are engaged in heavenly love breathe more freely and feel more alive the deeper into heaven they come.

We may gather from this that a heavenly and spiritual love is heaven for us because everything heavenly is written on that love; and that carnal and worldly love apart from heavenly and spiritual love is hell for us because everything hellish is written on that love.

We can see, then, that people come into heaven who have a heavenly and spiritual love, and people come into hell who have a carnal and worldly love without a heavenly and spiritual one.

The fact that *our faith does not stay with us unless it comes from a heavenly love* has been brought home to me by so much experience that if I were to relate what I have seen and heard about it, it would fill a book. I can attest to this: that there is no faith whatever and there can be none for people who are engrossed in carnal and worldly love apart from heavenly and spiritual love. There is only information, or a secondhand belief that something is true because it serves their own love. Further, a number of people who thought they had had faith were introduced to people of real faith; and once communication was established they perceived that they had no faith at all. They even admitted later that simply believing the truth or the Word is not faith; but faith is loving what is true from a heavenly love and intending and doing it from a deep affection. I was also shown that the secondhand belief they called faith was only like the light of winter in which everything on earth lies dormant, bound by the ice and buried in snow because there is no warmth to the light. As a result, the moment it is touched by rays of heaven's light, the light of their secondhand faith is not only extinguished but actually becomes a dense darkness in which people cannot even see themselves. At the same time, too, their deeper reaches are so darkened that they cannot discern anything and ultimately go mad because of their false convictions.

The result is that all the truths such people have learned from the Word and from the teaching of the church are taken away from them, all the things they claimed were part of their faith, and in their place they are filled with everything false that

482

accords with the evil of their life. They are actually all plunged into their loves and into the false notions that support them as well. Then, since truths contradict the false, malicious notions they are absorbed in, they hate the truths, turn their backs on them, and reject them.

I can bear witness from all my experiences of what happens in heaven and in hell that people who have confessed faith alone as a matter of doctrine and have engaged in evil as regards their lives are all in hell. I have seen thousands of them sent there and have described them in the booklet *The Last Judgment and Babylon Destroyed.*

483   The fact that *love in action, and therefore our life, is what remains* follows logically from what I have presented from experience and what I have just said about deeds and works. Love in action is the work and the deed.

484   We do need to know that all works and deeds are matters of moral and civic life and therefore focus on what is honest and right and what is fair and equitable. What is honest and right is a matter of moral life, and what is fair and equitable is a matter of civic life. The love these come from is either heavenly or hellish. The works and deeds of our moral and civic life are heavenly if we do them from a heavenly love, because things that we do from a heavenly love we do from the Lord, and everything we do from the Lord is good. On the other hand, the deeds and works of our moral and civic life are hellish if they come from a hellish love, since whatever we do from this love, which is a love for ourselves and the world, we do from ourselves, and whatever we do from ourselves is intrinsically evil. In fact, seen in our own right, or in terms of what is actually ours, we are nothing but evil.[f]

f. Our own nature is to love ourselves more than God and the world more than heaven, and to regard the neighbor as nothing in comparison to ourselves, so it is a love for oneself and for the world: 634 *[694]*, 731, 4317. This is the self into which we are born, and it is solid evil: 210, 215, 731, 874, 875, 876,

After Death, the Pleasures of Everyone's Life Are Turned into Things That Correspond

I EXPLAINED in the last chapter that our dominant affection or predominant love stays with us forever. Now, though, I need to explain that the pleasures of that affection or love change into things that correspond. "Changing into things that correspond" means changing into spiritual things that answer to the natural ones. We may gather that they change into spiritual things from the fact that as long as we are in our earthly bodies we are in the natural world; but once we leave that body behind, we arrive in the spiritual world and put on a spiritual body. (On angels having perfect human forms and being people after death, and on the bodies they wear being spiritual, see above, §§73–77 and 453–460; and for a description of the correspondence of spiritual things with natural ones, see §§87–115.)

All our pleasures stem from our dominant love, for the only things that feel pleasant to us are the ones that we love; so the most pleasant of all is what we love above all. Whether you say "our dominant love" or "what we love above all," it amounts to the same thing.

There are different pleasures—as many, generally speaking, as there are different dominant loves, which means as many as there are of us, and of spirits and angels, since no one's dominant love is entirely like that of anyone else. This is why no

485

486

987, 1047, 2307, 2318 *[2308]*, 3518, 3701, 3812, 8480, 8550, 10283, 10284, 10286, 10731 *[10832]*. From our self-image comes not only everything evil but also everything false: 1047, 10283, 10284, 10286. The evils that come from our self-image are contempt for others, hostility, hatred, vengefulness, cruelty, and deceit: 6667, 7372, 7373, 7374, 9348, 10038, 10742 *[10743]*. To the extent that our self-image rules, we either reject or stifle or pervert the goodness of love and the truth of faith: 2041, 7491, 7492, 7643, 8487, 10455, 10743. Our self-image is hell for us: 694, 8480. Anything good that we do because of our self-image is not good but is essentially evil: 8478 *[8480, 8487]*.

one's face is exactly like that of anyone else, since the face is the image of the mind, and in the spiritual world is an image of the dominant love. The pleasures of any specific individual are infinitely varied as well, with no pleasure ever entirely like any other. This applies both to the pleasures that come in sequence and to the ones that occur simultaneously. No two are ever alike. However, the specific pleasures of any given individual go back to that single love which is that individual's dominant love. In fact, they constitute it and therefore become one with it. In much the same way, all pleasures overall go back to one love that is universally dominant—in heaven, a love for the Lord, and in hell, a love for oneself.

487   The only way to know the kinds and qualities of the spiritual pleasures into which natural pleasures turn after death is through a knowledge of correspondences. This teaches in general that there is nothing natural to which something spiritual does not answer, and it teaches specifically the identity and nature of whatever does so correspond. This means that people who are engaged in this knowledge can recognize and know their state after death provided they know their love and how it relates in its nature to the universally dominant love to which, as we have just stated, all loves go back.

However, people who are involved in self-love cannot know what their dominant love is because they love whatever is theirs and call their evils good. They also call false things true, the false notions that support them and that they use to rationalize their evils. If they were willing, though, they could still know [their dominant love] from other people who are wise, because these latter see what they themselves do not. This does not happen, though, in the case of people who are so enmeshed in their self-love that they have nothing but contempt for any teaching of the wise.

[2] On the other hand, people who are in heavenly love do accept instruction and do see the evils into which they were

born when they are led into them. They see them from truths because truths make evils obvious. Anyone can in fact see what is evil and the distortion it causes by seeing from the truth that arises from what is good; but no one can see what is good and true from an evil standpoint. This is because the false notions that arise from evil are darkness and correspond to it. So people who are caught up in false notions that arise from evil are like blind people who do not see things that are in the light, and they avoid them the way owls avoid daylight.[a] On the other hand, the true perceptions that arise from good are light and correspond to light (see above, §§126–134). So people who are focused on the true perceptions that arise from good are sighted and open-eyed and can differentiate between things that are in light and shade.

[3] I have been granted confirmation of this too by experience. The angels who are in the heavens both see and grasp the evil and false promptings that well up in them from time to time; and they can also see the evil and false promptings that engage the spirits in the world of spirits who are in touch with the hells, though the spirits themselves cannot see their own evil and false promptings. They do not grasp what the virtue of heavenly love is, what conscience is, what is honest and fair (except as it is to their own advantage), or what it means to be led by the Lord. They say these things do not exist and therefore make no difference whatever.

All this has been presented to encourage people to examine themselves and to identify their dominant love on the basis of

---

a. By reason of correspondence, darkness in the Word means falsities, and dense darkness or gloom means falsities that stem from evil: 1839, 1860, 7688, 7711. Heaven's light is darkness to evil people: 1861, 6832, 8197. People who are in the hells are said to be in darkness because they are engrossed in false notions that stem from evil; with some discussion: 3340, 4418, 4531. In the Word, "the blind" means people who are engrossed in false convictions and do not want to be taught: 2383, 6990.

their pleasures, so that according to their grasp of the knowledge of correspondences, they may know their state of life after death.

It is possible to know from a knowledge of correspondences how our life pleasures are changed after death into what corresponds to them; but since this is not common knowledge, I should like to shed some light on the matter from experience.

People who are caught up in evil and who have formed fixed false convictions against the truths of the church, especially people who have rejected the Word, flee from heaven's light. They plunge into cellars that look murky through their openings and into crevices in the rocks and hide themselves there. This is because they have loved their false notions and hated true ones. Cellars like this, and crevices in the rocks as well,[b] and false things, correspond to darkness;[c] and light corresponds to things that are true. They find it pleasant to live there, and painful to live out in the open.

[2] People who took delight in covert plotting and in manufacturing deceptive schemes in secret also live in these cellars and move into rooms so dark that people can barely see each other. They whisper in each other's ears in the corners. This is what becomes of the pleasures of their love.

If people have loved the academic disciplines only in order to sound learned, without using them to develop their ability to reason, taking delight in their pride at the contents of their memories, they love sandy areas and prefer them to meadows and gardens because sandy areas correspond to these kinds of study.

[3] People who are wrapped up in knowing the doctrines of churches, their own and others', without applying them to life,

b. In the Word, rocky crevices and fissures mean what is dim and false in faith: 10582; because rocks mean faith from the Lord: 8581, 10580; and stone means truth of faith: 114, 643, 1298, 3720, 6426, 8608, 10376.
c. [Swedenborg's note at this point refers the reader back to the note in §487:2.]

love stony areas and live among rock piles. They avoid culti-
vated land because it is repulsive to them.

If people have given nature—and their own prudence—
credit for everything and have used various devices to gain high
office and a great deal of wealth, in the other life they study
magical arts that are misuses of the divine design, and find in
them the greatest pleasure of their life.

[4] People who have adapted divine truths to their own loves
and have therefore falsified them love urinary things because
urinary things correspond to the pleasures of this kind of love.[d]

People who were filthy misers live in cubicles and love the
filth of pigs and the foul odors they breathe out from half-
digested food in their stomachs.

[5] If people have devoted their lives wholly to pleasure, living elegantly, pandering to the gullet and the belly, loving this
as the greatest good of life, in the other life they love feces and
latrines and find them delightful. This is because pleasures like
these are spiritual filth. They avoid places that are clean and free
from filth because they find them distasteful.

[6] People who took pleasure in adultery pass their time in
brothels where everything is filthy and foul. They love these
places and avoid chaste homes. The moment they come near
such homes they feel faint. Nothing pleases them more than to
break up marriages.

People who have been bent on revenge and have therefore
taken on a savage and sadistic nature love places like morgues,
and are in hells of that sort.

Others fare differently.

In contrast, the life pleasures of people who have lived in
heavenly love in the world change into the kinds of corresponding things that exist in the heavens, things that come into being
from heaven's sun and from its light. The things which that
light renders visible have hidden within them divine realities.

489

---

d. Defilement of truth corresponds to urine: 5390.

What comes to view from this source moves the deeper reaches of angels' minds and the outer levels of their bodies as well; and since a divine light (which is divine truth emanating from the Lord) is flowing into their minds, which have been opened by heavenly love, it presents in outward form things that answer to the pleasures of their love. In the chapter that dealt with representations and appearances in heaven (§§170–176) and the chapter on the wisdom of heaven's angels (§§265–275), I have explained that the things presented to angels' sight in the heavens answer to their own deeper natures or to elements of their faith and love, and therefore to their intelligence [and] wisdom.

[2] Since I have begun supporting this general proposition by examples drawn from my experience, to shed light on what has been said so far on the basis of the causes of things, I should also like to bring in at this point something about the heavenly pleasures into which the natural pleasures turn for people who live in heavenly love in the world.

People who have loved divine truths and the Word from a deep affection, or from an affection for the truth itself, live in the light, in uplands that look like mountains, and are constantly bathed in the light of heaven there. They know nothing of the kind of darkness we have at night in the world, and they live in a springtime climate as well. Their scenery offers them views like fields ripe for harvest and vineyards. Everything in their houses gleams as though it were made of precious stones. Looking through their windows is like looking through pure crystal. These are their visual pleasures; but they are actually deeper pleasures because of their correspondence with divine heavenly qualities, since the truths from the Word that they have loved correspond to the harvest fields, vineyards, precious stones, windows, and crystals.ᵉ

e. A harvest in the Word means a state of acceptance and growth of what is true because of the good: 9291. Standing grain means truth being conceived: 9146. Vineyards mean the spiritual church and the truths of that church: 1069,

[3] People who have applied the teachings of the church from the Word directly to their lives are in the inmost heaven and more than anyone else are absorbed in the pleasures of wisdom. They see divine realities in particular objects. They actually do see the objects, but the corresponding divine realities flow directly into their minds and fill them with a sense of blessedness that affects all their sensory functions. As a result, everything they see seems to laugh and play and live (on this, see above, §270).

[4] If people have loved learning and have developed their rational ability accordingly and thereby gained intelligence, and if they have acknowledged the Divine Being at the same time, their delight in knowledge and pleasure in reasoning changes in the other life into a spiritual pleasure that is the delight of first-hand knowledge of what is good and true. They live in gardens where you can see flower beds and lawns beautifully marked off, surrounded by rows of trees with arcades and promenades. The trees and flowers change from day to day. Looking at all this brings pleasure to their minds generally, and the specific changes make it constantly new. Further, since all this corresponds to divine qualities, and since these people are drawn to their knowledge of correspondences, they are constantly being filled with new insights and thereby having their spiritual rational faculty perfected. They enjoy these pleasures because gardens, flower beds, lawns, and trees correspond to information, insights, and the intelligence that ensues.[f]

9139. Precious stones mean truths of heaven and of the church translucent from the good: 114, 9863, 9865, 9868, 9873, 9905. Windows mean the intellectual function of our inner sight: 655, 658, 3391.

f. Gardens, groves, and parks mean intelligence: 100, 103, 3220. Therefore the early people held their holy worship in groves: 2722, 4552. Flowers and flower beds mean truths of information and insight: 9553. Small plants, grasses, and lawns mean true information: 7571. Trees mean perceptions and insights: 103, 2163, 2682, 2722, 2972, 7692.

[5] If people have given the Divine credit for everything and regarded nature as relatively dead, simply subservient to spiritual concerns, and if they have convinced themselves of this, they are in heavenly light; and everything that presents itself to their eyes derives a kind of translucence from that light. In that translucency they see innumerable shadings of light that their inner sight seems to drink directly in. This is how they perceive deeper pleasures. The objects in their houses look like diamonds with similar variegations of light. I have been told that their walls look like crystal and are therefore also translucent, and that within them one can see what looks like fluid forms representative of heavenly things, again with constant variety. This is because this kind of translucence corresponds to an intellect that has been enlightened by the Lord, with the shadows that arise from faith in and love of natural things taken away. Things like this—and infinitely more—are what people who have been in heaven are talking about when they say that they have seen what the eye has never seen, and that from the grasp of divine things conveyed to them in this connection, they have heard what the ear has never heard.

[6] If people have not acted covertly but have wanted everything they were thinking to be out in the open to the extent that civil law allows, then since they have thought nothing but what was honest and fair because of the Deity, in heaven their faces are radiant. Because of that radiance, the details of their thoughts and affections are visible in their faces as though presented in a form; and in both speech and action they are virtual images of their feelings. They are more beloved than others. When they are talking, their faces dim a little, but after they have spoken, then the very things they have said can be fully and plainly seen in their faces. Further, since everything around them answers to their deeper natures, everything takes on a countenance that enables others to see clearly what they represent and mean. Spirits who have found pleasure in covert

activity get as far from them as they can, and seem to themselves to slither away from them like snakes.

[7] People who have regarded adultery as unspeakable and have lived in chaste love of their marriage are more in the pattern and form of heaven than anyone else. This gives them a total beauty and a constant flower of youth. The pleasures of their love are indescribable, and increase to eternity. This is because all the joys and delights of heaven flow into that love; and this in turn is because that love comes down from the Lord's union with heaven and with the church and in general from the union of the good and the true that is heaven in general and in every individual angel in particular (see above, §§366–386). Their external pleasures are so wonderful that they cannot be described in human words.

Still, what I have said about the correspondences of pleasures for people who are involved in heavenly love is only a little.

This enables us to know that after death our pleasures do change into corresponding ones, but that the love itself remains the same forever, especially marriage love, the love of what is fair, honest, good, and true, the love of information and insights, the love of intelligence and wisdom, and the rest. The things that flow from these loves like streams from their spring are pleasures that not only last but are raised to a higher level when they are changed from natural pleasures into spiritual ones.

490

ABOUT *DIVINE LOVE*
AND WISDOM

Divine Love and Wisdom is the most philosophical of Swedenborg's theological works. In it, he discusses the nature of God, the heavens, and life itself, laying out a number of ideas that are important to understanding his thought.

After publishing *Heaven and Hell* in 1758, Swedenborg immediately began work on a verse-by-verse commentary on the book of Revelation in a format similar to *Secrets of Heaven*. The draft manuscript was never published. Instead, Swedenborg abandoned the work and began writing four shorter pieces addressing different aspects of his theology: *The Lord*, *Life*, *Faith*, and *Sacred Scripture*. (These works are often published collectively as "The Four Doctrines.") *Divine Love and Wisdom* was published in the same year as those four books, 1763. Although the order in which the 1763 works were written is not known, it is thought that *Divine Love and Wisdom* was written last. A companion book, *Divine Providence*, appeared in 1764. Only once those works were finished did Swedenborg finally complete and publish his commentary on the book of Revelation. Swedenborgian scholar George F. Dole, who translated the following excerpt, speculates that Swedenborg had found himself sidetracked by a need to work through the philosophical issues raised in *Divine Love and Wisdom* and *Divine Providence*.

Whereas Swedenborg's previous works were written for people "of simple heart and simple faith"—that is to say, for the masses rather than church leaders or the intelligentsia—*Divine Love and Wisdom* seems to have been geared toward a more scholarly audience, using terminology aimed more at philosophers than theologians. Throughout the book, Swedenborg makes only minimal references to the Bible, instead appealing to reason, experience, and the laws of the physical world as authorities. Because of this more general approach, *Divine Love and Wisdom* has historically held a special appeal for artists and the philosophically inclined. For example, the poet William Blake (1757–1827) was so inspired by reading *Divine Love and Wisdom* that he attended one of the early meetings of the Church of the New Jerusalem—only to be disillusioned by organizers who focused on Swedenborg's more Bible-oriented works.

Divine Love and Wisdom starts with the proposition that God is, in essence, both love itself and life itself. Humans on earth and angels in heaven are all the recipients of that love, and therefore are all alive, albeit in different states of being. Swedenborg describes God as being human, not in the stereotypical sense of a bearded old man in the sky looking down on his creation, but in the sense that God's love and wisdom are the source of human love and wisdom, which are what make us all truly human. God is omnipresent throughout all of creation while existing outside of time and space.

There are levels to creation, writes Swedenborg, with the most perfect levels approaching God and the lowest levels in hell. These levels of creation also exist inside of us, and it is possible for those levels to open to the Lord, thus elevating us and expanding our spiritual lives. This process can continue after death, with angels perfecting themselves and moving eternally toward God. Evil spirits, on the other hand, reject God's love and make their home in hell.

In the following excerpt, Swedenborg tackles nothing less than the nature of God: how God is present in all things and all times without being present in space; how he is in essence love and wisdom and yet human in form; and how everything in the universe reflects that divine essence.

[The Lord's Love & Wisdom]

LOVE is our life. For most people, the existence of love is a given, but the nature of love is a mystery. As for the existence of love, this we know from everyday language. We say that someone loves us, that monarchs love their subjects, and that subjects love their monarch. We say that a husband loves his wife and that a mother loves her children, and vice versa. We say that people love their country, their fellow citizens, their neighbor. We use the same language about impersonal objects, saying that someone loves this or that thing.

Even though the word "love" is so commonly on our tongues, still hardly anyone knows what love is. When we stop to think about it, we find that we cannot form any image of it in our thoughts, so we say either that it is not really anything or that it is simply something that flows into us from our sight, hearing, touch, and conversation and therefore influences us. We are wholly unaware that it is our very life—not just the general life of our whole body and of all our thoughts, but the life of their every least detail. Wise people can grasp this when you ask, "If you take away the effects of love, can you think anything? Can you do anything? As the effects of love lose their warmth, do not thought and speech and action lose theirs as well? Do they not warm up as love warms up?" Still, the grasp of these wise people is not based on the thought that love is our life, but on their experience that this is how things happen.

We cannot know what our life is unless we know that it is love. If we do not know this, then one person may believe that life is nothing but sensation and action and another that it is thought, when in fact thought is the first effect of life, and sensation and action are secondary effects of life. Thought is the first effect of life, as just noted, but there are deeper and deeper forms of thought as well as more and more superficial ones. The deepest form of thought, the perception of ends, is actually the first effect of life. But more on this below [§§179–183] in connection with levels of life.

3 We can get some idea that love is our life from the warmth of the sun in our world. We know this warmth acts like the life shared by all earth's plants because when it increases in the spring, plants of all kinds sprout from the soil. They dress themselves in their leafy finery and then in their blossoms and eventually in fruit. This is how they "live." When the warmth ebbs away, though, as it does in fall and winter, they are stripped of these signs of life and they wither. Love works the same way in us because love and warmth correspond to each other. This is why love makes us warm.

4 *God alone—the Lord —is love itself, because he is life itself. Both we on earth and angels are life-receivers.* I will be offering many illustrations of this in works on divine providence and life. Here I would say only that the Lord, who is the God of the universe, is uncreated and infinite, while we and angels are created and finite. Since the Lord is uncreated and infinite, he is that essential reality that is called Jehovah and is life itself or life in itself. No one can be created directly from the Uncreated, the Infinite, from Reality itself and Life itself, because what is divine is one and undivided. We must be created out of things created and finite, things so formed that something divine can dwell within. Since we and angels are of this nature, we are life-receivers. So if we let ourselves be misled in thought so badly that we think we are not life-receivers but are actually life, there is no way to keep us from thinking that we are God.

Our sense that we are life and our consequent belief that we are life rests on an illusion: in an instrumental cause, the presence of its principal cause is only felt as something identical to itself. The Lord himself teaches that he is life in itself in John: "As the Father has life in himself, so too he has granted the Son to have life in himself" (John 5:26); and again in John (11:25 and 14:6) he teaches that he is life itself. Since life and love are one and the same, as we can see from the first two sections above, it follows that the Lord, being life itself, is love itself.

If this is to be intelligible, though, it is essential to realize that the Lord, being love in its very essence or divine love, is visible to angels in heaven as a sun; that warmth and light flow from that sun; that the outflowing warmth is essentially love and the outflowing light essentially wisdom; and that to the extent that angels are receptive of that spiritual warmth and spiritual light, they themselves are instances of love and wisdom—instances of love and wisdom not on their own, but from the Lord.

Spiritual warmth and spiritual light flow into and affect not only angels but also us, precisely to the extent that we become receptive. Our receptivity develops in proportion to our love for the Lord and our love for our neighbor.

That sun itself, or divine love, cannot use its warmth and light to create anyone directly from itself. If it did, the creature would be love in its essence, which is the Lord himself. It can, however, create people out of material substances so formed as to be receptive of its actual warmth and light. In the same way, the sun of our world cannot use its warmth and light to bring forth sprouts in the earth directly. Rather, the sun uses substances in the soil in which it can be present through its warmth and light to make plants grow. (On the Lord's divine love being seen as the sun in the spiritual world, with spiritual warmth and light flowing from it, giving angels their love and wisdom, see *Heaven and Hell* 116–142.)

Since we are life-receivers, not life, it follows that our conception from our parents is not the conception of life but simply the conception of the first and purest forms that can accept life. These forms serve as a nucleus or beginning in the womb, to which are added, step by step, material substances in forms suited, in their various patterns and levels, to the reception of life.

Divinity is not in space. Given the divine omnipresence—presence with everyone in the world, with every angel in heaven, and with every spirit under heaven—there is no way a merely physical image can compass the thought that Divinity, or God, is not in space. Only a spiritual image will suffice. Physical images are inadequate because they involve space. They are put together out of earthly things, and there is something spatial about absolutely every earthly thing we see with our eyes. Everything that is large or small here involves space, everything that is long or wide or high here involves space—in a word, every measurement, every shape, every form here involves space. This is why I said that a merely physical image cannot compass the fact that Divinity is not in space when the claim is made that it is everywhere.

Still, we can grasp this with our earthly thinking if only we let in a little spiritual light. This requires that I first say something about spiritual concepts and the spiritual thinking that arises from them. Spiritual concepts have nothing to do with space. They have to do solely with state, state being an attribute of love, life, wisdom, desires, and the delights they provide—in general, an attribute of what is good and true. A truly spiritual concept of these realities has nothing in common with space. It is higher and looks down on spatial concepts the way heaven looks down on earth.

However, since angels and spirits see with their eyes the way we do on earth, and since objects can be seen only in space, there does seem to be space in the spiritual world where angels and spirits are, space like ours on earth. Still, it is not space but an appearance of space. It is not fixed and invariant like ours. It can be lengthened and shortened, changed and altered; and since it cannot be defined by measurement, we here cannot grasp it with an earthly concept, but only with a spiritual one. Spiritual concepts are no different when they apply to spatial distances than when they apply to "distances" of what is good and "distances" of what is true, which are agreements and likenesses as to state.

It stands to reason, then, that with merely earthly con- **8**
cepts we cannot grasp the fact that Divinity is everywhere
and still not in space, and that angels and spirits understand
this quite clearly. This means that we too could understand
if we would only let a little spiritual light into our thinking.
The reason we can understand is that it is not our bodies that
think but our spirits; so it is not our physical side but our
spiritual side.

The reason so many people do not grasp this is that they love **9**
what is earthly and are therefore reluctant to lift their thinking
above it into spiritual light. People who are reluctant can think
only spatially, even about God; and thinking spatially about
God is thinking about the extended size of nature.

This premise is necessary because without a knowledge and
some sense that Divinity is not in space, we cannot understand anything about the divine life that is love and wisdom,
which are our present topic. This means there can be little if
any understanding of divine providence, omnipresence, omniscience, omnipotence, infinity, and eternity, which are to be
dealt with in sequence.

I have stated that in the spiritual world, just as in this physi- **10**
cal world, we can see space and therefore distances as well, but
that they are appearances, dependent on spiritual likenesses of
love and wisdom, or of what is good and true. This is why even
though the Lord is with angels everywhere in heaven, he still
appears high overhead, looking like a sun. Further, since it is
the acceptance of love and wisdom that causes likeness to him,
if angels have a closer resemblance because of their acceptance,
their heavens appear to be closer to the Lord than those of the
angels whose resemblance is more remote. This is also why the
heavens (there are three of them) are marked off from each
other, as are the communities of each heaven. It is also why the
hells underneath them are farther away in proportion to their
rejection of love and wisdom.

It is the same for us. The Lord is present in us and with us throughout the whole world; and the reason for this is simply that the Lord is not in space.

11 *God is the essential person.* Throughout all the heavens, the only concept of God is a concept of a person. The reason is that heaven, overall and regionally, is in a kind of human form, and Divinity among the angels is what makes heaven. Further, thinking proceeds in keeping with heaven's form, so it is not possible for angels to think about God in any other way. This is why all the people on earth who are in touch with heaven think about God in the same way when they are thinking very deeply, or in their spirit. It is because God is a person that all angels and spirits are perfectly formed people. This is because of heaven's form, which is the same in its largest and its smallest manifestations. (On heaven being in a human form overall and regionally, see *Heaven and Hell* 59–87 *[59–86]*, and on thought progressing in keeping with heaven's form, see §§203–204 there.)

It is common knowledge that we were created in the image and likeness of God because of Genesis 1:26, 27 and from the fact that Abraham and others saw God as a person.

The early people, wise and simple alike, thought of God only as a person. Even when they began to worship many gods, as they did in Athens and Rome, they worshiped them as persons. By way of illustration, here is an excerpt from an earlier booklet.

> Non-Christians—especially Africans—who acknowledge and worship one God as the Creator of the universe conceive of that God as a person. They say that no one can have any other concept of God. When they hear that many people prefer an image of God as a little cloud in the center, they ask where these people are; and when they are told that these people are among the Christians, they respond that this is impossible. They are told, however, that Christians get this idea from the

fact that in the Word God is called a spirit; and the only concept they have of spirit is of a piece of cloud. They do not realize that every spirit and every angel is a person. However, when inquiry was made to find out whether their spiritual concept was the same as their earthly one, it turned out that it was not the same for people who inwardly recognized the Lord as the God of heaven and earth.

I heard one Christian elder say that no one could have a concept of a being both divine and human; and I saw him taken to various non-Christians, more and more profound ones. Then he was taken to their heavens, and finally to a heaven of Christians. Through the whole process people's inner perception of God was communicated to him, and he came to realize that their only concept of God was a concept of a person— which is the same as a concept of a being both divine and human.

The ordinary concept of God among Christians is a concept of a person because God is called a person in the Athanasian doctrine of the Trinity. The better educated, though, claim that God is invisible. This is because they cannot understand how a human God could have created heaven and earth and filled the universe with his presence, along with other things that pass the bounds of understanding as long as people do not realize that Divinity is not in space. Still, people who turn to the Lord alone think of one who is both divine and human, and therefore think of God as a person. 12

We may gather how important it is to have a right concept of God from the fact that this concept is the very core of the thinking of anyone who has a religion. All the elements of religion and of worship focus on God; and since God is involved in every element of religion and worship, whether general or particular, unless there is a right concept of God there can be no communication with heaven. This is why every nation is 13

allotted its place in the spiritual world according to its concept
of a human God. This [understanding of God as human] is
where the concept of the Lord is to be found, and nowhere else.

We can see very clearly that our state after death depends on
our avowed concept of God if we consider the opposite, namely
that the denial of God, and in the Christian world, a denial of
the Lord's divinity, constitutes hell.

14 *In the Divine-Human One, reality and its manifestation are both
distinguishable and united.* Wherever there is reality, there is its
manifestation: the one does not occur without the other. In fact,
reality *exists* through its manifestation, and not apart from it.
Our rational capacity grasps this when we ponder whether there
can be any reality that does not manifest itself, and whether
there can be any manifestation except from some reality. Since
each occurs with the other and not apart from it, it follows that
they are one entity, but "distinguishably one."

They are distinguishably one like love and wisdom. Further,
love *is* reality and wisdom is its manifestation. Love occurs only
in wisdom, and wisdom only from love. So love becomes manifest when it is in wisdom. These two are one entity in such a
way that although they can be distinguished in thought they
cannot be distinguished in fact; and since they can be distinguished in thought and not in fact, we refer to them as "distinguishably one."

Reality and its manifestation are also distinguishably one in
the Divine-Human One the way soul and body are. A soul does
not occur without its body, nor a body without its soul. The
divine soul of the Divine-Human One is what we mean by the
divine reality, and the divine body of the Divine-Human One is
what we mean by the divine manifestation.

The notion that a soul can exist and think and be wise without a body is an error that stems from deceptive appearances.
Every soul is in a spiritual body after it has cast off the material
skin that it carried around in this world.

The reason reality is not reality unless it is manifested is that   **15**
before that happens it has no form, and if it has no form it
has no attributes. Anything that has no attributes is not really
anything. Whatever is manifest on the basis of its reality is one
with that reality because it stems from that reality. This is the
basis of their being united into a single entity, and this is why
each belongs to the other reciprocally, with each being wholly
present in every detail of the other, as it is in itself.

It therefore stands to reason that God is a person and in this   **16**
way is God manifest—not manifest from himself, but manifest
in himself. The one who is manifest in himself is the God who
is the source of all.

In the Divine-Human One, infinite things are distinguishably one.   **17**
It is recognized that God is infinite: he is in fact called the Infinite One. But he is called infinite because he is infinite. He
is not infinite simply because he is intrinsically essential reality and manifestation, but because there are infinite things in
him. An infinite being without infinite things within it would
be infinite in name only.

The infinite things in him should not be called "infinitely
many" or "infinitely all," because of our earthly concepts of
"many" and "all." Our earthly concept of "infinitely many" is
limited, and while there is something limitless about our concept of "infinitely all," it still rests on limited things in our universe. This means that since our concept is earthly, we cannot
arrive at a sense of the infinite things in God by some process
of shifting it to a higher level or by comparison. However, since
angels enjoy spiritual concepts they can surpass us by changing
to a higher level and by comparison, though they cannot reach
infinity itself.

Anyone can come to an inner assurance about the presence   **18**
of infinite things in God—anyone, that is, who believes that
God is a person; because if God is a person, he has a body and
everything that having a body entails. So he has a face, torso,

abdomen, upper legs, and lower legs, since without these he would not be a person. Since he has these components, he also has eyes, ears, nose, mouth, and tongue. He also has what we find within a person, such as a heart and lungs and the things that depend on them, all of which, taken together, make us human. We are created with these many components, and if we consider them in their interconnections, they are beyond counting. In the Divine-Human One, though, they are infinite. Nothing is lacking, so he has an infinite completeness.

We can make this comparison of the uncreated Person, who is God, with us who are created, because that God is a person. It is because of [his being a person] that we earthly beings are said to have been created in his image and in his likeness (Genesis 1:2, 27).

19 The presence of infinite things in God is even more obvious to angels because of the heavens where they live. The whole heaven, made up of millions of angels, is like a person in its overall form. Each individual community of heaven, large or small, is the same; and therefore an angel is a person. An angel is actually a heaven in its smallest form (see *Heaven and Hell* 51–87 *[51–86]*).

Heaven is in this form overall, regionally, and in individuals because of the divine nature that angels accept, since the extent to which angels accept the divine nature determines the perfection of their human form. This is why we say that angels are in God and that God is in them, and that God is everything to them.

The multiplicity of heaven is indescribable; and since it is Divinity that makes heaven, and therefore Divinity is the source of that indescribable multiplicity, we can see quite clearly that there are infinite things in that quintessential Person who is God.

20 We can draw the same inference from the created universe if we turn our attention to its functions and the things that

answer to them. However, this will not be comprehensible until some examples have been offered.

Since there are infinite things in the Divine-Human One, things that are, so to speak, reflected in heaven, in angels, and in us, and since the Divine-Human One is not in space (see §§7–10 above), we can see and understand to some extent how God can be omnipresent, omniscient, and omniprovident, and how, even as a person, he could have created everything, and how as a person he can forever keep everything he has created in its proper order.

Further, if we look at ourselves we can see a kind of reflection of the fact that these infinite things in the Divine-Human One are distinguishably one. There are many things within us—countless things, as already noted [§18]; yet we feel them as one. On the basis of our feelings, we have no sense of our brain or heart or lungs, of our liver or spleen or pancreas, of the countless components of our eyes, ears, tongue, stomach, sexual organs, and so on; and since we are not aware of them, we sense them as all one.

The reason is that all these organs are gathered into a form that precludes the absence of any one of them. It is a form designed to receive life from the Divine-Human One, as explained in §§4–6 above. The organization and connection of all these elements in this kind of form give rise to the feeling and therefore to the image of them not as many or countless but as one.

We may therefore conclude that the innumerably many components that constitute a kind of unity in us are distinguishably one—supremely so—in that quintessential Person who is God.

There is one human God who is the source of everything. All the elements of human reason unite in, and in a sense center on, the fact that a single God is the Creator of the universe. As a result, rational people, on the basis of their shared understanding, neither do nor can think in any other way. Tell people of sound reason that there are two creators of the universe and you will feel within yourself how they recoil from this notion, perhaps simply from the tone of their voice in your ear. This enables us to see that all the elements of human reason unite and center on the oneness of God.

There are two reasons for this. The first is that in its own right, our very ability to think rationally is not our own property. It is a property of God within us. Human rationality in general depends on this fact, and this general property causes our reason more or less spontaneously to see the oneness of God. The second is that through our rational ability either we are in heaven's light or we draw from it some general quality of its thought, and the all-pervading element of heaven's light is that God is one.

This is not the case if we have used our rational ability to skew our lower understanding. In this case we still possess the ability, but by the distortion of our lower abilities we have steered it off course, and our rationality is not sound.

24 We may not be aware of it, but we all think of an aggregation of people as a single individual. So we understand right away when someone says that monarchs are the head and that their subjects are the body, or when someone says that this or that individual has some particular role in the body politic, that is, in the realm. It is the same with the spiritual body as with the civil. The spiritual body is the church, whose head is the Divine-Human One. We can see from this what kind of person a church would look like under this construct if we were to think not of one God as creator and sustainer of the universe but of many gods instead. We would apparently be envisioning a single body with many heads on it—not a human being, then, but a monster.

If we were to claim that these heads have a single essence that made them all one head, then the only possible image would be either of a single head with many faces or of many heads with one face. In our perception, then, the church would look grotesque. In fact, one God is the head, and the church is the body that acts at the bidding of the head and not on its own, as is true of us as well.

This is also why there is only one monarch per realm. More than one would pull it apart; one holds it together.

It would be the same in the church that is spread throughout the world, which is called a communion because it is like a single body under a single head. It is recognized that the head governs the body beneath itself at will. The head is after all the locus of our discernment and our volition, and the body acts at the behest of our discernment and volition to the point that the body is pure obedience. The body is incapable of doing anything except at the behest of the discernment and volition in the head; and in similar fashion we of the church can do nothing apart from God. It does seem as though the body acts on its own—as though hands and feet move of their own accord when we do something, as though mouth and tongue vibrate of their own accord when we say something—and yet nothing whatever is done "on its own." It is prompted by the stimulus of our volition and the consequent thinking of the discernment in the head.

Just think. If one body had many heads, and each head had its own agenda based on its mind and its volition, could the body survive? There could be no unanimity among them the way there is with a single head.

It is the same in the heavens, which consist of millions of angels, as it is in the church. Unless every single angel focused on one God, one angel would move away from another and heaven would fall apart. So an angel who even thinks about many gods instantly disappears, exiled to the very edge of heaven, and collapses.

Since the whole heaven and everything in it depend on a single God, it is the nature of angelic speech to come to a close in a particular harmony that flows from heaven's own harmony.

25

26

This is a sign that it is impossible for angels to think of more than one God. Their speech follows from their thought.

27   Surely everyone of sound reason perceives the fact that Divinity is not divisible, that there is not a multiplicity of infinite, uncreated, omnipotent beings, or gods. Suppose some irrational soul were to say that there could be a multiplicity of infinite, uncreated, omnipotent beings, or gods, if only they had a single "same essence," and that this would result in one being who was infinite, uncreated, omnipotent, and god. Would not that single same essence have one "same identity"? And it is not possible for many beings to have the same identity. If this individual were to say that one is derived from the other, then the one that is derived from the other is not God in and of himself; yet God in and of himself is the source of all (see §16 above).

28   *The true divine essence is love and wisdom.* If you gather together everything you know, focus your mind's insight on it, and look through it carefully from some spiritual height to discover what is common to everything, the only conclusion you can draw is that it is love and wisdom. These two are essential to every aspect of our life. Everything we deal with that is civic, everything moral, and everything spiritual depends on these two things. Apart from them, there is nothing. The same holds true for everything in the life of that composite person who is (as already noted [§24]) our larger and smaller community, our monarchy or empire, the church, and also the angelic heaven. Take love and wisdom away from these collective bodies and ask whether there is anything left, and you will be struck by the fact that without love and wisdom as their source, they are nothing.

29   No one can deny that in God we find love and wisdom together in their very essence. He loves us all out of the love that is within him, and he guides us all out of the wisdom that is within him.

Further, if you look at the created universe with an eye to its design, it is so full of wisdom from love that you might say everything taken all together is wisdom itself. There are things without measure in such a pattern, both sequential and simultaneous, that taken all together they constitute a single entity. This is the only reason they can be held together and sustained forever.

It is because the very essence of the Divine is love and wisdom that we have two abilities of life. From the one we get our discernment, and from the other volition. Our discernment is supplied entirely by an inflow of wisdom from God, while our volition is supplied entirely by an inflow of love from God. Our failures to be appropriately wise and appropriately loving do not take these abilities away from us. They only close them off; and as long as they do, while we may call our discernment "discernment" and our volition "volition," essentially they are not. So if these abilities really were taken away from us, everything human about us would be destroyed—our thinking and the speech that results from thought, and our purposing and the actions that result from purpose.

We can see from this that the divine nature within us dwells in these two abilities, in our ability to be wise and our ability to love. That is, it dwells in the fact that we are capable of being wise and loving. I have discovered from an abundance of experience that we have the ability to love even though we are not wise and do not love as we could. You will find this experience described in abundance elsewhere.

It is because the divine essence itself is love and wisdom that everything in the universe involves what is good and what is true. Everything that flows from love is called good, and everything that flows from wisdom is called true. But more on this later [§§83–102].

It is because the divine essence itself is love and wisdom that the universe and everything in it, whether living or not,

30

31

32

depends on warmth and light for its survival. Warmth in fact corresponds to love and light corresponds to wisdom, which also means that spiritual warmth is love and spiritual light is wisdom. But more on this as well later [§§83–84, 89–92].

33   All human feelings and thoughts arise from the divine love and wisdom that constitute the very essence that is God. The feelings arise from divine love and the thoughts from divine wisdom. Further, every single bit of our being is nothing but feeling and thought. These two are like the springs of everything that is alive in us. They are the source of all our life experiences of delight and enchantment, the delight from the prompting of our love and the enchantment from our consequent thought.

Since we have been created to be recipients, then, and since we are recipients to the extent that we love God and are wise because of our love for God (that is, the extent to which we are moved by what comes from God and think as a result of that feeling), it therefore follows that the divine essence, the Creatress, is divine love and wisdom.

34   *Divine love is a property of divine wisdom, and divine wisdom is a property of divine love.* On the divine reality and the divine manifestation being distinguishably one in the Divine-Human One, see §§14–16 above. Since the divine reality is divine love and the divine manifestation is divine wisdom, these latter are similarly distinguishably one.

We refer to them as "distinguishably one" because love and wisdom are two distinguishable things, and yet they are so united that love is a property of wisdom and wisdom a property of love. Love finds its reality in wisdom, and wisdom finds its manifestation in love. Further, since wisdom derives its manifestation from love (as noted in §15 *[14]* above), divine wisdom is reality as well. It follows from this that love and wisdom together are the divine reality, though when they are distinguished we call love the divine reality and wisdom the divine manifestation.

This is the quality of the angelic concept of divine love and wisdom.

Because there is such a oneness of love and wisdom and of wisdom and love in the Divine-Human One, the divine essence is one. In fact, the divine essence is divine love because that love is a property of divine wisdom, and it is divine wisdom because that wisdom is a property of divine love. Because of this oneness, the divine life is a unity as well: life is the divine essence. The reason divine love and wisdom are one is that the union is reciprocal, and a reciprocal union makes complete unity. But there will be more to say about reciprocal union later [§§115–116].

There is a union of love and wisdom in every divine work as well. This is why it endures, even to eternity. If there were more divine love than divine wisdom or more divine wisdom than divine love in any created work, nothing would endure in it except what was equal. Any excess would pass away.

As divine providence works for our reformation, regeneration, and salvation, it shares equally in divine love and divine wisdom. We cannot be reformed, regenerated, and saved by any excess of divine love over divine wisdom or by any excess of divine wisdom over divine love. Divine love wants to save everyone, but it can do so only by means of divine wisdom. All the laws that govern salvation are laws of divine wisdom, and love cannot transcend those laws because divine love and divine wisdom are one and act in unison.

In the Word, "justice" and "judgment" mean divine love and divine wisdom, "justice" meaning divine love and "judgment" meaning divine wisdom; so in the Word justice and judgment are ascribed to God. For example, we read in David, "Justice and judgment are the foundation of your throne" (Psalms 79:15 *[89:14]*); and again, "Jehovah will bring out his justice like light and his judgment like noonday" (Psalms 37:6); in Hosea, "I will betroth myself to you forever in justice and judgment" (Hosea

2:19); in Jeremiah, "I will raise up a just branch for David who will rule as king and make judgment and justice in the land" (Jeremiah 23:5); in Isaiah, "He will sit on the throne of David and over his kingdom, to make it secure in judgment and in justice" (Isaiah 9:6 *[9:7]*); and again, "Let Jehovah be extolled, because he has filled the earth with judgment and justice" (Isaiah 33:5); in David, "When I shall have learned the judgments of your justice . . . seven times a day I will praise you over the judgments of your justice" (Psalms 119:7, 164). "Life" and "light" in John mean the same: "In him was life, and the life was the light of humanity" (John 1:4). "Life" here means the Lord's divine love, and "light" his divine wisdom. "Life" and "spirit" mean the same in John as well: "Jesus said, 'The words that I speak to you are spirit and life'" (John 6:63).

39 Even though love and wisdom seem to be two separate things in us, essentially they are distinguishably one. This is because the quality of our love determines the quality of our wisdom and the quality of our wisdom the quality of our love. Any wisdom that is not united to our love seems like wisdom, but it is not; and any love that is not united to our wisdom seems like wisdom's love even though it is not. Each gets its essence and its life from the other in mutual fashion.

The reason the wisdom and love within us seem to be two separate things is that our ability to understand can be raised into heaven's light, while our ability to love cannot, except to the extent that we act according to our understanding. So any trace of apparent wisdom that is not united to our love for wisdom relapses into the love with which it is united. This may not be a love for wisdom, and may even be a love for insanity. We are perfectly capable of knowing, from our wisdom, that we ought to do one thing or another, and then of not doing it because we have no love for it. However, to the extent that we do the bidding of our wisdom, from love, we are images of God.

Divine love and wisdom is substance and is form. The everyday   **40**
concept of love and wisdom is that they are something floating
around in, or breathed out by, thin air or ether. Hardly anyone
considers that in reality and in function they are substance and
form.

Even people who do see that love and wisdom are substance
and form sense them as something outside their subject, flowing from it; and they refer to what in their perceptions is outside the subject and flowing from it as substance and form even
though they sense it as floating around. They do not realize
that love and wisdom are the actual subject, and that what they
sense as floating out from the subject is only the appearance of
the inherent state of the subject.

There are many reasons why this has not come to light
before. One of them is that appearances are the first things the
human mind draws on in forming its understanding, and the
only way to dispel these appearances is through careful probing
into cause. If a cause is deeply hidden, we cannot probe into
it unless we keep our discernment in spiritual light for a pro-
tracted period of time; and we cannot hold it there for a long
time because of the earthly light that keeps pulling us back.

Still, the truth is that love and wisdom are the real and functional substance and form that make up the very subject.

Since this truth is counter to appearance, though, it may   **41**
seem unworthy of credence unless some evidence is supplied;
and since the only way to supply evidence is with the kind of
things we perceive with our physical senses, that is what I need
to draw on.

We have five external senses, called touch, taste, smell, hearing, and sight. The subject of touch is the skin that envelops us:
the very substance and form of the skin make it feel what comes
into contact with it. The sense of touch is not in the things that
come into contact with it but in the substance and form of the
skin. That is the subject, and the sense itself is simply the way

it is affected by contact. It is the same with taste. This sense is simply the way a substance and form, this time of the tongue, are affected. The tongue is the subject. It is the same with smell. We recognize that odors affect the nostrils and are in the nostrils, and that smell is the way impinging aromas affect them. It is the same with hearing. It seems as though hearing were in the place where the sound originates, but hearing is in the ear and is the way its substance and form are affected. It is only an appearance that hearing happens at a distance from the ear. This is true of sight as well. When we see objects at a distance, it seems as though our sight were where they are. However, sight is in the eye, which is the subject; and sight is the way the eye is affected, too. Distance is simply what we infer about space on the basis of intervening objects or on the basis of reduced size and consequent loss of clarity of an object whose image is being presented within the eye according to its angle of incidence. We can see from this that sight does not go out from the eye to the object, but that an image of the object enters the eye and affects its substance and form. It is the same for both sight and hearing. Hearing does not go out of the ear to seize on the sound, but the sound enters the ear and affects it. It stands to reason, then, that the affecting of substance and form that constitutes a sense is not something separate from the subject. It is simply the effecting of a change within the subject, with the subject remaining the subject throughout and thereafter. It then follows that sight, hearing, smell, taste, and touch are not things that go floating out from their organs. They are the organs themselves, in respect to their substance and form. Sensation happens when they are affected.

42 It is the same with love and wisdom, the only difference being that the substances and forms that are love and wisdom are not visible to our eyes as are the organs of our external senses. Still, no one can deny that those matters of love and wisdom that we call thoughts, perceptions, and feelings are substances and forms. They are not things that go floating out from nothing, remote from any functional and real substance and form that are their subjects. There are in fact countless substances and forms in the brain that serve as the homes of all the inner sensation that involves our discernment and volition. What has just been said about our external senses points to the conclusion that all our feelings, perceptions, and thoughts in those substances and forms are not something they breathe out; they themselves are functional and substantial subjects. They do not emit anything, but simply undergo changes in response to the things that touch and affect them. There will be more later [§§210, 273] on these things that touch and affect them.

This brings us to the point where we can see that divine love and wisdom in and of themselves are substance and form. They are essential reality and manifestation, and unless they were as much reality and manifestation as they are substance and form, they would be only theoretical constructs that in and of themselves are nothing.

43

Divine love and wisdom are substance and form in and of themselves, and are therefore wholly "itself" and unique. I have just given evidence that divine love and wisdom is substance and form, and I have also said that the divine reality and its manifestation is reality and manifestation in and of itself. We cannot say that it is reality and manifestation derived from itself, because that would involve a beginning, a beginning from something else that had within it some intrinsic reality and manifestation; while true reality and its manifestation in and of itself exists from eternity. Then too, true reality and manifestation in and of itself is uncreated; and nothing that has been created can exist except from something uncreated. What is created is also finite; and what is finite can arise only from what is infinite.

44

Anyone who can pursue and grasp inherent reality and its manifestation at all thoughtfully will necessarily come to grasp

45

the fact that it is wholly itself and unique. We call it wholly itself because it alone exists; and we call it unique because it is the source of everything else. Further, since what is wholly itself and unique is substance and form, it follows that it is the unique substance and form, and wholly itself; and since that true substance and form is divine love and wisdom, it follows that it is the unique love, wholly itself, and the unique wisdom, wholly itself. It is therefore the unique essence, wholly itself, and the unique life, wholly itself, since love and wisdom is life.

46   All this shows how sensually people are thinking when they say that nature exists in its own right, how reliant they are on their physical senses and their darkness in matters of the spirit. They are thinking from the eye and are unable to think from the understanding. Thinking from the eye closes understanding, but thinking from understanding opens the eye. They are unable to entertain any thought about inherent reality and manifestation, any thought that it is eternal, uncreated, and infinite. They can entertain no thought about life except as something volatile that vanishes into thin air, no other thought about love and wisdom, and no thought whatever about the fact that they are the source of everything in nature.

The only way to see that love and wisdom are the source of everything in nature is to look at nature on the basis of its functions in their sequence and pattern rather than on the basis of some of nature's forms, which register only on our eyes. The only source of nature's functions is life, and the only source of their sequence and pattern is love and wisdom. Forms, though, are vessels of functions. This means that if we look only at forms, no trace is visible of the life in nature, let alone of love and wisdom, and therefore of God.

47   *Divine love and wisdom cannot fail to be and to be manifested in others that it has created.* The hallmark of love is not loving ourselves but loving others and being united to them through love.

The hallmark of love is also being loved by others because this is how we are united. Truly, the essence of all love is to be found in union, in the life of love that we call joy, delight, pleasure, sweetness, blessedness, contentment, and happiness.

The essence of love is that what is ours should belong to someone else. Feeling the joy of someone else as joy within ourselves—that is loving. Feeling our joy in others, though, and not theirs in ourselves is not loving. That is loving ourselves, while the former is loving our neighbor. These two kinds of love are exact opposites. True, they both unite us; and it does not seem as though loving what belongs to us, or loving ourselves in the other, is divisive. Yet it is so divisive that to the extent that we love others in this way we later harbor hatred for them. Step by step our union with them dissolves, and the love becomes hatred of corresponding intensity.

Can anyone fail to see this who looks into the essential nature of love? What is loving ourselves alone, really, and not loving someone else who loves us in return? This is more fragmentation than union. Love's union depends on mutuality, and there is no mutuality within ourselves alone. If we think there is, it is because we are imagining some mutuality in others. **48**

We can see from this that divine love cannot fail to be and to be manifested in others whom it loves and who love it. If this is characteristic of all love, it must be supremely characteristic, infinitely characteristic, of love itself.

In regard to God, loving and being loved in return are not possible in the case of others who have some share of infinity or anything of the essence and life of intrinsic love or of Divinity. If there were within them any share of infinity or anything of the essence and life of intrinsic love—of Divinity, that is—it would not be *others* who would be loving God. He would be loving *himself.* What is infinite or divine is unique. If it were in others, it would still be itself; and it would be pure love for itself, of which there cannot be the slightest trace in God. **49**

This is absolutely opposite to the divine essence. For love to be mutual, then, it needs to be a love for others in whom there is nothing of intrinsic Divinity; and we will see below [§§55, 305] that it is a love for others who were created by Divinity.

For this to happen, though, there must be an infinite wisdom that is at one with infinite love. That is, there must be the divine love of divine wisdom and the divine wisdom of divine love discussed above (§§34–39).

50   On our grasping and knowing this mystery depends our grasping and knowing God's manifestation or creation of everything and God's maintenance or preservation of everything— that is, all the acts of God in the created universe that I will be talking about in the following pages.

51   Please, though, do not muddle your concepts with time and space. To the extent that there is time and space in your concepts as you read what follows, you will not understand it, because Divinity is not in time and space. This will become clear in the sequel to the present book, specifically on eternity, infinity, and omnipresence.

52   *Everything in the universe was created by the divine love and wisdom of the Divine-Human One.* The universe, from beginning to end and from first to last, is so full of divine love and wisdom that you could call it divine love and wisdom in an image. This is clearly evidenced by the way everything in the universe answers to something in us. Every single thing that comes to light in the created universe has such an equivalence with every single thing in us that you could call us a kind of universe as well. There is a correspondence of our affective side and its consequent thought with everything in the animal kingdom, a correspondence of our volitional side and its consequent discernment with everything in the plant kingdom, and a correspondence of our outermost life with everything in the mineral kingdom.

This kind of correspondence is not apparent to anyone in our physical world, but it is apparent to observant people in the spiritual world. We find in this latter world all the things that occur in the three kingdoms of our physical world, and they reflect the feelings and thoughts of the people who are there—the feelings that come from their volition and the thoughts that come from their discernment—as well as the outermost aspects of their life. Both their feelings and their thoughts are visible around them looking much like the things we see in the created universe, though we see them in less perfect representations.

From this it is obvious to angels that the created universe is an image depicting the Divine-Human One and that it is his love and wisdom that are presented, in image, in the universe. It is not that the created universe is the Divine-Human One: rather, it comes from him; for nothing whatever in the universe is intrinsic substance and form or intrinsic life or intrinsic love and wisdom. We are not "intrinsic persons." It all comes from God, who is the intrinsic person, the intrinsic wisdom and love, and the intrinsic form and substance. Whatever has intrinsic existence is uncreated and infinite; while what comes from it, possessing nothing within itself that has intrinsic existence, is created and finite. This latter presents an image of the One from whom it derives its existence and manifestation.

Created, finite things may be said to have reality and mani- 53 festation, substance and form, life, and even love and wisdom, but all of these are created and finite. The reason we can say they have these attributes is not that they possess any divinity but that they are in Divinity and there is Divinity in them. Anything that has been created is intrinsically without soul and dead, but it is given a soul and brought to life by the presence of Divinity in it, and by its dwelling in Divinity.

The divine nature is not different in one subject than it is in 54 another. Rather, one created subject is different from another: there are no two alike, so each vessel is different. This is why the divine nature seems to differ in appearance. I will be talking later [§275] about its presence in opposites.

55   *Everything in the created universe is a vessel for the divine love and wisdom of the Divine-Human One.* We acknowledge that everything in the universe, great and small, has been created by God. That is why the universe and absolutely everything in it is called "the work of Jehovah's hands" in the Word.

People do say that the whole world was created out of nothing, and they like to think of "nothing" as absolutely nothing. However, nothing comes from "absolutely nothing" and nothing can. This is an abiding truth. This means that the universe, being an image of God and therefore full of God, could be created by God only in God. God is reality itself, and everything that exists must come from that reality. To speak of creating something that exists from a "nothing" that does not exist is a plain contradiction of terms.

Still, what is created by God in God is not a continuation of him, since God is intrinsic reality and there is no trace of intrinsic reality in anything created. If there were any intrinsic reality in a created being, it would be a continuation of God, and any continuation of God is God.

The angelic concept involved is that anything created by God in God is like something within ourselves that we have put forth from our life, but the life is then withdrawn from it. It then agrees with our life, but still, it is not our life. In support of this, angels cite many things that happen in their heaven, where they say that they are in God and that God is in them, and yet that they have in their being no trace of God that is actually God. This may serve simply as information; more of the angels' evidence will be offered later [§116].

56   Everything created from this source is in its own nature suited to be receptive of God not by continuity but by contact. Union comes through contact, not through continuity. What is created is suitable for this contact because it has been created by God in God. Because it has been created in this way, it is an analog; and because of the union, it is like an image of God in a mirror.

This is why angels are not angels in their own right but are angels by virtue of their union with the Divine-Human One; and their union depends on their acceptance of what is divinely good and what is divinely true. What is divinely good and what is divinely true are God, and seem to emanate from him even though they are within him. Their acceptance depends on the way angels apply the laws of his design, which are divine truths, to themselves, using their freedom to think and intend according to their reason, a freedom given them by God as their own possession. This is what enables them to accept what is divinely good and divinely true in apparent autonomy; and this in turn is what makes possible the mutual element in their love, for as already noted [§48], love is not real unless it is mutual. It is the same with us here on earth.

All this enables us finally to see that everything in the created universe is a vessel for the divine love and wisdom of the Divine-Human One.

There are many things that need to be said about levels of life and levels of vessels of life before I can give an intelligible explanation of the fact that other things in the universe, things that are not like angels and people, are also vessels for the divine love and wisdom of the Divine-Human One—for example, things below us in the animal kingdom, things below them in the plant kingdom, and things below them in the mineral kingdom. Union with them depends on their functions. All useful functions have their only source in a related union with God that is, however, increasingly dissimilar depending on its level. As we come down step by step, this union takes on a nature in which there is no element of freedom involved because there is no element of reason. There is therefore no appearance of life

57

58

involved; but still these are vessels. Because they are vessels, they are also characterized by reaction. It is actually by virtue of their reactions that they are vessels.

I will discuss union with functions that are not useful after I have explained the origin of evil [§§264–270].

59   We can conclude from this that Divinity is present in absolutely everything in the created universe and that the created universe is therefore the work of Jehovah's hands, as it says in the Word. That is, it is a work of divine love and wisdom, for this is what is meant by "Jehovah's hands." Further, even though Divinity is present in all things great and small in the created universe, there is no trace of intrinsic divinity in their own being. While the created universe is not God, it is from God; and since it is from God, his image is in it like the image of a person in a mirror. We do indeed see a person there, but there is still nothing of the person in the mirror.

60   I once heard a number of people around me in the spiritual world talking and saying that they did in fact want to recognize that there was something divine in absolutely everything in the universe because they saw God's wonders there, and the deeper they looked, the more wonderful were the things they saw. However, when they heard someone say that there actually *was* something divine in absolutely everything in the created universe, they resented it. This was a sign that they claimed the belief but did not actually believe it.

They were therefore asked whether they could not see this simply in the marvelous ability in every seed of generating its growth in sequence all the way to new seeds. In every seed, then, there is an image of something infinite and eternal, an inherent effort to multiply and bear fruit without limit, to eternity.

Or they might see this in even the tiniest animals, realizing that they contain sensory organs, brains, hearts, lungs, and the like, along with arteries, veins, nerve fibers, muscles, and the activities that arise from them, to say nothing of incredible features of their basic nature that have had whole books written about them.

All these wonders come from God, though the forms that clothe them are of earthly matter. These forms give rise to plant life and, in due sequence, to human life. This is why humanity is said to have been created out of the ground, to be the dust of the earth with the breath of life breathed in (Genesis 2:7). We can see from this that the divine nature is not our possession but is joined to us.

All the things that have been created reflect the human in some **61** *respect.* There is evidence for this in every detail of the animal kingdom, in every detail of the plant kingdom, and in every detail of the mineral kingdom.

We can see ourselves reflected in every detail of the animal kingdom from the fact that all kinds of animal have in common with us members for locomotion, sensory organs, and the inner organs that support these activities. They also have their impulses and desires like our own physical ones. They have the innate knowledge proper to their desires, with an apparently spiritual element visible in some of them, more or less obvious to the eye in the beasts of the earth, the fowl of the heavens, bees, silkworms, ants, and the like. This is why merely earthly-minded people regard the living creatures of this kingdom as much like themselves, lacking only speech.

We can see ourselves reflected in every detail of the plant kingdom in the way plants grow from seeds and go through their successive stages of life. They have something like marriages with births that follow. Their vegetative "soul" is the function to which they give form. There are many other ways in which they reflect us, which some writers have described.

We can see ourselves reflected in every detail of the mineral kingdom simply in its effort to produce the forms that reflect us—all the details of the plant kingdom, as I have just noted—and to perform its proper functions in this way. The moment a seed falls into earth's lap, she nurtures it and from all around offers it resources from herself for its sprouting and emerging in a form representative of humanity. We can see this effort in solid mineral materials if we look at deep-sea corals or at flowers in mines, where they spring from minerals and metals. This effort toward becoming plant life and thereby performing a useful function is the outermost element of Divinity in created things.

62   Just as there is an energy in earth's minerals toward plant growth, there is an energy in plants toward movement. This is why there are various kinds of insect that are responsive to the fragrances they give off. We will see later [§§157–158] that this is not caused by the warmth of our world's sun but comes through it, from life, according to the recipient vessels.

63   What has been cited thus far tells us that there is some reference to the human form in everything in the created universe, but it enables us to see this fact only obscurely. In the spiritual world, though, people see this clearly. Everything in the three kingdoms exists there as well, surrounding each angel. Angels see these things around themselves and also are aware that they are pictures of their own selves. In fact, when the very heart of their understanding is opened, they recognize themselves and see their own image in their surroundings, almost like a reflection in a mirror.

64   We can be quite certain, on the basis of all this and of many other things consistent with it (which it would take too long to include) that God is a person and that the created universe is an image of him. The overall totality offers a reflection of him, just as specific aspects offer reflections of us.

65   *The useful functions of everything created tend upward, step by step, from the lowest to us, and through us to God the Creator, their source.* As already stated [§52], these "lowest things" are all

the elements of the mineral kingdom—various forms of matter, some stony substances, some saline, some oily, some mineral, some metallic, with the constant addition of a humus composed of plant and animal matter reduced to minute particles. Here lie hidden the goal and the beginning of all the functions that arise from life. The goal of all useful functions is the effort to produce [more] functions; the beginning of all functions is an active force that comes out of that effort. These are characteristics of the mineral kingdom.

The intermediate things are all the elements of the plant kingdom—grasses and herbs of all kinds, plants and shrubs of all kinds, and trees of all kinds. Their functions are in support of everything in the animal kingdom, whether flawed or flawless. They provide food, pleasure, and life. They nourish [animal] bodies with their substance, they delight them with their taste and fragrance and beauty, and they enliven their desires. This effort is inherent in them from their life.

The primary things are all the members of the animal kingdom. The lowest of these are called worms and insects, the intermediate ones birds and animals, and the highest humans; for there are lowest, intermediate, and highest things in each kingdom. The lowest are for the service of the intermediate and the intermediate for the service of the highest. So the useful functions of all created things tend upwards in a sequence from the lowest to the human, which is primary in the divine design.

There are three ascending levels in the physical world and three ascending levels in the spiritual world. All animals are life-receivers, the more perfect ones receiving the life of the three levels of the physical world, the less perfect receiving the life of two levels of that world, and the least perfect the life of one level. Only we humans are receptive of the life not only of the three levels of the physical world but also of the three levels of the spiritual world. This is why we, unlike animals, can be lifted up above the physical world. We can think analytically

66

and rationally about civil and moral issues within the material world and also about spiritual and heavenly issues that transcend the material world. We can even be lifted up into wisdom to the point that we see God. I will discuss in their proper place, though, the six levels by which the functions of all created things rise up all the way to God, their Creator.

This brief summary enables us to see that there is a ladder of all created things to that First who alone is life and that the functions of all things are the actual vessels of life, and so too, therefore, are the forms of those functions.

67   I need also to explain briefly how we climb—or rather, are lifted—from the last level to the first. We are born on the lowest level of the physical world, and are lifted to the second level by means of factual knowledge. Then as we develop our discernment through this knowledge, we are lifted to the third level and become rational. The three ascending levels in the spiritual world are within this, resting on the three physical levels, and do not become visible until we leave our earthly bodies. When we do, the first spiritual level is opened for us, then the second, and finally the third. However, this last happens only for people who become angels of the third heaven. These are the ones who see God.

Angels of the second heaven and of the lowest heaven are people in whom the second and the lowest level can be opened. The opening of each spiritual level within us depends on our acceptance of divine love and wisdom from the Lord. People who accept some of this love and wisdom reach the first or lowest spiritual level; people who accept more reach the second or intermediate spiritual level; and people who accept a great deal reach the third or highest level. However, people who do not accept any divine love and wisdom stay on the physical levels, deriving from the spiritual levels only enough to allow them to think and therefore to talk and to intend and therefore to act—but not intelligently.

There is something else that we need to know about this lift- **68** ing of the inner levels of our minds. Reaction is characteristic of everything created by God. Only life is action, while reaction is prompted by the action of life. This reaction seems to be proper to the created being because it becomes perceptible when that being is stirred; so when it happens in us, it seems to be our own. The reason is that even though we are only life-receivers, we have no sense that our life is anything but our own.

This is why we react against God as a result of our inherited evil. However, to the extent that we believe that all our life comes from God and that everything good about it comes from an act of God and everything bad about it from our own reaction, our reaction becomes a property of the action and we are then acting with God with apparent autonomy. The equilibrium of all things comes from action and immediate reaction, and everything must necessarily be in an equilibrium.

I mention these things to prevent any belief that we ourselves climb up to God on our own power. It is done by the Lord.

Divinity fills all space in the universe nonspatially. Nature has two **69** basic properties: space and time. In this physical world, we use them to form the concepts of our thinking and therefore the way we understand things. If we stay engaged with them and do not raise our minds above them, there is no way we can grasp anything spiritual and divine. We entangle such matters in concepts drawn from space and time, and to the extent that we do, the light of our discernment becomes merely earthly. When we use this light to think logically about spiritual and divine matters, it is like using the dark of night to figure out things that can be seen only in the light of day. Materialism comes from this kind of thinking.

However, when we know how to raise our minds above images of thought derived from space and time, we pass from darkness into light and taste things spiritual and divine.

Eventually we see what is inherent in them and what they entail; and then we dispel the darkness of earthly lighting with that [new] light and dismiss its illusions from the center to the sides.

People who possess discernment can think on a higher level than these properties of nature—can think realistically, that is—and see with assurance that Divinity, being omnipresent, is not within space. They can also see with assurance the other things already mentioned. If they deny divine omnipresence, though, and attribute everything to nature, then they do not want to be lifted up even though they could be.

70   These two properties of nature—the space and time just mentioned—are left behind by everyone who dies and becomes an angel. At that time, people come into a spiritual light in which the objects of their thought are truths, and the objects of their vision—even though those objects look like things in this physical world—are actually responsive to their thoughts.

The objects of their thought, which as just noted are truths, are not at all dependent on space and time. While the objects of their sight do seem to be in space and in time, angels do not use them as the basis for their thinking. The reason is that in the spiritual world intervals of space and time are not fixed the way they are in our physical world, but are changeable in response to their states of life. This means that states of life take the place of space and time in the concepts of their thinking. Issues related to states of love are in place of spatial intervals and issues related to states of wisdom are in place of temporal intervals. This is why spiritual thought and the consequent spiritual speech are so different from earthly thought and its speech that they have nothing in common. They are alike only as to the deeper aspects of their subject matter, which are entirely spiritual. I need to say more about this difference later [§§163, 295, and 306].

Since angels' thoughts do not depend at all on space and time, then, but on states of life, we can see that angels do not understand when someone says that Divinity fills space. They do not know what spatial intervals are. They understand perfectly, though, when someone says that Divinity fills everything, with no reference to any image of space.

The following example should illustrate how merely earthly people think in spatial terms about matters spiritual and divine, while spiritual people do so without reference to space. When merely earthly people think, they use images they have garnered from things they have seen. There is some shape to all of these involving length, breadth, and height, some angular or curved form bounded by these dimensions. These dimensions are clearly present in the mental images people have of visible, earthly things; and they are present as well in their mental images of things they do not see, such as civic and moral matters. They do not actually see these dimensions, but they are still present implicitly.

71

It is different for spiritual people, and especially for heaven's angels. Their thinking has nothing to do with form and shape involving spatial length, breadth, and height. It has to do with the state of the matter as it follows from a state of life. This means that in place of length they consider how good something is as a result of the quality of the life from which it stems; in place of breadth they consider how true something is because of the truth of the life from which it stems; and in place of height they consider the level of these qualities. They are thinking on the basis of correspondence, then, which is the mutual relationship between spiritual and earthly things. It is because of this correspondence that "length" in the Word means how good something is, "breadth" means how true it is, and "height" means the level of these qualities.

We can see from this that the only way heaven's angels can think about divine omnipresence is that Divinity fills everything, but nonspatially. Whatever angels think is true, because the light that illumines their understanding is divine wisdom.

72 This is a foundational thought about God, since without it, while readers may understand what I am going to say about the creation of the universe by the Divine-Human One and about God's providence, omnipotence, omnipresence, and omniscience, they still will not retain it. This is because even when merely earthly people do understand these things, they still slip back into the love of their life that is their basic volition. This dissipates their previous thought and plunges their thinking into space, where they find the light that they call "rational." They do not realize that to the extent that they deny what they have understood, they become irrational.

You may confirm the truth of this by looking at the concept of the truth that God is human. Please read carefully what I wrote above in §§11–13 and thereafter, and you will understand that it is true. Then bring your thoughts back into the earthly lighting that involves space. Will these things not seem paradoxical to you? And if you bring your thoughts all the way back, you will deny them.

This is why I said that Divinity fills all space in the universe and did not say that the Divine-Human One does. If I were to say this, merely earthly light would not accept it, though it can accept the notion that Divinity fills all space because this agrees with the standard language of theologians. They say that God is omnipresent, and hears and knows everything. There is more on this subject in §§7–10 above.

73 *Divinity is in all time, nontemporally.* Just as Divinity is in all space nonspatially, it is in all time nontemporally. Nothing proper to the physical world can be attributed to Divinity, and space and time are proper to the physical world. Space in the physical world can be measured, and so can time. Time is measured in days, weeks, months, years, and centuries; days are measured in hours; weeks and months in days; years in the four seasons; and centuries in years. The physical world gets these measurements from the apparent circuit and rotation of earth's sun.

It is different in the spiritual world. Life does seem to go on in time there in much the same way. People live with each other the way we do on earth, which cannot happen without some appearance of time. However, time there is not divided into segments the way it is in our world because their sun is always in its east. It never moves. It is actually the Lord's divine love that angels see as their sun. This means that they do not have days, weeks, months, years, or centuries, but states of life instead. It provides them with divisions that cannot be called divisions into time segments, only divisions of state. This is why angels do not know what time is, and why they think of state when time is mentioned. Further, when it is state that determines time, time is only an appearance. A pleasant state makes time seem brief, and an unpleasant one makes it seem long. We can therefore see that time in the spiritual world is simply an attribute of state.

This is why hours, days, weeks, months, and years in the Word mean states and their sequences, viewed either serially or comprehensively. When the church is described in terms of time, its morning is its initial state, its noon is its fulfillment, its evening is its decline, and its night is its end. The same holds true for the four seasons of the year: spring, summer, fall, and winter.

We can see from this that time is the equivalent of thought from feeling. This is in fact the source of our basic quality as people. **74**

There are many examples of the fact that as people move through space in the spiritual world, distances are equivalent to progress through time. Paths there are actually or correspondingly lengthened, in response to eagerness, which is a matter of thought from affection. This is also why we speak of "stretches of time." In other situations, though, such as in dreams, where thought is not coordinated with our actual feelings, time is not in evidence.

Now, since the segments of time that are proper to nature in its world are nothing but states in the spiritual world, and **75** since these states come to view sequentially because angels and spirits are finite, it stands to reason that they are not sequential in God, because God is infinite. The infinite things in God are all one, in keeping with what has been explained above in §§17–22. It then follows from this that Divinity is present in all time, nontemporally.

76   If people do not know about God beyond time, if they cannot think about such a God with some insight, then they are totally incapable of seeing eternity as anything but an eternity of time. They cannot help getting caught in crazy thoughts about God from eternity, thinking about some beginning; and a beginning has to do with nothing but time. This leads to the fantasy that God emerged from himself, and promptly degenerates into nature originating from itself. The only way out of this notion is through a spiritual or angelic concept of eternity, one that does not involve time. Once time is excluded, eternity and Divinity are one and the same; Divinity is Divinity in and of itself, and not from itself. Angels say that while they can conceive of God from eternity, there is no way they can conceive of nature from eternity, let alone nature from itself; by no means whatever can they conceive of nature that is intrinsically nature. This is because anything that has intrinsic existence is the reality itself that is the source of everything else. That intrinsic reality is the "life itself" that is the divine love that belongs to divine wisdom and the divine wisdom that belongs to divine love.

This, for angels, is eternity, which transcends time the way the Uncreated transcends the creature or the Infinite one transcends the finite. There is no ratio whatever between them.

77   *Divinity is the same in the largest and smallest things.* This follows from the two preceding sections, from Divinity being nonspatially present in all space and nontemporally present in all time. There are larger and larger and smaller and smaller spaces; and since as already noted [§74] space and time are indistinguishable, the same holds true for segments of time.

The reason Divinity is the same in all of them is that Divinity is not changeable or inconsistent like everything that involves space and time, or nature. It is constant and unchanging, so it is everywhere and always the same.

It does seem as though Divinity were not the same in one person as in another, as though it were different in a wise person than in a simple one, for example, or different in an elderly one than in a child. This is just the deceptive way things seem, though. The person may be different, but Divinity within is not. The person is a receiver, and the receiver or vessel will differ. A wise person is a more adequate receiver of divine love and wisdom than a simple one, and therefore a fuller receiver. An elderly and wise individual is more receptive than a child or youth. Still, Divinity is the same in the one as in the other.

Outward appearance also gives rise to the illusion that Divinity is different in heaven's angels than it is in people on earth because heaven's angels enjoy indescribable wisdom and we do not. However, this apparent difference is in the subjects and depends on their openness to Divinity. It is not in the Lord.

We may also use heaven and an individual angel to illustrate the fact that Divinity is the same in the largest and smallest things. Divinity in the whole heaven and Divinity in an individual angel is the same. This is why all heaven can be seen as a single angel.

The same holds true for the church and for the individual member of it. The largest entity in which Divinity is present is all of heaven and the whole church together; the smallest is an individual angel or an individual member of the church. On occasion I have seen a whole heavenly community as a single angelic person, and I have been told that this may look like an immense, gigantic individual or like a little, childlike one. This is because Divinity is the same in the largest and smallest things.

Divinity is also the same in the largest and smallest of inanimate created things. It is actually present in every benefit of the function that they serve. The reason they are not alive is that

78

79

80

they are forms of functions rather than forms of life, and the form will vary depending on the benefit of the function. I will be explaining how Divinity is present in them later, when we get to the subject of creation.

81 Take away space and absolutely rule out vacuum, and then think about divine love and wisdom as ultimate essence once space has been taken away and vacuum has been ruled out. Then think in terms of space, and you will see that Divinity is the same in the largest and the smallest instances of space. Once you remove space from essence, there is no "large" or "small." It is all the same.

82 I need to say something about vacuum at this point. I once heard some angels talking with Newton about vacuum, saying that they could not stand the notion of vacuum. This was because in their world, which is a spiritual one, within or above the space and time of our earthly world, they were still feeling, thinking, being moved, loving, intending, and breathing, and still talking and acting, which could not possibly happen in a vacuum that was "nothing" because nothing is nothing, and we cannot attribute anything to nothing.

Newton said he knew that Divinity, the One who is, fills everything, and that he was aghast at the notion of a vacuum as nothing because this was a totally destructive notion. He urged the angels who were discussing vacuum with him to beware the notion of nothing, calling it a fantasy because there is no mental activity in nothing.

ABOUT *DIVINE PROVIDENCE*

Divine Providence was published in 1764, immediately after *Divine Love and Wisdom*, and in many ways can be seen as a companion volume to it. Where *Divine Love and Wisdom* is primarily concerned with the nature of God and the way that God manifests in the universe, *Divine Providence* talks about the spiritual laws that govern God's creation. In the process, Swedenborg tackles a difficult theological question: why suffering and evil are allowed to exist in the world.

In *Divine Providence*, he lays out five spiritual laws. First, human beings have free will to choose their actions. Second, the only way that we can begin to live spiritually is to consciously reject evil. Third, we must have faith and love of our own accord; we can't be forced into a particular set of beliefs. Fourth, the Lord is guiding and teaching us constantly, even when it doesn't appear so. And finally, we are not compelled by the workings of divine providence, and we often are not aware that it is affecting us, but we should still acknowledge its action in our lives.

It can be hard to see the Lord's presence in a personal loss like the death of a family member, or a large-scale disaster. Swedenborg says that good can come out of any situation, no matter how bad things seem, but how much good can come out of a given situation partly depends on the individual's response to it. Throughout the book—indeed, throughout all of his books—Swedenborg emphasizes that just as we have no life apart from God, we also have no ability to do good except to the extent that we allow God's goodness to live inside of us. We must freely choose the right path in order for that to happen.

Structurally, *Divine Providence* is a more or less continuous work, unlike *Divine Love and Wisdom*, which is divided into five distinct sections. *Divine Providence*, in other words, is presented as a single continuous idea or train of thought on divine governance of the universe.

In the following excerpt, Swedenborg describes human beings as being born with evil inclinations, and explains that those evils need to be confronted before we can be rid of them. The Lord never stops trying to lead evil people to a better path, he says, or providing opportunities for good to come out of the evil they do.

Evils Are Permitted for a Purpose: Salvation

IF we were born loving, as we were when we were created, we would not be prone to any evil. We would not even know what evil is, because if we have not been drawn to evil and therefore are not inclined to evil, there is no way we can know what it is. If we were told that one thing or another was evil, we would not believe that it was possible. This is the state of innocence that Adam and his wife Eve were in; the nakedness that did not embarrass them portrayed that state. Familiarity with evil after the fall is meant by eating from the tree of the knowledge of good and evil.

275

The love we were created with is a love for our neighbor that makes us as generous with our neighbor as we are with ourselves, and even more so. We find ourselves full of the joy of that love when we do something good for others, very much the way parents feel toward their children.

This love is truly human. There is something spiritual within it that makes it different from the earthly love that the lower animals have. If we were born loving like this, we would not be born into the darkness of ignorance the way all of us are nowadays, but into some light of knowledge and intelligence; and before long we would actually be informed and intelligent. At first we would go on all fours like animals, but would have an inborn urge to walk on our feet, because even though we were on all fours we would not be looking down toward the ground, but forward toward heaven; and we would be straightening up so that we could look upward.

However, when our love for our neighbor turned into love for ourselves and this love grew stronger, then our human love turned into an animal love and we became animals instead of humans. The only difference was that we could think about what our bodies were sensing and tell one thing from another rationally and could be taught and become civic and moral people and eventually spiritual people. That is, as already noted

276

[§275], we do have a spiritual nature that distinguishes us from the lower animals. That nature enables us to learn what is evil and good on the civic level, what is evil and good on the moral level, and even, if we are willing, what is evil and good on the spiritual level.

Once love for our neighbor had changed into love for ourselves, we could no longer be born into the light of knowledge and intelligence but only into the darkness of ignorance. This is because we were born into that lowest level of life that we call sensory and bodily. We are led from there into the deeper functions of our earthly mind by being taught, always with spirituality close at hand. We shall see later why we are born into that lowest level of life that we call sensory and bodily and therefore into the darkness of ignorance.

[2] Everyone can see that love for our neighbor and love for ourselves are opposing loves. Love for our neighbor wants to do good to everyone, while love for ourselves wants everyone to do good to us alone. Love for our neighbor wants to serve everyone, and love for ourselves wants everyone to be our servants. Love for our neighbor sees all people as our family and friends, while love for ourselves sees all people as our slaves, and if people are not subservient, it sees them as our enemies. In short, it focuses on ourselves alone and sees others as scarcely human. At heart it values them no more than our horses and dogs, and since it regards them as basically worthless, it thinks nothing of doing them harm. This leads to hatred and vengeance, adultery and promiscuity, theft and fraud, deceit and slander, brutality and cruelty, and other evils like that. These are the evils to which we are prone from birth.

To explain that they are permitted for the purpose of salvation, I need to proceed in the following sequence.

1. We are all involved in evil and need to be led away from it in order to be reformed.

2. Evils cannot be set aside unless they come to light.

3. To the extent that our evils are set aside, they are forgiven.

4. So evil is permitted for the purpose of salvation.

1. *We are all involved in evil and need to be led away from it in order to be reformed.* It is well known in the church that we all have an inherited evil nature and that this is the source of our obsession with many evils. This is also why we can do nothing good on our own. The only kind of good that evil can do is good with evil within it. The inner evil is the fact that we are doing it for selfish reasons, and solely for the sake of appearances.

277a

We know that we get this inherited evil from our parents. Some do say that it comes from Adam and his wife, but this is wrong. We all get it by birth from our parents, who got it from their parents, who got it from theirs. So it is handed down from one to another, growing greater and stronger, piling up, and being inflicted on the offspring. That is why there is nothing sound within us, why everything in us is so evil. Does anyone feel that there is anything wrong with loving oneself more than others? If not, then who knows what evil is, since this is the head of all evils?

[2] We can see from much that is common knowledge in our world that our heredity comes from our parents, grandparents, and great-grandparents. For example, we can tell what household and larger family and even nation people belong to simply from their faces; the face bears the stamp of the spirit, and the spirit is determined by our desires of love. Sometimes the face of an ancestor crops up in a grandchild or great-grandchild. I can tell simply from their faces whether people are Jewish or not, and I can tell what family group others belong to. I have no doubt that others can do the same.

If our desires of love are derived and passed down from our parents in this way, then it follows that their evils are as well, since these are matters of desire.

I need now to state where this similarity comes from. [3] For all of us, the soul comes from the father and simply puts on a body in the mother. The fact that the soul comes from the father follows not only from what has just been said but also from a number of other indications. One of these is the fact that the baby of a black or Moorish man by a white or European woman will be born black, and the reverse. In particular, the soul dwells in the semen, for this is what brings about impregnation, and this is what the mother clothes with a body. The semen is the elemental form of the father's characteristic love, the form of his dominant love and its immediate derivatives, the deepest desires of that love.

[4] In all of us, these desires are veiled by the decencies of moral life and the virtues that are partly matters of our civic life and partly matters of our spiritual life. These make up the outward form of life even for evil people. We are all born with this outer form of life. That is why little children are so lovable; but as they get older or grow up, they shift from this outer form toward their deeper natures and ultimately to the dominant love of their fathers. If the father was evil, and if this nature is not somehow softened and deflected by teachers, then the child's love becomes just like that of the father.

Still, evil is not uprooted, only set aside, as we shall see below [§279]. We can tell, then, that we are all immersed in evil.

277b

No explanation is necessary to see that we need to be led away from our evils in order to be reformed, since if we are given to evil in this world, we will be given to evil after we leave this world. This means that if our evil is not set aside in this world, it cannot be set aside afterwards. The tree lies where it falls; and so too our life retains its basic quality when we die. We are all judged according to our deeds. It is not that these deeds are tallied up but that we return to them and behave the same. Death is a continuation of life, with the difference that then we cannot be reformed.

All our reformation is thorough—that is, it includes both first things and last things. The last things are reformed in this world in harmony with the first ones. They cannot be reformed afterwards, because the outermost things of our lives that we take with us after death become dormant and simply cooperate or act in unison with the inner ones.

2. *Evils cannot be set aside unless they come to light.* This does **278a** not mean that we have to act out our evils in order to bring them to light but that we need to look carefully not only at our actions but also at our thoughts, at what we would do if it were not for our fear of the laws and of ill repute. We need to look especially at which evils we see as permissible in our spirit and do not regard as sins, for eventually we do them.

It is for this self-examination that we have been given discernment, a discernment separate from our volition, so that we can know, discern, and recognize what is good and what is evil. It is also so that we can see what the real nature of our volition is—that is, what we love and what we desire. It is to enable us to see this that our discernment has been given both higher and lower thought processes, both more inward and more outward thought processes. It is so that we can use the higher or more inward thoughts to see what our volition is up to in our lower or outer thoughts. We see this the way we see our face in a mirror; and when we see and recognize what a sin is, then if we want to and ask the Lord for help, we can stop intending it, abstain from it, and later act against it. If we cannot go through this process easily, we can still make it happen by trying to go through it so that finally we reject that evil and detest it. Then for the first time we actually sense and feel that evil is evil and good is good.

This is what it means to examine ourselves, to see and acknowledge our evils, and to confess them and then refrain from them. However, there are so few who know that this is the essence of the Christian religion (because the only people who do so are ones who have charity and faith and are led by the Lord and do what is good in his strength) that I need to say something about the people who do not do this and still think that they are religious. They are (a) people who confess that they are guilty of all sins but do not look for any single sin in themselves; (b) people who for religious reasons do not bother to look; (c) people who for worldly reasons do not think about sins and therefore do not know what they are; (d) people who cherish their sins and therefore cannot know what they are. (e) In all these cases, the sins do not come to light and therefore cannot be set aside. (f) Finally, I need to expose a previously unrecognized reason why evils could not be set aside apart from this examination, this bringing to light, this recognition, this confession, and this resistance.

278b   These items need to be looked at one at a time, though, because they are the basic elements of the Christian religion on our part.

(a) *They are people who confess that they are guilty of all sins but do not look for any single sin in themselves.* They say, "I am a sinner! I was born in sins; there is no soundness in me from head to toe! I am nothing but evil! Gracious God, look on me with favor, forgive me, purify me, save me, make me walk in purity, in the way of the righteous," and the like. Yet they do not look into themselves and therefore do not identify any particular evil; and no one who does not identify an evil can abstain from it, let alone fight against it. They think that they are clean and washed after these confessions when in fact they are unclean and unwashed from their heads to the soles of their feet. This blanket confession is nothing but a lullaby that leads finally to blindness. It is like some grand generalization with no details, which is actually nothing.

[2] (b) *They are people who for religious reasons do not bother to look.* These are primarily people who separate charity from faith. They say to themselves, "Why should I ask whether something is evil or good? Why should I ask about evil when

it does not damn me? Why should I ask about goodness when it does not save me? It is my faith alone, the faith that I have thought about and proclaimed with trust and confidence, that justifies me and purifies me from all sin; and once I have been justified I am whole in God's sight. Of course I am immersed in evil, but God wipes this away the moment it happens so that it is no longer present," and more of the same sort.

Can anyone whose eyes are open fail to see that these are meaningless words, words that have no content because they have no worth in them? Anyone can think and talk like this, and can do so "with trust and confidence," when thinking about hell and eternal damnation. Do people like this want to know anything further, whether anything is really true or good? As to truth, they say, "What is truth other than whatever reinforces my faith?" As to goodness, they say, "What is good other than what I have because of my faith? In order to have it within me, though, I do not need to do it as though I were doing it myself, because that would be for credit, and good done for credit is not truly good." So they skip over the whole subject so completely that they do not know what evil is. What will they look for and see in themselves, then? What is their state but a fire of obsessions with evil that is confined within them, devouring the inner substance of their minds and destroying everything right up to the door? All they are doing is guarding the door so that no one can see the fire; but the door is opened after death, and then everyone can see.

[3] (c) *They are people who for worldly reasons do not think* ~~LGBTQ~~ *about sins and therefore do not know what they are.* These are people who love the world above all and will not give a hearing to any truth that might deflect them from the false principles of their religion. They say to themselves, "What do I care about this? This is not the way I think." So they reject it as soon as they hear it; or if it does get through at all, they suppress it. They do much the same thing when they hear sermons, retaining only a few words and no substance.

Since this is how they treat truths, they do not know what good is, since the two act in unison; and there is no way to identify evil on the basis of any good that is not based on truth. All they can do is call evil "good" by rationalizing it with their distortions.

These are the people meant by the seeds that fell among thorns. The Lord said of them, "Other seeds fell among thorns, and the thorns grew up and choked them. These are people who hear the Word, but the cares of this world and the deceptiveness of riches choke the Word so that it becomes unfruitful" (Matthew 13:7, 22; Mark 4:7, 14 *[4:7, 18, 19]*; Luke 8:7, 14).

[4] (d) *They are people who cherish their sins and therefore cannot know what they are.* These are people who believe in God and worship him with the usual rituals and yet rationalize for themselves that some evil that is a sin is really not a sin. They camouflage it with disguises and cosmetics that conceal how grotesque it is; and once they have accomplished this they cherish it and make it their friend and constant companion.

I have said that these people believe in God because only people who believe in God are capable of regarding evil as sin: all sin is sin against God.

But some examples may make this clear. When people who are bent on profit make different kinds of cheating permissible by inventing rationalizations, they are saying that an evil is not a sin. People who rationalize taking vengeance on their enemies are doing the same thing, as are people who rationalize plundering people who are not their enemies in times of war.

[5] (e) *In these cases, the sins do not come to light and therefore cannot be set aside.* Any evil that is not brought to light feeds on itself. It is like fire in wood buried in ashes. It is like poison in a wound that has not been lanced; for any evil that is shut away keeps growing and growing until everything has been brought to an end. So to prevent any evil from being shut away, we are allowed to think in favor of God and against God, in favor of

the holy practices of the church or against them, without being punished for it in this world.

The Lord speaks of this in Isaiah:

> From the soles of the feet to the head there is no soundness; there is wound and scar and fresh beating, not squeezed out or bound up or anointed with oil. Wash yourselves, purify yourselves. Take away the evil of your deeds from before my eyes. Stop doing evil, learn to do good. Then if your sins have been like scarlet, they will be white as snow; if they have been ruddy as a purple robe, they will be like wool. If you refuse and rebel, you will be devoured by the sword. (Isaiah 1:6, 16, 18, 10 [*1:6, 16, 17, 18, 20*])

"Being devoured by the sword" means being destroyed by our malicious distortions.

[6] (f) *There is a previously unrecognized reason why evils could not be set aside apart from this examination, this bringing to light, this recognition, this confession, and this resistance.* I have already mentioned [§§62, 65, 217] that heaven overall is arranged in communities according to [people's desires for what is good, and that hell overall is arranged in communities according to] desires for what is evil that are opposite to those desires for what is good. As to our spirits, each of us is in some community—in a heavenly one when our good desires are in control, and in a hellish one when our evil desires are in control. We are unaware of this while we are living in this world, but in spirit that is where we are. We could not go on living otherwise, and that is how the Lord is guiding us.

If we are in a hellish community, the only way the Lord can lead us out is under the laws of his divine providence. One of them says that we must see that we are there, must want to get out, and must ourselves make an effort with what seems to be our own strength. We can do this while we are in this world but not after death. Then we stay forever in the community we joined in this world. This is why we need to examine ourselves, see and acknowledge our sins, repent, and remain constant for the rest of our lives.

I could support this with enough experience to warrant complete belief, but this is not the place to bring in proofs from experience.

279   3. *To the extent that our evils are set aside, they are forgiven.* One currently popular misconception is that our evils are taken from us and discarded when they are forgiven, and that the state of our life can be changed instantly, even totally reversed, so that we become good instead of evil. This would be leading us out of hell and transporting us instantly into heaven, all by some direct mercy of the Lord.

However, people who hold this kind of belief or thought have no idea whatever of what evil and good really are or what the state of our own life is. They are utterly unaware that the feelings of our volition are simply shifts and changes of state of the purely organic substances of our minds, that the thoughts of our discernment are simply shifts and changes of their forms, and that memory is the ongoing effect of these changes. This enables us to see clearly that evil can be taken away only gradually and that the forgiveness of evil is not the same as its removal. This, though, is presenting the ideas in condensed form. If they are not explained at greater length, they can be recognized but not grasped; and if they are not grasped, that is like a wheel that we turn by hand. I need to explain these propositions, then, one at a time in the order just given.

[2] (a) *One currently popular misconception is that our evils are taken from us and discarded when they are forgiven.* I have been taught in heaven that no evil that we are born with or that we ourselves adopt by our behavior is taken completely away from us. Evils are set aside so that they are no longer visible. Like so many other people in this world, I used to believe that when

our evils are forgiven they are thrown away just as dirt is rinsed and washed away from our faces by water. That is not what it is like with our evils or sins, though. They are all still there, and when they are forgiven after we have repented, they are moved from the center to the sides. Whatever is in the middle is right in front of our eyes and seems to be out in broad daylight. What is off to the sides seems to be in the shade, or at times, even in the dark of night. Since our evils are not taken completely away, then, but are only displaced or put off to the side, and since we can be transported from the center to the boundaries, it can happen that we once again get involved in evils we thought we had left behind. It is part of our own nature that we can move from one desire to another, and sometimes into an opposite one. This means that we can move from one center to another. A desire determines our center as long as we are caught up in it. Then we are absorbed in its pleasure and its light.

[3] There are some people who are raised into heaven by the Lord after death because they have lived good lives but who bring with them a belief that they are free and clean from sins and therefore wholly without guilt. At first they are given white robes that reflect this belief, since white robes portray a state of having been purified from evils. Later, though, they begin to think the way they did in the world, to think that they have been washed clean from all evil; so they boast that they are no longer sinners like everyone else. It is almost impossible to separate this from a kind of mental "high" that includes a measure of looking down on others. So at this point, in order to free them from the faith they imagine they have, they are sent down from heaven and back into the evils they had fallen prey to in the world. This shows them that they have inherited evils that they had not known about before. This brings them to admit that their evils have not been taken away from them but only set aside, and that they themselves are still unclean, and in fact nothing but evil; that it is the Lord who is protecting them

from their evils and keeping them focused on those good qualities; and that all this seems to be their own doing. Once this has happened, the Lord brings them back up into heaven.

[4] (b) *A second popular misconception is that the state of our life can be changed instantly, so that we become good instead of evil. This would be leading us out of hell and transporting us instantly into heaven, all by some direct mercy of the Lord.* This is the misconception of people who separate charity from faith and attribute salvation to faith alone. That is, they think that the mere thought and utterance of a statement of that faith, performed with trust and confidence, will justify and save them. Many of them also think that this can happen instantaneously, either before the hour of death or as it approaches. They cannot avoid believing that the state of our life can be changed in an instant and that we can be saved by direct mercy. We shall see in the last section of this book, though, that the Lord's mercy does not operate in this direct way, that we cannot become good instead of evil in an instant and be led out of hell and transported into heaven except by the ongoing efforts of divine providence from our infancy to the end of our lives.

At this point we may rest the case simply on the fact that all the laws of divine providence are aimed at our reformation, and therefore at our salvation, which means inverting the hellish state into which we are born into its opposite, a heavenly state. This can be done only gradually as we move away from evil and its pleasure and move into what is good and its pleasure.

[5] (c) *People who hold this kind of belief have no idea whatever of what evil and good really are.* They do not really know that evil is the pleasure we find in the urge to act and think in violation of the divine pattern, and that goodness is the pleasure we feel when we act and think in harmony with the divine pattern. They do not realize that there are thousands of individual impulses that go to make up any particular evil, and that there are thousands of individual impulses that go to make up any

particular good tendency. These thousands of impulses are so precisely structured and so intimately interconnected within us that no single one of them can be changed without changing all the rest at the same time.

If people are unaware of this, they can entertain the belief or the thought that an evil that seems to be all by itself can be set aside easily and that something good that also seems to be all by itself can be brought in to replace it. Since they do not know what good and evil are, they cannot help thinking that there are such things as instantaneous salvation and direct mercy. The last section of this book will show that this is not possible.

[6] (d) *People who believe in instantaneous salvation and direct mercy are utterly unaware that the feelings of our volition are simply changes of state of the purely organic substances of our minds, that the thoughts of our discernment are simply changes and shifts of their forms, and that memory is the ongoing effect of those changes and shifts.* Once someone mentions it, everyone will realize that feelings and thoughts can happen only with substances and their forms as subjects. Since they happen in our brains, which are full of substances and forms, we say that these forms are purely organic. If we think rationally, we cannot help laughing at the wild idea that feelings and thoughts do not happen in substantial subjects but are breezes affected by warmth and light, like illusions seen in the air or the ether. In fact, thought can no more happen apart from its substantial form than sight can happen apart from its substantial form, the eye, or hearing from its ear, or taste from its tongue. Look at the brain and you will see countless substances and fibers, and nothing there that is not structured. What need is there of more proof than this visual one?

[7] Just what is this "feeling," though, and just what is this "thought"? We can figure this out by looking at the body overall and in detail. There are many internal organs there, all set

in their own places, all carrying out their functions by shifts and changes in their states and forms. We know that they are occupied with their tasks. The stomach has its task, the intestines have theirs, the kidneys have theirs, the liver, pancreas, and spleen have theirs, and the heart and lungs have theirs. All of them are inwardly activated solely for their tasks, and this inward activation happens by shifts and changes of their states and forms.

This leads us to the conclusion that the workings of the purely organic substances of the mind are no different, except that the workings of the organic substances of the body are physical and the workings of the organic substances of the mind are spiritual. The two act as a unity by means of responsiveness [to each other].

[8] There is no way to offer visual evidence of the nature of the shifts and changes of state and form of the organic substances of the mind, the shifts and changes that constitute our feelings and thoughts. We can see them in a kind of mirror, though, if we look at the shifts and changes of state of our lungs in the acts of speech and singing. There is a parallelism, since the sounds of speech and song as well as the differentiations of sound that make the words of speech and the melodies of song are produced by the lungs. The sound itself answers to our feeling and the language to our thought. That is what causes them; and it is accomplished by shifts and changes of the state and form of the organic substances in our lungs, from the lungs into the trachea or windpipe in the larynx and glottis, then in the tongue, and finally in our lips.

The first shifts and changes of state and form of sound happen in the lungs, the second in the trachea and larynx, the third in the glottis by opening its aperture in various ways, the fourth by the tongue by touching the palate and teeth in various places, and the fifth by our lips through taking different shapes. We can see from this that both the sound and its modifications that constitute speech and song are produced solely by sequential and constant shifts and changes in the states of these organic forms.

Since the only source of sound and speech is our mental feelings and thoughts—that is where they come from, and there is no other source—we can see that the feelings of our volition are shifts and changes of state of the purely organic substances of our minds, and that the thoughts of our discernment are shifts and changes of the forms of those substances, just the way it happens in our lungs.

[9] Further, since our feelings and thoughts are simply changes of state of the forms of our minds, it follows that our memory is nothing but their ongoing effect. It is characteristic of all the shifts and changes of state in organic substances that once they have been learned they do not disappear. So the lungs are trained to produce various sounds in the trachea and to modify them in the glottis, articulate them with the tongue, and shape them with the mouth; and once these organs have been trained to do these things, the actions are ingrained and can be repeated.

Material presented in *Divine Love and Wisdom* 119–204 *[199–204]* shows that the shifts and changes in the organic substances of the mind are infinitely more perfect than those in the body. There it is explained that all processes of perfection increase and rise by and according to levels. There is more on the subject in §319 below.

Another popular misconception is that when sins have been forgiven they are also set aside. This misconception is characteristic of people who believe that their sins are forgiven through the sacrament of the Holy Supper even though they have not set them aside by repenting from them. It is characteristic also of people who believe they are saved by faith alone or by papal dispensations. They all believe in direct mercy and instant salvation.

280

When the sequence is reversed, though, it is true: when sins have been set aside, they are forgiven. Repentance must precede forgiveness, and apart from repentance there is no forgiveness. That is why the Lord told his disciples to preach repentance for the forgiveness of sins (Luke 24:27) and why John preached the baptism of repentance for the forgiveness of sins (Luke 3:3).

The Lord forgives everyone's sins. He does not accuse us or keep score. However, he cannot take our sins away except by the laws of his divine providence; for when Peter asked him how many times he should forgive someone who had sinned against him, whether seven was enough, he said that Peter should forgive not seven times but seventy times seven times (Matthew 18:21, 22). What does this tell us about the Lord, who is mercy itself?

281   4. *So the permission of evil is for the purpose of salvation.* We know that we are quite free in our thinking and intentions, but are not free to say and do whatever we think and intend. We can be atheists in our thoughts, denying the existence of God and blaspheming the holy contents of the church's Word; we can even want to destroy them utterly by what we say and do; but civil and moral and ecclesiastical laws hold us back. So we indulge in these ungodly and criminal practices in our thoughts and our wishes and even in our intentions, but still not in our actions. People who are not atheists are still quite free to harbor any number of evil thoughts, thoughts about cheating, lust, vengeance, and other senseless things, and even act them out at times.

Is it credible that if we did not have this complete freedom we would not only be beyond salvation but would completely perish? [2] Listen to the reason. We are all immersed in many kinds of evil from birth. They are in our volition, and we love whatever is in our volition. That is, we love all the intentions that come from within; and we intend whatever we love. This love of our volition flows into our discernment and makes itself felt there as pleasure. It moves from there into our thoughts and into our conscious intentions. So if we were not allowed to think the way the love of our volition wants us to, the love that is within us by heredity, that love would stay closed in and never come out where we could see it. Any such hidden love for evil is like an enemy plotting against us, like pus in a sore, like a toxin in the blood, and like an infection in the chest. If they are kept hidden, they hasten us to our end.

On the other hand, when we are allowed to think about the evils of our life's love even to the point of wanting to act them out, they are healed by spiritual means the way a life-threatening illness is cured by physical means.

[3] I need to explain what we would be like if we were not allowed to think in keeping with the pleasures of our life's love. We would no longer be human. We would have lost the two abilities called freedom and rationality that are the essence of our humanity. The pleasures of those loves would take control of the inner reaches of our minds so completely that the door would be opened wide. We then would not be able to avoid talking and acting in similar fashion, displaying our madness not only to ourselves but to the whole world. Eventually we would not know enough to cover our private parts. It is to keep this from happening that we are allowed to think about and to intend the evils we have inherited, but not to utter and do them. In the meanwhile, we learn civic, moral, and spiritual principles that also work their way into our thinking and displace these insane principles. The Lord heals us by this means, though only to the extent that we know how to guard the door, and not unless we believe in God and ask for his help to resist our evils. Then to the extent that we resist them, he does not let them into our intentions, and eventually not into our thoughts.

[4] We do therefore have a freedom to think as we wish, in order that our life's love may come out of hiding into the light

of our discernment; otherwise we would have no knowledge of our evil and could not abstain from it. It would then follow that the evil would gain strength within us to the point that there was no space for recovery within us and, since the evil of parents is passed on to their progeny, hardly any space for recovery in any children we might beget. The Lord makes sure, however, that this does not happen.

282   The Lord could heal everyone's discernment and make us incapable of thinking evil, capable only of thinking good. He could do this by various fears, by miracles, by messages from the dead, and by visions and dreams. However, healing only our discernment is healing us only superficially. Our discernment and its thought processes are the outside of our life, while our volition and its desire is the inside of our life. This means that healing only our discernment would be curing nothing but the symptoms. The deeper malignance, closed in and with no way out, would first devour what was nearest to it and then what was farther away until finally everything was dying. It is our volition itself that needs to be healed, not by our discernment flowing into it but by being taught and encouraged by our discernment.

If our discernment alone were healed we would be like an embalmed body or a corpse bathed in fragrant perfumes and roses. Before long the perfumes would draw forth from the body such a stench that none of us could put our nose anywhere near it. That is what it would be like for heavenly truths in our discernment if the evil love of our volition were repressed.

283   As already noted [§281], the purpose of letting us think about our evils even to the point of intending them is so that they can be displaced by civic, moral, and spiritual principles. This happens when we consider that something is in opposition to what is lawful and fair, what is sincere and decent, what is good and true, and therefore what is peaceful, happy, and blessed in our lives. The Lord heals the love of our volition by these three sets of principles as means, using our fears at first but our loves later.

Still, our evils are not taken away from us and discarded, they are only displaced and relegated to the sides. Once they are there and goodness is in the center, the evils are out of sight, since whatever is in the center is right in front of our eyes, visible and perceptible. We need to realize, though, that even though goodness may be in the center, this still does not mean we are devoted to it unless the evils that are off to the sides are tending downward and outward. If they are turned upward and inward they have not been displaced, because they are still trying to get back to the center. They are tending and turned downward and outward when we are abstaining from our evils as sins, and even more so when we find them distasteful. Then we are condemning them and consigning them to hell, which turns them in that direction.

Our discernment can accept what is good and what is evil, what is true and what is false, but our essential volition cannot. This must be focused on what is evil or what is good and not on both, because our volition is our essential self. It is where our life's love is. In our discernment, what is good and what is evil are kept apart like an inside and an outside, so we can be inwardly focused on evil and outwardly on good. However, when we are being reformed, the goodness and the evil are brought face to face. Then a clash occurs, a battle that is called a temptation if it is severe. If it is not severe, though, it happens like the fermentation of wine or beer. If the goodness wins, then the evil and its distortion are moved to the sides much as dregs settle to the bottom of the bottles. The goodness comes to be like a wine that has become vintage wine after fermentation, or beer that has become clear. If the evil wins, though, then the goodness and its truth are moved to the sides and become murky and dark like half-fermented wine or half-fermented beer.

The comparison with fermentation is based on the fact that in the Word, yeast means the falsity that comes from evil, as it does in Hosea 7:4; Luke 12:1; and elsewhere.

284

Divine Providence Is for Evil People and Good People Alike

285 WITHIN each of us, good and evil alike, there are two abilities. One of them makes up our discernment and the other our volition. The ability that makes up our discernment is our ability to differentiate and think, so we call it "rationality." The ability that makes up our volition is our ability freely to do these things—think, and therefore speak and act as well—as long as they do not violate our reason or rationality. Acting freely is doing whatever we want to whenever we want to do it.

These two abilities are constant. They are unbroken from beginnings to endings overall and in detail in everything we think and do. They are not intrinsic to us but are in us from the Lord. It therefore follows that when the Lord's presence is in these abilities it is a presence in details as well, even in the very smallest details of our discernment and thought, of our volition and desire, and therefore of our speech and action. Take these abilities out of any least detail and you could not think it or speak of it like a human being.

[2] I have already offered abundant evidence that it is by virtue of these two abilities that we are human, that we can think and talk, that we can sense what is good and discern what is true not only in civic and moral issues but in spiritual ones as well, and that we can be reformed and regenerated—in short, it is by virtue of these two abilities that we can be united to the Lord and therefore live forever. I have also explained that not only good people but evil ones as well have these two abilities. Since these abilities are given us by the Lord and we are not to claim them as our own, we are not to claim anything divine as our own either, though something divine can be attached to us so that it seems to be ours. Since this divine gift to us is in the smallest details of our nature, it follows that the Lord is in control of these smallest details in evil people as well as in good people; and the Lord's control is what we call divine providence.

Now since it is a law of divine providence that we can act freely and rationally (that is, availing ourselves of the two abilities called freedom and rationality), and since it is also a law of divine providence that whatever we do seems to be done by us and therefore to be ours, and since we can infer from these laws that evils have to be permitted, it follows that we can misuse these abilities. We can freely and rationally justify anything we please. We can take anything we please and make it rational, whether it is inherently rational or not. This leads some people to say, "What is truth? Can't I make anything true that I choose? Isn't that what the world does?" People do this by rationalizing if they can.

Take the most false proposition you can and tell clever individuals to justify it, and they will. For example, tell them to prove that we are nothing but animals, or that the soul is like a spider in its web, controlling the body by its filaments, or that religion is nothing but a restraint, and they will prove whichever you choose so that it actually seems true. Nothing could be easier, because they cannot identify an appearance or a false proposition that is taken in blind faith to be true. [2] This is why people cannot see the truth that divine providence is at work in the smallest details of everyone's discernment and volition, the smallest details of everyone's thoughts and impulses (which amounts to the same thing), in evil and good people alike.

The main thing that misleads them is that this seems to make the Lord responsible for evil when in fact no trace whatever of evil comes from the Lord. It all comes from us through our accepting as fact the appearance that we think, intend, talk, and act autonomously, as we shall shortly see. To make it clear, I need to proceed in the following sequence.

   1. Divine providence is at work in the smallest details everywhere, not only with the good but with the evil as well; but it is not in their evils.

2. Evil people are constantly leading themselves into evils, and the Lord is constantly leading them away from evils.

3. The Lord cannot fully lead evil people away from their evils and guide them in what is good as long as they believe that their own intelligence is everything and that divine providence is nothing.

4. The Lord controls the hells by means of opposites. As for evil people who are still in this world, he controls them in hell as to their deeper natures, but not as to their more outward natures.

287 1. *Divine providence is at work in the smallest details everywhere, not only with the good but with the evil as well, but it is not in their evils.* I have already explained that divine providence is in the smallest details of our thoughts and desires, which means that we cannot think or intend anything on our own. Everything we think and intend, and therefore everything we say and do, is the result of an inflow. If it is good, something is flowing in from heaven; if it is bad, something is flowing in from hell. In other words, if it is good it is flowing in from the Lord, and if it is bad it is flowing in from our own sense of self-importance.

I do realize, though, that all this is hard to grasp because it differentiates between what flows in from heaven or from the Lord and what flows in from hell or from our own sense of self-importance, and at the same time it says that divine providence is at work in the smallest details of our thoughts and desires to the point that we cannot think or intend anything on our own. Since I am saying that we can think and intend from hell, or from our sense of self-importance, there does seem to be a contradiction. However, there is none, as we shall see below [§294], once a few points are prefaced that will shed some light on the matter.

All of heaven's angels admit that no one can originate a **288** thought, that all thinking comes from the Lord, while all the spirits of hell claim that thought cannot originate in anyone but themselves. Actually, these spirits have been shown any number of times that none of them are originating their own thoughts, that they cannot, and that it is all flowing in, but to no effect— they are unwilling to accept it.

However, experience will teach first of all that even for spirits in hell, every bit of thought and feeling is flowing in from heaven. The problem is that the inflowing good is being turned into evil in hell, and the truth is being turned into falsity. Everything becomes its opposite. This is how it was shown to me. Something true from the Word was let down from heaven and taken hold of by people in the upper levels of hell. They sent it on down to the lower hells all the way to the lowest. Step by step along this path the truth turned into falsity, finally into a falsity absolutely opposite to the truth. The people who were changing it thought they themselves were thinking up this falsity. That was all they knew, and yet the falsity was that truth flowing down from heaven on its way to the lowest hell, that truth falsified and distorted. Three or four times I have heard of this happening. The same thing happens to what is good. When this flows down from heaven it is turned step by step into the evil that is opposite to it.

This has enabled me to see that when what is true and good emanates from the Lord and is taken up by people who are devoted to what is false and evil, it is changed. It takes on another form so completely that its original form can no longer be seen. That is just what is going on with all who are evil, because in spirit they are in hell.

I have often been shown that no one in hell originates a **289** thought. They all depend on others around them, who again are not originating their thoughts but depend on still others. Thoughts and desires move from community to community in a pattern without people realizing that they are not thinking autonomously.

Some individuals who believed that they thought and intended autonomously were assigned to a particular community. They were cut off from communication with those neighbors to whom their thoughts usually spread and were held where they were. Then they were told to think differently from the way the spirits of that community were thinking, to force themselves to think along contradictory lines; but they admitted that it was impossible for them. [2] This has happened to any number of people, including Leibniz. Even he was convinced that no one thinks independently, only from others, who in turn are not thinking independently. We are all thinking as a result of an inflow from heaven, and heaven depends on an inflow from the Lord.

Some people who have thought deeply about this have declared that it is so stunning that hardly anyone could be compelled to believe it, it is so contrary to the way things seem. However, they could not deny it, because it had been fully demonstrated. Still, in their wonderment they claimed that it meant that they were not to blame for thinking evil and that it seemed as though evil came from the Lord. They did not understand how the Lord alone could work things out so that we all think differently, either. These three issues need to be unfolded next.

290   I need to add the following to the experiences already cited. When the Lord first allowed me to talk with spirits and angels, this secret was immediately made known to me. I was told from heaven that, like others, I believed that I was thinking and intending on my own, when in fact nothing was coming from me. If it was good, it was coming from the Lord, and if it was bad, it was coming from hell. I was shown this at first hand by having various thoughts and desires imposed on me so that eventually I could feel and sense it. So later, as soon as anything

evil impinged on my volition or anything false on my thoughts, I asked where it was coming from and was shown. I was also allowed to talk with the people it came from, to rebut them, and to make them go away. This meant that they took their evil and falsity back and kept it to themselves, no longer instilling anything of the sort into my thoughts. This has happened thousands of times; and I have been in this state now for a number of years and still am to the present time. Nevertheless, I seem to myself to be thinking and intending on my own just like everyone else, with no difference at all. It seems like this to everyone because of the Lord's divine providence, as explained at the appropriate point above.

Some newly arrived spirits were bewildered by my state. It looked to them exactly as though I was not thinking or intending anything on my own, and that I was therefore like something empty. However, I explained the mystery to them. I added that I was thinking more deeply and sensing what was flowing into my more outward thinking, seeing whether it was coming from heaven or from hell, rejecting the one and accepting the other. It still seemed to me as though I was thinking and intending on my own, just like them.

It is not entirely unknown in this world that everything good comes from heaven and everything evil from hell. Everyone in the church knows it. Is there anyone who has been ordained into the ministry who does not teach that everything good comes from God and that we cannot gain anything that is not given us from heaven? Ministers teach also that the devil puts evils into our thoughts and leads us astray by prompting us to do them. So the ministers who believe they are preaching with holy zeal pray that the Holy Spirit will teach them and guide their thoughts and their speech. Some of them say they have a sense of being led. When their sermons are praised they answer devoutly that they have not been speaking from their own resources but from God. 291

So too, when they see people speaking and behaving well they describe them as led to it by God, and conversely when they see people speaking and behaving badly, they describe them as led to it by the devil. Everyone knows that this is how people talk in the church, but who really believes it?

292 Everything we think and intend and therefore everything we say and do flows in from the only fount of life; and yet that one fount of life, the Lord, is not the cause of our thinking things that are evil and false.

There are enlightening parallels in the physical world. Warmth and light radiate from its sun, and these two flow into all the subjects and objects that we see with our eyes, not only good subjects and beautiful objects, but also bad subjects and ugly objects; and they bring forth different effects in each. They flow not only into trees that bear good fruit but into trees that bear bad fruit, flowing into the actual fruit itself and helping it to develop. They flow into the good seed and into the weeds, into useful, healthful shrubs and into harmful, toxic shrubs. Yet it is the same warmth and the same light; and there is no cause of evil in it, only in the subjects and objects that receive it.

[2] The same can be said of the warmth that hatches the eggs of owls or vipers and the eggs of doves, beautiful birds, and swans. Putting both kinds of egg under a hen and her warmth, which in and of itself is harmless, will hatch them. What does this warmth have in common with these evil and noxious creatures?

The same applies to the warmth that flows into swamps, manure, decay, and decomposition and into things that are winelike, fragrant, sparkling, and alive. Can anyone fail to see that the cause is not in the warmth but in the receptive subject?

The very same light, too, makes beautiful colors when it flows into one object and unpleasant colors when it flows into another. Actually, it is displaying itself and glowing in bright objects and dimming itself as objects become blacker, darkening itself.

[3] The same thing happens in the spiritual world. There are also warmth and light there from its sun, which is the Lord, flowing from him into their subjects and objects. The subjects and objects there are angels and spirits, specifically their processes of volition and discernment. The warmth there is the radiating divine love and the light there is the radiating divine wisdom. They are not responsible for the fact that different people receive them differently, for the Lord says, "He makes his sun rise on the evil and the good and sends rain on the righteous and the unrighteous" (Matthew 5:45). In its highest spiritual meaning the sun means divine love and the rain means divine wisdom.

I may add what angels think about volition and intelligence. It is their opinion that none of us has even a grain of volition or prudence that is actually ours. If there were such a grain in anyone, neither heaven nor hell could stand and the whole human race would perish. The reason they give is that heaven and hell are made up of millions of people, all the people who have been born since the creation of the world. Heaven and hell are arranged from top to bottom in a design that makes each a unity, heaven a beautiful person and hell a grotesque person. If there were a single grain of volition or intelligence that belonged to anyone, that unity would not be possible. It would be torn apart, and with it would go the divine form that can stand and endure only when the Lord is absolutely everything, and everything else is absolutely nothing.

Another reason they give is that thinking and intending autonomously is divinity itself, while thinking and intending from God is humanity itself. Divinity itself cannot be claimed by any of us: that would mean that we would be God. Remember this; and if you want to, you will find it corroborated by angels when you arrive in the spiritual world after you die.

I mentioned in §289 above that when some people were shown convincingly that we do not think on our own but receive thoughts from others, all of whom in turn are not

293

294

thinking on their own but from an inflow from the Lord, in their wonderment they claimed that it meant that they were not to blame for doing evil and that it seemed as though evil came from the Lord. They did not understand how the Lord alone could work things out so that we all think differently, either.

Since these three thoughts are bound to occur to people who think about effects as coming solely from effects and not from causes, I need to pick these up and look at them in terms of causes.

[2] *First, it meant that they were not to blame for doing evil.* If everything we think is flowing in from others, it does seem as though the blame rests on those others as the source. However, the real blame rests on us who accept what is flowing in, since we accept it as our own. That is all we know and all we want to know. We all want to be our own people and find our own way. Particularly, we want to think our own thoughts and make our own decisions. This is the essence of that freedom we enjoy that seems to be our very own. If we knew, then, that what we are thinking and intending was flowing in from someone else, we would feel caught and caged, no longer under our own control, and all the joy would go out of our lives. Eventually, our very humanity would go, too.

[3] I have often seen this demonstrated. When some individuals were allowed to feel and sense that they were being led by others, their rage blazed up so that they could no longer think straight. They said that they would rather be chained and imprisoned in hell than not be allowed to think what they wanted to think and intend what they were thinking. They called this restriction having their life itself bound, which was harsher and more intolerable than being bound physically. They did not say the same about being restrained from saying and doing what they were thinking and intending, because what held them in check was the pleasure of civil and moral life, and this made the restraint easier to bear.

[4] Since we do not want to know that others are leading us to think what we think, then, but want to think on our own and believe that we do, it necessarily follows that we ourselves are to blame and cannot avoid that blame as long as we are in love with our own thinking. If we are not in love with our own thinking, though, we extricate ourselves from our engagement with these others. This happens when we realize that something is evil and want therefore to abstain and refrain from it. Then the Lord rescues us from the community that is focused on this evil and moves us to a community that is not. However, if we recognize that something is evil and do not abstain from it, then we are held responsible for it and become guilty of that evil.

Whatever we believe we are doing autonomously, then, is said to come from us and not from the Lord.

[5] *Second, it therefore seemed as though evil came from the Lord.* This can seem as though it follows from what I said in §288, namely, that in hell, the goodness that flows in from the Lord is turned into evil and the truth into falsity. Surely, though, anyone can see that the evil and falsity do not come from what is good and true and therefore from the Lord. They come from the receiving subject or object that is focused on what is evil and false and that distorts and inverts what it is receiving, as has been amply demonstrated in §292. I have already explained several times [§§15, 204, 286] how the evil and falsity in us originate.

There have been experiments in the spiritual world with people who believed that the Lord could take the evils out of evil people and replace them with good qualities, thereby taking all hell into heaven and saving everyone. You may see that this is impossible, though, at the end of this book [§§331–340] where I deal with instant salvation and direct mercy.

[6] *Third, they did not understand how the Lord alone could work things out so that we all think so differently.* The Lord's divine love is infinite, and his divine wisdom is infinite, and

infinite forms of love and infinite forms of wisdom radiate from the Lord and flow into everyone in heaven and everyone in hell. From heaven and hell they flow into everyone in the world. This means that none of us can lack the ability to think and intend, since infinite forms are everything infinitely.

The infinite things that radiate from the Lord flow in not only in a general way but in full detail, since divinity is all-inclusive because of those smallest details, and the divine smallest details are what we call "the totality," as already explained [§202]. Further, every divine detail is also infinite.

We can tell from this that it is the Lord alone who makes each one of us think and intend in keeping with our own natures and in keeping with the laws of his providence. I have explained in §§46–69 and in *Divine Love and Wisdom* 17–22 that everything that is in the Lord and that radiates from the Lord is infinite.

295 2. *Evil people are constantly leading themselves into evils, and the Lord is constantly leading them away from evils.* It is easier to understand how divine providence works with good people than to understand how it works with evil people. Since this latter is our present concern, I shall proceed in the following sequence. (a) There are countless elements in every evil. (b) Evil people are constantly and intentionally leading themselves deeper into their evils. (c) For evil people, divine providence is a constant permission of evil with the ultimate goal of constantly leading them out. (d) The Lord does this leading out of evil in a thousand ways, some of them quite mysterious.

296 For a clear sense and grasp of the way divine providence works with evil people, I need to explain these statements in the order in which they are listed.

(a) *There are countless elements in every evil.* Every evil looks to us like a simple unit. That is how we see hatred and vengefulness, theft and fraud, adultery and promiscuity, pride and arrogance, and the like. We do not realize that there are countless elements in every evil, more than there are fibers and vessels in the human body. An evil person is a miniature form of hell, and hell is made up of millions of individuals, each one in a form that is human even though it is grotesque. All the fibers and all the vessels in that person are inverted. Essentially, a spirit is an evil that looks to itself like a single entity, but there are as many elements in it as there are compulsions that arise from it. We are all our own good or our own evil from our heads to the soles of our feet. So if evil people are like this, we can see that each one is an evil made up of countless different things that are distinct varieties of evil, things we refer to as the compulsions of that evil.

It then follows that if we are to be reformed, the Lord has to repair and turn around all these elements in the sequence in which they occur, and that this cannot be accomplished except by the Lord's divine providence working step by step from the beginning of our lives to the end.

[2] In hell, every compulsion to evil looks like a vicious animal when it is made visible, like a dragon, for example, or some kind of poisonous snake, or some kind of owl, and so on. This is what the compulsions of our own evil look like when angels see them. All these forms of compulsion have to be turned around one at a time. The task is to take people who in spirit look like gargoyles or devils and turn them around to look like beautiful angels, and each single compulsion has to be turned around so that it looks like a lamb, a sheep, a dove, or a turtle-dove. This what the desires for good of angels in heaven look like when they are made visible. Changing a dragon into a lamb or a serpent into a sheep or an owl into a dove can only happen gradually, by uprooting the very seed of the evil and planting good seed in its place.

This has to be done in the way a scion is grafted onto a tree that is nothing but some roots and a trunk. Even so, the branch that has been grafted gets some sap from the old root and turns it into good, juicy fruit. The scion that is to be grafted has to be taken from the Lord, who is the tree of life. This is the intent of the Lord's words in John 15:1–7.

[3] (b) *Evil people are constantly and intentionally leading themselves deeper into their evils.* We say they are doing this intentionally because everything evil comes from us. We turn the goodness that comes from the Lord into evil, as already noted [§294]. The basic reason evil people lead themselves deeper into evil is that they are making their way farther and farther into hellish communities, getting in deeper and deeper as they intend and do what is evil. This increases their pleasure in evil as well, and it takes possession of their thoughts to the point that nothing feels more gratifying. Furthermore, when we have made our way farther and deeper into hellish communities, we are wrapped up in chains, so to speak, though as long as we are living in this world, we do not feel them as chains. They feel like soft linen or slender threads of silk that we like because they caress us. After death, though, the softness of the chains turns hard, and the caresses start to chafe.

[4] If we consider theft, robbery, plunder, vengeance, domineering, profiteering, and the like, we can recognize this growth of the pleasure we find in evil. Do not the people who are committing these evils feel surges of pleasure as things go well and as obstacles to their efforts vanish? It is well known that thieves get such pleasure from theft that they cannot stop stealing; and strange as it sounds, they love one stolen coin more than ten coins freely given. It would be the same for adulterers if things were not so arranged that the power to commit this evil decreases as it is abused. Still, though, for many people the pleasure of thinking and talking about it is still there, and if nothing else, there is the insistent urge to touch.

[5] What people do not realize is that this is happening because they are making their way farther and farther, deeper and deeper, into hellish communities as they commit these

evils intentionally and consciously. If the evils occur in our thoughts only and not in our volition, we are not with the evil in some hellish community yet. We enter such a community when the evils are in our volition as well. If at that time we are also conscious that this evil is against the laws of the Ten Commandments, and if we regard these laws as divine, and still deliberately do it, this sends us down so deep that the only way we can be rescued is by active repentance.

[6] We need to realize that all of us, in spirit, are in some community in the spiritual world, in a hellish one if we are evil, and a heavenly one if we are good. Sometimes we are even visible there when we are deep in meditation. Further, just as sound and speech spread through the air in the physical world, desire and thought spread out in the communities in the spiritual world. There is a correspondential relationship here because desire answers to sound and thought to speech.

[7] (c) *For evil people, divine providence is a constant permission of evil with the ultimate goal of constantly leading them out.* The reason divine providence is a constant permission for evil people is that nothing can come out of their life except evil. Whether we are devoted to good or evil, we cannot be devoted to both at the same time, or even alternately, unless we are lukewarm. It is not the Lord who lets evil living into our volition and from there into our thought, it is we ourselves; and this is called permission.

[8] Now since everything evil people intend and think is a matter of permission, the question arises as to what divine providence is in this situation, the providence that we say is at work in the smallest details within all of us, evil and good alike. Divine providence consists of the fact that it is constantly allowing things to happen for a purpose and is permitting only things that serve that purpose, nothing else. It is constantly examining the evils that are allowed to emerge, separating them, purifying them, banishing the ones that do not suit its purpose,

and lifting them away in ways we cannot see. This is going on primarily in our deeper volition and secondarily in our deeper thought. Divine providence is also constantly at work to see that we do not welcome back into our volition the things that have been banished and lifted from us, because everything we accept into our volition becomes part of us. Things we have accepted in thought but not in volition, though, are separated and sent away.

This is the constant effort of the Lord's providence for evil people—as just noted, a constant permission with a view to constant rescue.

[9] We know very little about this because we do not feel it. The main reason we do not feel it is that our evils are inherent in the cravings of our life's love, and we do not feel these as evil but as pleasant. No one pays them any heed. Do we pay any attention to the pleasures of our love? Our thoughts drift along in them like a little boat in the current of a river. We sense them like a breath of fragrant air that we breathe in deeply. All we can do is sense a little of them in our outer thought, but we still take no notice of them there unless we have a clear knowledge of what evil is. There will be more on this later, though [§298].

[10] (d) *The Lord does this leading out of evil in a thousand ways, some of them quite mysterious.* I have been shown only a few of these, and only some of the commonest ones at that. What happens is that pleasures of our compulsions, of which we are utterly unaware, are emitted in close-knit groups into the inner thought processes of our spirit and from there into its outer thought processes. There they take on the guise of a kind of feeling that something is gratifying or pleasing or desirable. These inner pleasures mingle there with our lower and sensory pleasures. In this arena there are means of separation and purification and routes of dismissal and relief. The means are primarily the pleasure we find in contemplation, thought, and

reflection for various purposes that are constructive; and there are as many purposes that are constructive as there are elements and details of our various jobs and offices. There are also just as many constructive purposes as there are attractive thoughts about how we can seem to be civic-minded and moral individuals and spiritual individuals—as well as some unattractive ones that intrude themselves. Because these pleasures are effects of our love in our outer self, they serve as means by which the pleasures of the compulsions to evil of our inner self can be separated, purified, excreted, and withdrawn.

[11] For example, take dishonest judges, who see money or cronyism as the goals or functions of their office. Inwardly, they are constantly focused on these goals, but this comes out in an effort to act competently and fairly. They find a constant pleasure in pondering, thinking, reflecting, and intending ways to bend, turn, adapt, and finagle the legal system so that their decisions seem to conform to the laws and to mimic justice. They are not aware that this inner pleasure is made up of plots, pretences, deceit, undercover theft, and much more of the same kind, and that a pleasure comprising all these pleasures of obsessions with evil is the controlling element in everything that goes on in their outward thinking where they find pleasure in seeming to be fair and honest.

The inner pleasures are allowed to come down into the outer ones and mingle there the way food is churned in the stomach. That is where they are separated, purified, and withdrawn. This applies, though, only to the more serious pleasures of our compulsions to evil. [12] For evil people, only this separation, purification, and withdrawal of the more serious pleasures from the less serious ones is possible. For good people, however, there can be a separation, purification, and withdrawal of the less serious evils as well as the more serious ones. This is accomplished by means of the pleasures of our attraction to what is good and true, what is fair and honest, pleasures that we experience to the extent that we see our evils as sins and therefore abstain from them and turn away from them, and even more if we actively fight against them. These are the means the Lord uses to purify everyone who is being saved. He also purifies our evils by outward means that have to do with our reputation and respect and sometimes our finances. Even so, the Lord is planting in these means the pleasures of desires for what is good and true that guide and adapt them so that they become pleasures of a love for our neighbor.

[13] If we were to see the pleasures of our compulsions to evil in some kind of visible form or feel them clearly with any other sense, we would see and sense that there are so many that they cannot be delimited. Hell in its totality is nothing but a form of all our compulsions to evil; and in hell there is no single compulsion to evil that is exactly like any other. There cannot be one exactly like another to eternity. We know almost nothing about these countless elements, let alone how they are connected; and yet in his divine providence the Lord is constantly letting them come forth so that they can be withdrawn, doing this in a perfect pattern and sequence. An evil person is a miniature hell, and a good person is a miniature heaven.

[14] There is no better way to see and be assured that the Lord accomplishes this withdrawal from evils in a thousand ways, some most mysterious, than to look at the mysterious workings of the soul in the body. Here are some that we know about.

We know that when we are going to eat something we look at it, smell it, want it, taste it, break it up with our teeth, and use our tongues to send it down the esophagus into the stomach. However, there are mysterious workings of the soul of which we are totally unaware because we do not feel them. The stomach churns the food it has received, breaks it down and sorts it out with its secretions—that is, digests it—and assigns the elements to the appropriate open pores and veins that take them in, carrying some elements off into the blood, some into the lymphatic vessels, and some into the lacteal vessels of the mesentery, while some are sent down into the intestines. Then the chyle that comes from its reservoir in the mesentery is brought down through the thoracic duct into the vena cava and from there into the heart, and from the heart into the lungs. From there it passes through the left ventricle of the heart into the aorta, and from there through the whole branching system into the organs of the whole body. Material is also brought to the kidneys, in both of which there take place separation, purification, and withdrawal from the blood of elements that are not suitable. Allow me to leave out how the heart sends the blood that has been purified in the lungs up to the brain, which it does through the carotid arteries, and how the brain sends energized blood back into the vena cava just above the place where the thoracic duct injects the chyle, and from there back to the heart.

[15] These are some of the mysterious workings of the soul in the body, and there are many others. Most people are unaware of them, and people who are not trained in anatomy know nothing about them. Yet things like this are going on in the deeper reaches of our own minds, since nothing can happen in the body unless it comes from the mind. The mind is our spirit, and the spirit is just as much a person as we are. The only difference is that the things that happen in the body happen on the physical level and the things that happen in the mind happen on the spiritual level. There is a perfect parallelism.

We can see from this that divine providence works in a thousand ways, some most mysterious, in each of us, and that its constant effort is to purify us. This is because it is focused on the goal of saving us; and all that is required of us is that we set aside the evils in our outer self. The Lord takes care of the rest, if we ask.

3. *The Lord cannot fully lead evil people away from their evils and guide them in what is good as long as they believe that their own intelligence is everything and that divine providence is nothing.*   297

It seems as though we can lead ourselves away from evil if we only think that it is against the common good, impractical, and against national and international law. Evil people can do this just as well as good people if by birth or by training they are the kind of people who can think to themselves with analytic and rational clarity. However, we still cannot lead ourselves away from evil.

This is because while the Lord gives the ability to understand and appreciate things abstractly to everyone, evil and good alike (as already noted any number of times [§§86, 96, 99, 223, 285]), such understanding still does not enable us to lead ourselves away from evil. Evil is a matter of our volition, and our discernment does not flow into our volition except to give it light, to illuminate it, and to instruct it. If the warmth of our volition (that is, our life's love) is hot because of obsessions with evil, it is cold toward any desire for what is good. This means that it does not accept the light, but reflects it back, or stifles it, or turns it into evil by inventing some distortion. Winter sunlight, which is just as bright as summer sunlight, does the same thing when it flows into frozen trees.

However, it will be easier to see this in the following sequence. (a) When our volition is devoted to evil, our own intelligence sees nothing but falsity. It neither wants to see anything else nor is able to. (b) If our own intelligence does see anything true at such times, it either turns away or falsifies it. (c) Divine providence is constantly making sure we see what is true and giving us a desire to both appreciate it and accept it. (d) In this way we are led away from evil not by ourselves but by the Lord.

298 These items need to be explained in sequence, though, so that whether rational people are evil or good, whether their light is winter sunlight or summer sunlight, they will see them in the same colors.

(a) *When our volition is devoted to evil, our own intelligence sees nothing but falsity. It neither wants to nor is able to see anything else.* I have often been shown this in the spiritual world. When we become spirits, which happens after death, all of us take off our physical bodies and put on spiritual ones. We are then led alternately into our two basic states of life, the outer one and the inner one. When we are in the outer state we talk and act rationally and wisely just like any rational and wise individual in this world. We can tell others a tremendous number of things about moral and civic living. If we were ministers, we can teach about spiritual living as well. However, when we leave that outer state and come into the inner one, when the outer one becomes dormant and the inner one is awakened, then if we are evil people it is a different scene. We become sense-centered instead of rational, and insane instead of wise. Our thinking is prompted by the evil of our volition and its pleasure, which means that we are thinking with our own intelligence. We cannot see anything except what is false or do anything except what is evil. We believe that malice is wisdom and that craft is prudence. Our own intelligence convinces us that we are demigods, and our whole mind is thirsty for appalling skills.

[2] I have seen this kind of insanity any number of times. I have also seen people shift back and forth between these two states two or three times in a single hour, which enabled them to see and recognize their insanity; but they still did not want to stay in their rational and moral state. Of their own accord they turned back to their inner sensory and insane state. They loved it more than the other because that was where they found the pleasure of their life's love.

Who would think that evil people are like this under the surface and that they experience such a metamorphosis when they go within? This experience alone shows what our own intelligence is like when its evil intent is in control of our thinking and actions.

It is different for good people. When they shift from their outer to their inner state, they become even wiser and more decent.

[3] (b) *If our own intelligence does see anything true at such times, it either turns away or falsifies it.* We have both an emotional and a cognitive sense of identity. Our emotional sense of identity is evil and our cognitive sense of identity is the falsity that it prompts. The latter is what is meant by "the will of man" and the former by "the will of the flesh" in John 1:13.

Essentially, our voluntary side is a love for ourselves and our cognitive side is a pride born of that love. They are like two married partners, and their marriage is called the marriage of what is evil and what is false. Every evil spirit is consigned to this marriage before entering hell; and once people are there they do not know what is good, since they call their evil good and experience it as pleasant. They turn away from truth as well and do not want to see it. This is because they see the falsity that agrees with their evil the way the eye sees beauty, and they hear it the way the ear hears harmony.

[4] (c) *Divine providence is constantly making sure we see what is true and giving us a desire to both appreciate it and accept it.* This happens because divine providence is acting from the inside and flowing through to the outside, from the spiritual level into things in our lower self. Then it enlightens our discernment with heaven's light and gives life to our volition with heaven's warmth. Essentially, heaven's light is divine wisdom and heaven's warmth is divine love; and nothing can flow in from divine wisdom except what is true, and nothing can flow in from divine love except what is good. This is how the Lord gives our discernment a desire to see what is true and to appreciate and accept it; and this is how we become human not only as to our outer face but as to our inner one as well.

Is there anyone who does not want to seem like a rational and spiritual individual? Is anyone not aware of the desire to be regarded by others as truly human? If we are rational and spiritual only in outward form, then, and not inwardly as well, are we human? Are we anything but an actor on the stage or an ape with an almost human face? Does this not show that we are human only when we are inwardly as human as we seem to others? If we recognize the one kind of humanity, we must recognize the other.

The only thing our own intelligence can do is adopt a human form outwardly, but divine providence can adopt one inwardly and give us an outward form through the inner. When this is done, then we not only look human, we are human.

[5] (d) *In this way we are led away from evil not by ourselves but by the Lord.* The reason we can be led away from evil when divine providence enables us to see what is true and gives us a desire for it as well is that truth points out and indicates things. When our volition does these things, it unites with truth and transforms it to something good within itself. It becomes a matter of its love, and whatever is a matter of love is good. All our reformation is accomplished by means of truth and not apart from it, since in the absence of truth our volition stays dedicated to evil. If it does look to our discernment it is not taught anything. Instead, its evil is justified by falsities.

[6] As for our intelligence, it seems to be ours, really to belong to us, whether we are good or evil. Good people are kept in a state of acting from their intelligence as though it belonged to them, just as evil people are. If we believe in divine providence, though, we are kept from evil; but if we do not believe, we are not kept from it. When we recognize that an evil is a sin and want to be kept from it, we believe; when we do not recognize and want this, we do not believe. The difference between the two kinds of intelligence is like the difference between something we believe to be inherently real and something we believe is not inherently real but which still seems to be. It is like an outer surface that does not have an inner substance consistent with it, and an outer surface that does have such an inner substance. So it is like the speech and actions of mimes and actors who play the parts of royal and noble persons

on the one hand, and the royals and nobles themselves on the other. The latter are the same inwardly as they are outwardly. The others have only the outward guise, and when they lay that aside we call them comics, actors, and impersonators.

299

4. *The Lord controls the hells by means of opposites. As for evil people who are still in this world, he controls them in hell as to their deeper natures, but not as to their more outward natures.* People who do not know what heaven and hell are like have no way whatever of knowing what the human mind is like. Our mind is our spirit, the spirit that lives after death. This is because the whole form of our mind or spirit is like the form of heaven or hell. There is no difference whatever except that the one is immense and the other minute, or that the one is the model and the other the impression. As far as our minds or spirits are concerned, then, we are either a miniature heaven or a miniature hell, a heaven if we are being led by the Lord and a hell if we are leading ourselves.

Since I have been allowed to know what heaven is like and what hell is like, and since it is important that we know our nature as to mind or spirit, I want to offer a brief description of each.

300

All the people who are in heaven are simply desires for what is good and the consequent recognition of what is true; and all the people who are in hell are simply obsessions with evil and the consequent illusions of falsity. These are arranged on each side so that the obsessions with evil and illusions of falsity in hell are exactly opposite to the desires for what is good and recognition of what is true in heaven. So hell is under heaven and diametrically opposed to it, as diametrically opposed as two people lying in opposite directions or stationed foot to foot, one upside down, and both united at the soles of their feet, heel against heel. Sometimes hell can be seen in this kind of location or direction relative to heaven.

The reason is that for people in hell, obsessions with evil constitute the head, and desires for what is good constitute the

feet, while for people in heaven desires for what is good constitute the head, and obsessions with evil constitute the soles of
the feet. This means that they are opposites of each other.

To say that there are desires for what is good and therefore
recognition of truth in heaven, and that there are obsessions
with evil and therefore illusions of falsity in hell, is actually to
say that there are spirits and angels of this quality, because we
are all our own desire or our own obsession. Heaven's angels
are their own desires and hell's spirits are their own obsessions.

The reason heaven's angels are desires for what is good   **301**
and a consequent recognition of truth is that they are receptive of divine love and wisdom from the Lord, and all desires
for what is good come from divine love, and all recognition
of truth comes from divine wisdom. On the other hand, the
reason all spirits of hell are obsessions with evil and consequent
illusions of falsity is that they are wrapped up in their self-love
and in their own intelligence, and all obsessions with evil come
from self-love, and all illusions of falsity come from our own
intelligence.

The arrangement of desires in heaven and of obsessions in   **302**
hell is astonishing: only the Lord knows it. In each case, they
are differentiated into genera and species and so coordinated
that they act as a unit. Since they are differentiated into genera
and species, they are divided into larger and smaller communities; and since they are coordinated so as to act as a unit, they
are coordinated the way everything in a person is. As a result,
heaven in its form is like a beautiful person whose soul is divine
love and wisdom, or the Lord. Hell in its form is like a grotesque person whose soul is self-love and self-intelligence, or the
devil. There is actually no "Devil" who is the sole lord in hell;
that is a name for self-love.

For a better understanding of what heaven and hell are like,   **303**
substitute "pleasures in what is good" for "desires for what is
good" and "pleasures in evil" for "obsessions with evil." After all,
there is no desire or obsession that does not have its pleasures:

in each case, it is the pleasures that provide the life. They are differentiated and united just the way desires for what is good and obsessions with evil are differentiated and united, as already described [§302]. Every angel in heaven is filled with and surrounded by the pleasure of his or her particular desire. So too, a shared desire fills and surrounds every community in heaven, and the pleasure shared by all, the most pervasive pleasure, fills and surrounds heaven as a whole. In the same way, every spirit in hell is filled with and surrounded by the pleasure of her or his particular obsession, a shared pleasure fills and surrounds every community in hell, and the shared pleasure of all, the most pervasive pleasure, surrounds hell as a whole.

Since heaven's desires and hell's obsessions are diametrically opposed to each other, as already noted [§300], we can see that heaven's pleasure is so painful in hell that people there cannot bear it, and conversely that hell's pleasure is so painful in heaven that people there cannot bear it. This gives rise to hostility, repulsion, and separation.

304   Since these pleasures constitute the life of each individual and of everyone in general, they are not sensed by the people who have them; but the opposite ones are sensed when they come near. This happens especially when they are turned into odors. Every pleasure has a corresponding odor, and in the spiritual world it can be turned into its odor. When this happens in heaven, a shared pleasure smells like a garden, varying depending on the scents of the particular flowers and fruits it contains. A shared pleasure in hell smells like stagnant water into which different kinds of sewage have been discharged, varying depending on the particular stenches of the decaying and putrid matter in it.

I have been shown how people feel the pleasure of each particular desire for what is good in heaven and the pleasure of each obsession with evil in hell, but it would take too long to present that now.

I have heard any number of newcomers from our world complain that they did not know that their lot in life would depend on the desires of their love. They said they had not thought about them in this world, let alone about the pleasures associated with them. They had loved whatever gave them pleasure and had simply believed that our lot depended on what we thought intellectually, especially what we thought in matters of devotion and therefore of faith.

However, they were told that if they had wanted to, they might have known that an evil life is unwelcome in heaven and displeasing to God, but welcome in hell and pleasing to the devil. By the same token, a good life is welcome in heaven and pleasing to God, but unwelcome in hell and displeasing to the devil. By the same token, evil is inherently foul smelling and good is inherently fragrant. Since they could have known this if they had wanted to, why had they not abstained from evils as hellish and demonic, and why had they approved of them simply because they felt good? Since they now knew that the pleasures of evil had such an acrid smell, they could also know that they could not come into heaven smelling like that.

When they had been given this answer, they made their way to people who were devoted to the same kinds of pleasure, because that was the only place where they could breathe.

Given this picture of heaven and hell, the nature of the human mind is clear. As already stated [§§296, 299], our mind or spirit is either a miniature heaven or a miniature hell. Its contents are simply desires and the thoughts that they prompt, differentiated into genera and species the way heaven is differentiated into larger and smaller communities and united so that they act as a unity. The Lord oversees our desires and thoughts in the same way that he oversees heaven and hell.

On the human being as either a miniature heaven or a miniature hell, see *Heaven and Hell* 51–87 *[51–86]* (published in London in 1758).

307   We may turn now to the basic proposition that the Lord controls the hells by means of opposites, and that with evil people who are still in this world, he controls them in hell as to their deeper natures, but not as to their more outward natures.

As to the first, that *the Lord controls the hells by means of opposites,* I explained in §§288–289 that heaven's angels do not get their love and wisdom, or desire for what is good and resultant thought about what is true, from themselves, but from the Lord. I noted that the goodness and truth flow from heaven into hell, and that the goodness there is turned into evil and the truth into falsity because the inner reaches of people's minds there are turned in the opposite direction. Since everything in hell is the opposite of everything in heaven, it follows that the Lord is controlling the hells by means of these opposites.

[2] Second, the reason that *with evil people who are still in this world, the Lord controls them in hell* is that as to our spirits we are in the spiritual world, each in some community. We are in a hellish community if we are evil, and in a heavenly community if we are good. Since our minds are inherently spiritual, they can be with spiritual people only, people we will join after death. I have also mentioned and explained this above [§§298, 299].

We are not located there the way spirits are who have been enrolled in a community, though. We are in a constant state of reforming, so depending on our life and the way it changes, the Lord moves us from one community in hell to another if we are evil, while if we are allowing ourselves to be reformed, he leads us out of hell and up into heaven. There too, we are moved from one community to another. This goes on until we die, at which point we are no longer transferred from community to community, because we are no longer in a state of reforming. Instead, we settle in the one where our life places us; so when we die, we are enrolled in our own location.

[3] Third, *the Lord controls evil people in this world one way as to their inner natures and another way as to their outer natures.*

The Lord controls the inner levels of the mind as just described, but he controls the outer levels in the world of spirits that is halfway between heaven and hell. This is because most of us are not the same outwardly as we are inwardly. Outwardly we can impersonate angels of light even though inwardly we may be spirits of darkness. As a result, our outer and inner natures are controlled differently; the outer are controlled in the world of spirits and the inner are controlled either in heaven or in hell as long as we are in this world. Consequently, when we die we arrive first in the world of spirits and are conscious in our outer nature. We lay that nature aside in the world of spirits, and once we have done so we are taken to the place where we are enrolled.

On the world of spirits and its nature, see *Heaven and Hell* 421–535 (published in London in 1758).

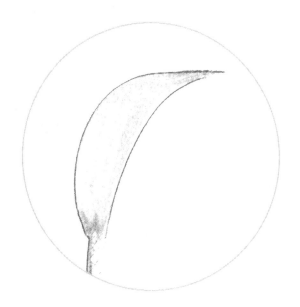

ABOUT *TRUE CHRISTIANITY*

True Christianity (1771) was the last book that Swedenborg published; in the months following its publication, his health went into decline, and he died in 1772. Its Latin subtitle describes the work as "a comprehensive theology of the new church," which might be misleading. It is not a summary of all Swedenborg's teachings, or surely it would have included chapters on life after death and marriage; but it is a bold statement of the new church position on fourteen key topics in Protestant (and especially Lutheran) theology of the time.

Note that the "new church" he mentions here does not refer to an earthly institution, although the church founded by followers of Swedenborg later became known as the New Church. Rather, Swedenborg was envisioning a new spiritual era for humanity as a whole, and a completely new kind of Christianity.

Swedenborg probably began work on *True Christianity* in late 1768 while in Amsterdam. In the spring of 1769, he learned that two good friends of his in Sweden were on trial for heresy for promoting his writings. Although Swedenborg was widely known to be the author of the works in question, he had published them abroad and for the most part anonymously; Sweden's strict censorship laws forbade publishing or teaching anything that contradicted the doctrines of the Lutheran state church.

A comparison of a projected outline of *True Christianity* published in 1769 with the final work as printed in 1771 suggests that Swedenborg substantially revised the work as a response to this attack: he expanded the chapters on the Trinity, retitled a chapter on the Ten Commandments to include a reference to the Catechism, added chapters on repentance and assignment of spiritual credit or blame, and deleted chapters on the nature of heaven and hell. All of these changes were geared very specifically toward addressing the key issues in Protestant thought at that time, particularly in the Lutheran church. *True Christianity*, in other words, was Swedenborg's response to his critics in Sweden and elsewhere—a statement of his inner convictions that in places is defiant.

True Christianity covers a wide range of issues, drawing in part from Swedenborg's previous works. The first chapter, on God as Creator, contains material first presented in *Divine Love and Wisdom*; the second, fourth, fifth, and sixth chapters discuss topics first presented in Swedenborg's short works *The Lord, Sacred Scripture, Life,* and *Faith*. Other portions are a fresh presentation of topics covered in other works, including chapters on freedom of choice, regeneration, and the rites of baptism and Communion.

The following excerpt was taken from a chapter on goodwill, a concept that in some editions is referred to as "charity." This chapter immediately follows the one on faith, and Swedenborg emphasizes that faith and goodwill are mutually dependent— good deeds that are not motivated by a genuine love of others are empty, while faith in God that is not expressed in actions is not true faith.

Note that this excerpt was edited for length; a series of asterisks indicates where a section was removed.

Goodwill (or Loving Our Neighbor) and Good Actions

HAVING addressed faith, we now turn to goodwill, because 392 faith and goodwill are united, just as truth and goodness are united. And truth and goodness are united like light and heat in springtime. I say this because spiritual light, which is the light that emanates from the sun in the spiritual world, is essentially truth. Therefore wherever the truth appears in that world it shines with a brightness that depends on how pure the truth is. The spiritual heat that emanates from that sun is essentially goodness. I state this because the same things apply to goodwill and faith that apply to good and truth. Goodwill is all the forms of good that we do for our neighbor combined. Faith is all the forms of truth that we think about God and about divine things combined.

[2] Since the truth that comes from faith is spiritual light and the goodness that comes from goodwill is spiritual heat, it follows that spiritual heat and light have properties similar to those of physical heat and light. Just as everything on earth blossoms when heat and light are united on earth, so everything in the human mind blossoms when heat and light are united in it. There is a difference, however: on earth the heat and light that cause blossoming are physical, but in the human mind the heat and light that cause blossoming are spiritual. Because the latter is a spiritual blossoming, it leads to wisdom and intelligence.

In addition to a similarity, there is also a correspondence between the two forms of heat and light. Therefore in the Word a human mind that contains goodwill united to faith and faith united to goodwill is compared to a garden. In fact, this is the meaning of the Garden of Eden (the truth of this has been fully shown in *Secrets of Heaven,* published in London).

[3] It is also important to realize that if there were no discussion of goodwill following the discussion of faith, the true nature of faith would be incomprehensible since, as I have said

and shown in the previous chapter, faith without goodwill is not faith; goodwill without faith is not goodwill; and neither of them is living unless it comes from the Lord, §§355–361. Also, the Lord, goodwill, and faith form a unity in the same way our life, our will, and our intellect form a unity; if we separate them, each one crumbles like a pearl that is crushed to powder, §§362–367. And furthermore, goodwill and faith come together in good actions, §§373 and following.

393   It is an abiding truth that faith and goodwill cannot be separated if we are to have a spiritual life and be saved. The truth of this is understandable to everyone, even people without the refinement of a costly education.

Suppose someone says, "People who live good lives and have proper beliefs are saved." No one could hear that without seeing it with an inner perception and therefore agreeing to it intellectually. Suppose someone says, "People who believe the right things but do not live good lives are also saved." Any people who heard this statement would reject it from their intellect as they would remove a piece of dirt that had fallen in their eye. Their inner perception would immediately cause them to think, "People cannot have good beliefs when they do not live good lives. What would those beliefs be except a painted model of faith rather than a living image of it?"

Likewise, if people were to hear, "Those who live good lives but have no beliefs are saved," they would turn this over a few times and then perceive and think that this does not make sense either. They would think, "Every good thing that is truly and intrinsically good comes from God; therefore living a good life comes from God. A good life without beliefs, then, is like clay in a potter's hand that can be molded into forms that are only useful in the earthly kingdom, not in the spiritual kingdom." Besides, there is an obvious contradiction in these statements, especially if you put them side by side: people are saved if they have beliefs but do not live good lives, and people are saved if they live good lives but have no beliefs.

What it is to live well, which is an aspect of goodwill, is partly known, partly unknown these days—people know what it is to live a good earthly life but not what it is to live a good spiritual life. Therefore I need to cover this point, inasmuch as it is an aspect of goodwill. The discussion will be broken into a series of individual topics.

There Are Three Universal Categories of Love: Love for Heaven; Love for the World; and Love for Ourselves

WE are starting with these three categories of love because they are universal and fundamental to all types of love and because goodwill has something in common with each of the three.

Love for heaven means love for the Lord and also love for our neighbor. Love for heaven could be called love for usefulness, because both love for the Lord and love for our neighbor have usefulness as their goal.

Love for the world is not only love for wealth and possessions but also love for all the things that the world provides that please our physical senses: beauty pleases our eye, harmony pleases our ear, fragrances please our nose, excellent food pleases our palate, soft touches please our skin. It also includes beautiful clothes, spacious accommodations, and social groups to belong to—all the pleasures that we get from these and many other things.

Love for ourselves is not only a love for respect, glory, fame, and status but also a love for seeking and getting high positions and becoming a leader.

Goodwill has something in common with each of these categories of love, because goodwill is by definition a love for usefulness of all kinds. Goodwill wants to do what is good for our neighbor, and *goodness* is the same as *usefulness*. Each of the categories of love just mentioned have usefulness as their goal: love for heaven has the goal of being useful in spiritual ways; love for the world has the goal of being useful in earthly ways, which

394

could also be called forms of civil service; and love for ourselves
has the goal of being useful in physical ways, which could also
be labeled benefits at home for ourselves and our loved ones.

395 The next part of this discussion [§§403–405] will show that
these three categories of love are in each one of us from creation
and by birth; when they are prioritized in the right way they
improve us, but when they are not prioritized in the right way
they damage us. At present it is enough to mention that these
three loves are prioritized in the right way when our love for
heaven plays the part of the head; our love for the world, the
part of the chest and abdomen; and our love for ourselves, the
part of the lower legs and feet.

As I have mentioned several times before [§§34, 42, 69, 147,
186, 296], the human mind is divided into three regions. From
our highest region we focus on God; from our second or middle
region we focus on the world; and from our third or lowest
region we focus on ourselves. Because our mind has this structure, it can be lifted up or can lift itself up to focus on God and
heaven; it can be spread out or spread itself out in every direction to focus on the world and its nature; and it can be lowered
down or can lower itself down to focus on the earth and hell.
In these respects physical sight emulates mental sight—physical
sight too can look up, around, and down.

[2] The human mind is like a three-story house with stairs
that provide transitions between levels. There are angels from
heaven living on the top floor, people of the world on the middle floor, and demons on the bottom floor. People for whom
these three categories of love have been prioritized in the right
way can go up or down whenever they want. When they go up
to the top floor, they are like angels among the angels there.
When they go down to the middle floor, they are like angelic
people with the people there. When they go even farther down,
they are like worldly people with the demons there—they give
the demons instructions, confront them, and tame them.

[3] When these three categories of love are properly prioritized in us, they are also coordinated in such a way that the highest love, our love for heaven, is present in the second love, our love for the world, and through that in the third or lowest love, our love for ourselves. In fact, the love that is inside steers the love that is outside wherever it wants. Therefore if a love for heaven is present in our love for the world and through that in our love for ourselves, with each type of love we accomplish useful things that are inspired by the God of heaven.

In operation these three loves function like the will, the intellect, and action: the will flows into the intellect, where it finds the means of producing action. There will be more on these last points in the next part of the discussion [§§403–405], which shows that if these three loves are prioritized in the right way, they improve us, but if they are not prioritized in the right way, they damage us and turn us upside down.

To present the points that follow in this chapter in such a way that they can be seen clearly (not to mention the points in chapters to follow on free choice [§§463–508], reformation and regeneration [§§571–625], and so on), I first need to present some points on *the will and the intellect; goodness and truth; love in general; love for the world and love for ourselves in specific; our outer and inner selves;* and *people who are merely earthly and sense-oriented.*

396

These points will be brought to light so that when readers see the things that come later, their rational sight will not feel as if it were in a fog, rushing along city streets until it had no idea of the way home. What is theology without understanding or with an intellect that remains unenlightened while we read the Word? It is like having a lamp in our hand but not lighting the candle inside it, like the lamps held by the five foolish young women who had no oil. Therefore these individual topics will be taken up in sequence.

397

1. *The will and the intellect.*

(a) There are two faculties that constitute our life. One is called the will, the other the intellect. They are distinct from each other, yet they were created to be one. When they are one, they are called "the mind." Therefore they are the human mind, where all of our life has its first beginnings, from which life then comes into our body.

(b) Just as everything in the universe—everything that is in the divine design—relates to goodness and truth, so everything in us relates to our will and our intellect. Goodness in us belongs to our will and truth in us belongs to our intellect. In fact, these two faculties or "lives" within us are vessels and abodes for goodness and truth. Our will is the vessel and abode for all things related to goodness, and our intellect is the vessel and abode for all things related to truth. Forms of good and truth exist nowhere else inside us. And since forms of good and truth exist nowhere else, love and faith do not exist anywhere else either, since love relates to goodness and goodness relates to love, and faith relates to truth and truth relates to faith.

(c) The will and the intellect also constitute our spirit. That is where our wisdom and intelligence, our love and goodwill, and our life in general reside. The body is merely an obedient servant.

(d) Nothing is more important to know than how the will and the intellect become a single mind. They become a single mind the way goodness and truth become one. The marriage between the will and the intellect is in fact similar to the marriage between goodness and truth. As will be shown in the next passage, which concerns goodness and truth, the nature of this marriage is that goodness is the underlying reality of a thing and truth is the resulting manifestation of the thing. Therefore in us our will is the underlying reality of our life and our intellect is the resulting manifestation of our life, because the goodness in our will takes shape and presents itself to be seen in our intellect.

2. *Goodness and truth.*

(a) Everything in the universe that is in the divine design relates to goodness and truth. Nothing that exists in heaven or on earth does not relate to these two. The reason is that both goodness and truth emanate from God, the source of all things.

[2] (b) Clearly then it is necessary for people to know what goodness is, what truth is, how they relate to each other, and how the one is united to the other. This is especially necessary for the people of the church. As everything in heaven relates to goodness and truth, so does everything in the church, since the goodness and truth of heaven are also the goodness and truth of the church.

[3] (c) The divine design is that goodness and truth are to be united, not separated. They are to be one thing, not two. They are united when they emanate from God, and they are united in heaven. Therefore they should be united in the church. In heaven the union of goodness and truth is called "the heavenly marriage." All who are in heaven have this marriage. This is why heaven is compared to a marriage in the Word, and the Lord is called Bridegroom and Husband while heaven is called Bride and Wife, as is the church. Heaven and the church are called this because the people in heaven and in the church receive divine goodness in their truths.

[4] (d) All the intelligence and wisdom that angels have comes from this marriage. None of it comes from goodness that is separate from truth or truth that is separate from goodness. The same is true for people of the church as well.

[5] (e) Since the union of goodness and truth is like a marriage, goodness clearly loves truth and truth loves goodness in return. Each one desires to be united to the other. People of the church who do not have this love or desire do not have the heavenly marriage. The church is not yet in them, since a union of goodness and truth constitutes the church.

[6] (f) There are many kinds of goodness. In general there is goodness that is spiritual and goodness that is earthly. Both

types come together in goodness that is genuinely moral. Just as there are different types of goodness, there are different types of truth, since truth belongs to goodness and is the form of goodness.

[7] (g) The situation with goodness and truth has an opposite in evil and falsity. As everything in the universe that is in the divine design relates to goodness and truth, so everything that is against the divine design relates to evil and falsity. As goodness loves to be united to truth, so evil loves to be united to falsity and the reverse. As the union of goodness and truth gives birth to all intelligence and wisdom, the union of evil and falsity gives birth to all insanity and foolishness. If you look deeply at the union of evil and falsity, you will see that it is not a marriage but an act of adultery.

[8] (h) The fact that evil and falsity are the opposite of goodness and truth makes it clear that truth cannot be joined to evil and that goodness cannot be joined to the falsity that comes from evil. If truth is joined to evil it becomes false and no longer true because it has been falsified. If goodness is joined to the falsity that comes from evil the goodness becomes evil and no longer good because it has been contaminated. Falsity that does not come from evil, however, can be joined to goodness.

[9] (i) No people who are focused on evil and falsity as a result of their convictions and their lives are able to know what goodness and truth are, because they believe that their evil is good and their falsity is true. On the other hand, all who are focused on goodness and truth as a result of their convictions and their lives are able to know what evil and falsity are, because all goodness and truth are essentially heavenly, but all evil and falsity are essentially hellish; and everything heavenly is in the light but everything hellish is in the dark.

399

3. *Love in general.*

(a) Our love is our very life itself. The nature of our love determines the nature of our life and in fact our entire nature as a human being. Our dominant or leading love, however, is the love that constitutes us.

Our dominant or leading love has many other loves; they are derived from it in a hierarchy beneath it. No matter how these other loves may look or seem, each one of them is part of our leading love. With it they make one government, so to speak. Our dominant love is like the monarch and leader of the rest: it guides our other loves and uses them as intermediate purposes through which it focuses on and aims for its goal. Both directly and indirectly, this goal is the primary and ultimate objective for them all.

[2] (b) The focus of our dominant love is what we love above all else. What we love above all else is constantly present in our thinking, because it is in our will and ultimately constitutes our life.

For example, if we love wealth above everything else, whether that means money or property, we are constantly contemplating how to get more. When we do get more we are profoundly over-joyed. When we lose wealth we are profoundly grief-stricken. Our heart is in it.

If we love ourselves above all else, we keep ourselves in mind at all times. We think about ourselves, talk about ourselves, and act for our own benefit, because our life is a life of self.

[3] (c) Our purpose is what we love above all else. We focus on it in each and every thing we do. It exists in our will like a hidden current in a river that moves and carries things along, even when we are doing something else, because it is what motivates us. It is the factor that people look for and identify in others; then they use it either to influence the others or to cooperate with them.

[4] (d) Our nature is completely shaped by the dominant force in our lives. That force is what differentiates us from other people. If we are good, our heaven is created to accord with it. If we are evil, our hell is created to accord with it. It is our will,

our self, and our nature. It is the underlying reality of our life. It cannot be changed after we die, because it is our true self.

[5] (e) For each of us, all our pleasure, joy, and happiness comes from our dominant love and depends on it. This is because whatever we love we say is enjoyable, since we feel it that way. What we think about but we do not love we are also capable of calling enjoyable, but it is not the central enjoyment of our life. What our love enjoys we experience as good, and what our love does not enjoy we experience as evil.

[6] (f) There are two types of love that act as a source for all forms of goodness and truth. There are two types of love that act as a source for all forms of evil and falsity. The two loves that originate all forms of goodness and truth are love for the Lord and love for our neighbor. The two loves that originate all forms of evil and falsity are love for ourselves and love for the world. When the latter two loves are dominant, they are completely opposite to the former two loves.

[7] (g) Love for the Lord and love for our neighbor are the two loves that constitute heaven in us, as I said. They are the dominant types of love in heaven. Since they constitute heaven in us, they also constitute the church in us.

The two loves that originate all forms of evil and falsity, which as I said are love for ourselves and love for the world, constitute hell in us, since they are the dominant types of love in hell. Therefore they also destroy the church in us.

[8] (h) The two types of love that originate all forms of goodness and truth, which are the types of love in heaven, open and form our inner spiritual self, because that is where these loves reside. The two types of love that originate all forms of evil and falsity, which as I have said are the types of love in hell, close and destroy our inner spiritual self when they are dominant. They make us earthly and sense-oriented, depending on how extensively and powerfully dominant they are.

400

4. *Love for ourselves and love for the world in specific.*

(a) Love for ourselves is wanting good things for ourselves

alone and not wanting good things for others unless we benefit—not even if the others are the church, our country, any human community, or other people who live in the area. Love for ourselves also entails doing something good for others only if it benefits our own reputation, honor, and glory. If we do not see these benefits in the good things we are doing for others, we say at heart, "What's the point? Why should I do this? What's in it for me?" and we no longer bother to do them. Clearly then, if we are wrapped up in loving ourselves we do not love the church, our country, our community, other people in our area, or anything else that is truly good. We love only ourselves and our own things.

[2] (b) When we are not focusing on our neighbor or the public in the things that we think about and do, let alone the Lord, we are wrapped up in loving ourselves. We are thinking only about ourselves and our own people. To put it another way, this is our nature when everything we do is for ourselves and our own people; if we do anything for the public, we do it only to look good; if we do anything for our neighbors, we do it only so they will like us.

[3] (c) I say "for ourselves *and our own people*" because if we love ourselves we also love our own people—specifically our own children and grandchildren, and generally all the people around us whom we call our own. Loving them is the same as loving ourselves, because we look at them as if we were looking at ourselves and we see them in relation to ourselves. "Our own people" also includes all the people who praise us, respect us, and look up to us. The rest may look human to our physical eyes, but with the eyes of our spirit we more or less see them as phantoms.

[4] (d) Love for ourselves is what we have if we despise our neighbors in comparison with ourselves. It is what we have if we think of people as our enemies because they do not favor, revere, or adore us. We are deeper in this love if we hate and persecute our neighbors for feeling that way. And we are deeper

still in this love if we have a burning desire for revenge against our neighbors and long for their destruction. If we have this nature, we eventually love to be savage.

[5] (e) We can see the nature of love for ourselves by comparing it with heavenly love. Heavenly love is a love for usefulness because it is useful; it is a love for the good things that we do for our church, our country, human society, and people in our area because they are good things to do. If, however, it is for our own sake that we love usefulness and good actions, we love them only as our drudges, because they serve us. Therefore if we love ourselves, we want our church, our country, human communities, and the people around us to serve us; we do not want to serve them. We place ourselves above them; we put them beneath ourselves.

[6] (f) Furthermore, the more we have a heavenly kind of love (we love actions that are useful and good and are moved with heartfelt pleasure when we do them), the more we are led by the Lord. This heavenly kind of love is the kind of love the Lord has; it is the kind of love that comes from him.

The more we love ourselves, the more we are led by ourselves and by our own self-centeredness. Our self-centeredness is nothing but evil. It is our hereditary evil. It is loving ourselves more than God and loving the world more than heaven.

[7] (g) The nature of love for ourselves is that the more the reins are let out—that is, the more its external constraints are removed, which are a fear of the law and its penalties and a fear of losing our reputation, respect, advantage, position, and life—the more our love for ourselves rushes on, until it wants to control not only the entire planet but also heaven and even God himself. It never has a limit or an end.

This limitless desire for control lies hidden within all people who are in love with themselves, although it is not visible to the world as long as the reins and constraints just mentioned hold them back. The nature of all people like this is that whenever further progress upward becomes impossible for them, they stay where they are until moving up becomes possible again. This explains why people who love themselves like this are unaware that there is an insane and limitless obsession hiding inside them.

No one can avoid seeing the truth of this, however, when looking at powerful people and monarchs—people who lack reins, constraints, and impossibilities. They rush on and overpower whole provinces and countries as long as they keep succeeding. They aspire to power and glory beyond all limits. This is particularly the case with people who extend their domain into heaven and transfer all the Lord's divine power to themselves. They always crave more.

[8] (h) There are two kinds of ruling power: one comes from love for our neighbor; the other comes from love for ourselves. They are opposite to each other. If we have ruling power because we love our neighbors, we want what is good for all. We love nothing more than being useful and serving others. Serving others is doing good and useful things for them because we wish them well. This is what we love to do and what gives pleasure to our heart. In this case, the more we are promoted to high positions, the happier we are, not because of the high positions but because of the useful things we can then do with a wider scope and greater magnitude. This is the nature of ruling power in the heavens.

On the other hand, if we have ruling power because we love ourselves, we want what is good for no one except ourselves and our own. The useful things we do are for our own honor and glory. As far as we are concerned, honor and glory are the only really useful things. If we serve others, it is for the purpose of being served and honored and having power. We pursue high positions not for the good things we could do but to have importance and glory and the heartfelt pleasure they bring us.

[9] (i) The particular love for ruling power that people have had stays with them after their life in the world. People who

had power because they loved their neighbor are entrusted with power in the heavens. In that situation, they do not have the power: the good and useful causes they love have the power. And when good and useful causes have the power, the Lord has the power.

People who had ruling power in the world because they loved themselves are thrown out of office after their life in the world comes to an end. They are then forced into slavery.

The points above make it now possible to recognize which people have love for themselves. It does not matter how they seem in outer form, whether haughty or obsequious. The attributes discussed above are in their inner selves, and the inner self is hidden from most other people. Their outer selves are taught to pretend to love the public and their neighbors—the opposite of what they feel. This too they do for their own sake. They are aware that loving the public and their neighbors deeply affects people and increases people's respect for them. This strategy works because heaven flows into a love for the public and for one's neighbor.

[10] (j) The evil qualities generally found in people who love themselves are contempt for others, jealousy, unfriendliness toward people who do not favor them; a resulting hostility; and various kinds of hatred, vengefulness, guile, deceit, ruthlessness, and cruelty. Where you find evils like this, you also find contempt for God and for the divine things that are the true insights and good actions taught by the church. If such people honor these things, their respect is only verbal, not heartfelt. Because evils like these are present, related falsities are also present, since falsities come from evils.

[11] (k) *Love for the world,* on the other hand, is wanting to redirect other people's wealth to ourselves with whatever skill we have. It is putting our heart in riches and letting the world distract us and steer us away from spiritual love (love for our neighbor) and heaven. We have a love for the world if we long

to redirect other people's possessions to ourselves by various methods, especially if we use trickery and deception, and have no concern for how our neighbor is doing. If we have this type of love, we have a strong and growing craving for good things other people have. Provided we do not fear the law or losing our reputation, we take people's things away, and in fact rob people blind.

[12] (l) Yet love for the world is not as opposite to heavenly love as love for ourselves is—the evils hidden in it are not as enormous.

[13] (m) Love for the world takes many forms. It can be a love we have for wealth in order to be promoted to higher positions. It can be a love for honor and high position for the sake of increasing our wealth. It can be a love for wealth for the sake of various benefits that gratify us in the world. It can be a love for wealth for the sake of wealth itself: this kind is miserly. And so on. Our purpose in gaining the wealth is the use we hope to get out of it. This purpose or use determines the quality of the love. The nature of any love is the nature of the purpose it has; everything else about it serves as a means.

[14] (n) To summarize, love for ourselves and love for the world are completely opposite to love for the Lord and love for our neighbor. Therefore love for ourselves and love for the world, as I have just described them, are hellish loves. In fact, they rule in hell. They also create a hell in us.

Love for the Lord, however, and love for our neighbor are heavenly loves. In fact, they rule in heaven. They also create a heaven in us.

5. *Our inner and outer selves.*

(a) We have been created to be in the spiritual world and the physical world at the same time. The spiritual world is where angels are. The physical world is where people are. Because we have been created that way, we have been given an inner and an outer level: an inner level so we can be in the spiritual world

401

and an outer level so we can be in the physical world. The inner level is called our inner self, and the outer level is called our outer self.

[2] (b) Everyone has an inner and an outer self, but they are different in good people than in evil people. The inner level of good people is in heaven and its light. Their outer level is in the world and its light; and the light of heaven within them illumines the light of the world. Their inner and outer levels are united like cause and effect or like something prior and something subsequent. With evil people, however, their inner level is in hell and its light. Compared to heaven's light, the light of hell is pitch darkness. The outer level of evil people can be in the same light that good people are in. Therefore they are upside-down. This explains how evil people are capable of speaking and teaching *about* faith, goodwill, and God, but not *from* faith, goodwill, and God the way good people can.

[3] (c) Our inner self is called our spiritual self because it is in the light of heaven, a light that is spiritual. Our outer self is called our earthly self because it is in the light of the world, a light that is earthly. People whose inner level is in the light of heaven and whose outer level is in the light of the world are spiritual on both levels, since spiritual light from within enlightens their earthly light and makes it its own. The reverse is true for evil people.

[4] (d) The inner self that is spiritual is actually an angel of heaven. Even while it is alive in our body, it is in a community with angels, although it does not realize that. After it is released from the body, it comes to live among those angels. The inner self among evil people, however, is a satan. Even while it is living in our body, it is in a community with satans. After it is released from the body, it comes to live among those satans.

[5] (e) In people who are spiritual, the inner parts of their mind are actually raised up toward heaven, because heaven is their predominant focus. In people who are merely earthly, however, the inner parts of their mind are turned away from

heaven toward the world, because the world is their predominant focus.

[6] (f) People who have only a general concept of the inner and outer self believe that the inner self is the part that thinks and wills while the outer self is the part that speaks and acts, since thinking and willing are internal while speaking and acting are external. One thing is important to realize, however. When we are thinking and willing good things in relation to the Lord and all that is the Lord's, and when we are thinking and willing them in relation to our neighbor and all that is our neighbor's, then our thinking and willing are coming from an inner self that is spiritual. This is so because they are coming from true faith and a love for what is good. On the other hand, when we have evil thoughts about the Lord and our neighbor and evil intentions toward them, then our thinking and willing are coming from an inner self that is hellish, because they are coming from a false faith and a love for what is evil. Briefly put, the more we focus on loving the Lord and our neighbor, the more spiritual our inner self is. From that inner self we think and will, and from it we even speak and act as well. On the other hand, the more we focus on loving ourselves and the world, the more our thinking and willing come from hell, although we speak and act otherwise.

[7] (g) The Lord has provided and arranged that the more our thinking and willing come from heaven, the more our spiritual self opens and adapts. This opening is an opening to heaven, all the way to the Lord; and this adaptation is an adaptation to things that are in heaven.

On the other hand, the more our thinking and willing come from the world, not heaven, the more our inner spiritual self closes and our outer self opens and adapts. This opening is an opening to the world and this adaptation is an adaptation to the things that are in hell.

[8] (h) People whose inner spiritual selves have opened to heaven and the Lord are in the light of heaven. They have

enlightenment from the Lord and a resulting intelligence and wisdom. They see truth from the light of truth. They sense what is good from a love for what is good.

People whose inner spiritual selves have closed, however, do not know what the inner self is. They do not believe in the Word, life after death, or anything related to heaven or the church. Because they have a light that is merely earthly, they believe that nature arises from itself, not from God. They see what is false as true and sense what is evil as good.

[9] (i) The inner and outer levels discussed here are the inner and outer levels of our spirit. Our body is only an element added on the outside as a container for all the above. Our body does nothing on its own—it acts on behalf of the spirit that is inside it.

It is important to know that after our spirit parts company with our body, it still thinks, wills, speaks, and acts. Thinking and willing remain our inner level and speaking and acting then become our outer level.

402

6. *People who are merely earthly and sense-oriented.*

Only a few know what "sense-oriented people" are and what they are like, even though it is an important thing to know. Therefore I will describe them.

(a) "Sense-oriented people" are people who judge everything on the basis of their physical senses—people who will not believe anything unless they can see it with their eyes and touch it with their hands. What they can see and touch they call "something." Everything else they reject. Sense-oriented people, then, are earthly in the lowest way.

[2] (b) The inner levels of their mind, levels that see in heaven's light, are closed inside people like this to the point where they see nothing true related to heaven or the church. This is because their thinking occurs on an outermost level and not inside, where the light is spiritual.

[3] (c) Since the light they have is dense and earthly, people like this are inwardly opposed to things related to heaven and

the church, although they are outwardly able to speak in favor of them. If things related to heaven and the church give these people ruling power, they are even capable of speaking ardently in favor of them.

[4] (d) Sense-oriented people are able to reason sharply and skillfully, because their thinking is so close to their speech as to be practically in it—almost inside their lips; and because they attribute all intelligence solely to the ability to speak from memory.

[5] (e) Some of them can defend whatever they want. They have great skill at defending things that are false. After they have defended falsities convincingly, they themselves believe those falsities are true. They base their reasoning and defense on mistaken impressions from the senses that the public finds captivating and convincing.

[6] (f) Sense-oriented people are more deceptive and ill-intentioned than others.

[7] (g) The inner areas of their mind are foul and filthy because they use them to communicate with the hells.

[8] (h) The inhabitants of hell are sense-oriented. The deeper in hell they are, the more sense-oriented they are. The sphere of hellish spirits is connected to our sense impressions through a kind of back door.

[9] (i) Sense-oriented people do not see anything that is genuinely true in the light. Instead, on every topic they debate and argue whether it is so. From a distance their arguments sound like the grinding of teeth. The sounds of teeth grinding are actually the result of falsities colliding with each other, and falsity and truth in collision as well. This makes it clear what "the grinding" or "gnashing of teeth" means in the Word. Teeth correspond to reasoning based on mistaken impressions from our senses.

[10] (j) The educated and the scholarly who are deeply convinced of falsities—especially people who oppose the truths in the Word—are more sense-oriented than others, although

that is not how they seem to the world. People who are sense-oriented are the foremost developers of heresies.

[11] (k) For the most part, hypocrites, deceitful people, hedonists, adulterers, and misers are sense-oriented.

[12] (l) The ancients had a term for people who debate on the basis of sense impressions alone and speak against genuine truths in the Word and the church: they called them serpents of the tree of the knowledge of good and evil.

Sense impressions mean things that impinge on our physical senses and are experienced by those senses. This point leads to a number of others:

[13] (m) We are in touch with the world by means of sense impressions and with heaven by means of impressions on our rationality, which transcend sense impressions.

[14] (n) Sense impressions supply things from the physical world that serve the inner realms of the mind in the spiritual world.

[15] (o) There are sense impressions that feed the intellect: they are various earthly objects that are labeled "material." There are sense impressions that feed the will: they are called the pleasures of the senses and the body.

[16] (p) Unless our thought is lifted above the level of our sense impressions, we have very little wisdom. Wise people think above the level of sense impressions. When our thinking rises above sense impressions, it enters a clearer light and eventually comes into the light of heaven. From this light we get the awareness of truth that constitutes real intelligence.

[17] (q) The ancients knew how to lift their minds above sense impressions and take their minds away from them.

[18] (r) If sense impressions have the lowest priority, they help open a pathway for the intellect. We then extrapolate truths by a method of extraction. On the other hand, if sense impressions have the highest priority, that pathway is closed and truths are not visible to us except as if they were in a fog or in the dark of night.

[19] (s) For wise people, sense impressions have the lowest priority and are subservient to things that are deep inside. For unwise people, sense impressions have the highest priority and are in control. This type of person can truly be called sense-oriented.

[20] (t) There are sense impressions that we have in common with animals and sense impressions that we do not have in common with animals. The more we lift our thinking above sense impressions, the more human we are. Without acknowledging God and living by his commandments, however, none of us can lift our thinking above sense impressions and see the truths that relate to the church. It is God who lifts and enlightens us.

When the Three Universal Categories of Love Are Prioritized in the Right Way They Improve Us; When They Are Not Prioritized in the Right Way They Damage Us and Turn Us Upside Down

FIRST I will say something about the prioritization of the three universal categories of love: love for heaven, love for the world, and love for ourselves. Then I will talk about the inflow and integration of one into the other. Finally I will discuss the effect of their prioritization on our state.

403

These three loves relate to each other as do the three areas of the body: the highest is the head; the middle is the chest and abdomen; and our thighs, lower legs, and feet make up the third. When our love for heaven constitutes the head, our love for the world constitutes the chest and abdomen, and our love for ourselves constitutes the lower legs and feet, then we are in the perfect state we were created to be in. In this state the two lower categories of love serve the higher category the way the body and everything in it serves the head.

Therefore when a love for heaven constitutes the head, this love flows into our love for the world, which is chiefly a love for wealth, and takes advantage of that wealth to do useful things; our love for heaven also flows through our love for the world into our love for ourselves, which is chiefly a love for having a high position, and takes advantage of that high position to do useful things. Therefore an inflow from one love into the next allows the three categories of love to join forces in order to do useful things.

[2] Surely everyone realizes that when people intend to do useful things because they are moved by spiritual love coming from the Lord (which is what "love for heaven" means), their earthly self uses its wealth and other goods to achieve those useful things, and their sense-oriented self carries them out as part of its position and derives honor from so doing.

Surely everyone also realizes that all the things we do with our body we do from the state of mind in our head. If our mind has a love for acts of service, our body uses its limbs to perform acts of service. Our body will do this because our will and intellect have their primary structures in our head and the derivations of those primary structures in our body, so that our will is present in what we do and our thinking is present in what we say.

Likewise the reproductive impetus in a seed affects each and every part of a tree and uses those parts to produce pieces of fruit as its acts of service. Or for another example, fire and light inside a clear container make the container hot and bright. In people whose three categories of love have been prioritized in the right and proper way, their mind's spiritual sight and their body's physical sight are translucent to the light that flows in through heaven from the Lord, just as a pomegranate is translucent all the way through to the center where the seeds are stored.

Something comparable is meant by the following words of the Lord: "Your eye is the lamp of your body. If your eye is whole, that is, good, your entire body is full of light" (Matthew 6:22; Luke 11:34).

[3] No one whose reason is sound could condemn wealth. Wealth in the general body politic is like blood in us. No one whose reason is sound could condemn the levels of status that go with different jobs—they are the monarch's hands and the pillars of society, provided a spiritual love for status takes priority over an earthly and sense-oriented love for it. In fact, there are government positions in heaven and there is status that goes with them; but because the people who fill these positions are spiritual, the thing they love the most is to be useful.

We take on a completely different condition if love for the world or for wealth constitutes the head, meaning that this is our dominant love. Then love for heaven leaves the head and goes into exile in the body. People who are in this state prefer the world to heaven. They do indeed worship God, but they do so from a love that is merely earthly, a love that leads them to take credit for all their acts of worship. They also do good things for their neighbor, but they do them to get something back in return.

In the case of people like this, heavenly things are like the clothes in which they strut about, garments that we see as shining but angels see as drab. When love for the world inhabits our inner self and love for heaven inhabits our outer self, then love for the world dims all things related to the church and hides them as if they were behind a piece of cloth.

Love for the world or for wealth comes in many forms, however. It gets worse the closer it approaches to miserliness. At the point of miserliness the love for heaven becomes dark. This love also gets worse the closer it approaches to arrogance and a sense of superiority over others based on love for oneself. It is not as detrimental when it tends toward wasteful indulgence. It is even less damaging if its goal is to have the finest things the world has to offer, like a mansion, fine furniture, fashionable clothing, servants, horses and carriages in grand style, and things like that. With any love, its quality depends on the goal that it focuses on and intends to reach.

404

Love for the world and for wealth is like a dark crystal that suffocates light and breaks it only into colors that are dull and faded. It is like fog or cloudiness that blocks the rays of the sun. It is also like wine in its first stages—the liquid tastes sweet, but it upsets your stomach.

From heaven's point of view, people like this look hunchbacked, walking with their head bent down looking at the ground. When they lift their head toward the sky, they strain their muscles and quickly go back to looking downward. The ancient people who were part of the church called people of this kind "Mammons." The Greeks called them "Plutos."

405 If, however, love for ourselves or love of power constitutes the head, then love for heaven goes down the body to the lower legs. The more this love grows, the more love for heaven moves through the ankles into the feet. If love for ourselves grows even more, love for heaven passes through the shoes and is trampled.

There is a love for power that comes from loving our neighbor and a love for power that comes from loving ourselves. People who have a love for power that comes from loving their neighbor are ambitious for power for the purpose of benefiting both the general public and individual citizens. In the heavens, in fact, power is entrusted to people like this. [2] If emperors, monarchs, and generals who were born and raised to be leaders humble themselves before God, they sometimes have less self-love than people who come from a lowly family and whose pride makes them long for superior status over others.

On the other hand, people who have a love for power that comes from loving themselves use love for heaven as their footstool. They put their feet on it in view of the crowd. If there is no crowd in sight, they either toss it in the corner or throw it out the door. Why? Because they love only themselves. As a result, they plunge the willing and thinking of their minds into self-absorption. Self-absorption is in fact a hereditary evil; it is the polar opposite of love for heaven.

[3] If we have a love for power that comes from loving ourselves, we also have evils that accompany that love. They are generally the following: despising others, jealousy, viewing people as our enemies if they do not show us special favor, hostility, hatred, vengefulness, mercilessness, savagery, and cruelty. Despising God is another such evil, as is despising the divine things that are the true insights and good actions taught by the church. If we give these things any honor, we only pay them lip service to prevent the church hierarchy from attacking our reputation and to stave off verbal abuse from everyone else.

[4] Love for power is different for the clergy than it is for the laity. In the clergy this love surges upward, as long as it is given the reins, until they want to be gods. Lay people, on the other hand, want to be monarchs. That is how far the imagination of that love takes their minds.

[5] In spiritually well-developed people, love for heaven occupies the highest place and constitutes the head of what follows it; love for the world is beneath it and is like the torso below the head; love for themselves is below this love in the role of the lower legs. It follows then that if love for ourselves constitutes the head, we are completely upside-down. In that case we look to the angels like people sleeping with their heads on the ground and their rear ends up in the air. When people like this are worshiping, they look as if they are frolicking on all fours like panther cubs. Furthermore, they look like various kinds of two-headed creatures—the head on top has the face of a wild animal, while the other below it has a human face that is continually pushed down from above and forced to kiss the ground.

All people of this type are sense-oriented. They are like the people described above in §402.

All Individual Members of Humankind Are the Neighbor We Are to Love, but [in Different Ways] Depending on the Type of Goodness They Have

406 WE are not born for our own sake; we are born for the sake of others. That is, we are not born to live for ourselves alone; we are born to live for others. Otherwise society would not be cohesive and there would be no good in it.

There is a common saying that we are all neighbor to ourselves. The body of teaching on goodwill, however, shows how we should understand this. We are all supposed to provide ourselves with the necessities of life, such as food, clothing, a place to live, and many other things that are required by the civic life in which we participate. And we provide these things not only for ourselves but also for our loved ones, not only for the present but also for the future. If we do not provide ourselves with the necessities of life, we are in no state to practice goodwill, because we lack everything.

How we are to be neighbors to ourselves, however, can be shown through the following analogy: We should all provide our bodies with food. This has to come first, but the goal is to have a sound mind in a sound body. We also ought to provide our mind with its food, that is, things that build intelligence and judgment; but the goal is to be in a state in which we can serve our fellow citizens, our community, our country, the church, and therefore the Lord. People who pursue this goal are providing well for themselves to eternity.

These points make clear what is primary from the standpoint of time and what is primary from the standpoint of purpose. What is primary from the standpoint of purpose is the true overall goal.

This situation is like people building a house. They have to lay the foundation first, but the foundation is for the house, and the house is for living in. People who hold being neighbors to themselves as their first and foremost objective are like people whose main purpose is building the foundation rather than living in the house. Yet living in the house is the primary and ultimate purpose overall; the house and its foundation are only a means to an end.

Now I need to say what it is to love our neighbor. Loving our neighbor is intending and doing good not only to neighbors, friends, and good people but also to strangers, enemies, and evil people. But we exercise goodwill in our dealings with the latter in different ways than we do in our dealings with the former. We exercise goodwill in our dealings with our neighbors and friends by benefiting them directly. We exercise goodwill in our dealings with our enemies and evil people by benefiting them indirectly through our warnings, corrective action, punishments, and therefore efforts to improve them. 407

This could be illustrated as follows. Judges who punish wrongdoers because it is the just and legal thing to do have love for their neighbor. By so doing the judges are straightening out the wrongdoers and are caring for people in the area by preventing the wrongdoers from doing them harm.

Everyone knows that parents who punish their children for doing what is wrong are showing them love; and on the other hand, parents who do not punish their children for doing what is wrong are showing love for evil traits in their children, which has nothing to do with goodwill.

For another example, suppose someone under the attack of an enemy repels the attacker and either strikes in self-defense or turns the attacker over to a judge to avoid being harmed. Say the victor maintains an intention nonetheless of becoming the attacker's friend. Then the victor is acting on the strength of goodwill. Even wars for the purpose of keeping the country and the church safe are not against goodwill. The ultimate purpose shows whether a given act is an expression of goodwill or not.

408 Fundamentally speaking, goodwill is wanting what is best for others. This desire resides in the inner self. When people of goodwill resist an enemy, punish a guilty person, or discipline evil people, clearly they do so through the medium of their outer selves. Therefore after the situation comes to an end, they go back to the goodwill that is in their inner selves. As much and as usefully as they can, they then wish the others well and benefit those others in a spirit of goodwill.

409 People who have genuine goodwill have a passion for what is good. In their outer selves that passion can look like rage and blazing anger, but it dies away and becomes calm as soon as their opponents come back to their senses. It is very different for people who have no goodwill. Their passion is a rage and a hatred that heat and ignite their *inner* selves.

Before the Lord came into the world, almost no one knew what the inner self was or what goodwill was. That is why in so many passages the Lord teaches love and goodwill. This is a distinguishing feature between the Old Testament or Covenant and the New.

In Matthew the Lord teaches that we are to do good to our adversaries and enemies and have goodwill toward them:

> You have heard the statement made to the ancients, "You are to love your neighbor and hate your enemy." But I am saying to you, love your enemies, bless the people who are cursing you, do good to the people who are hating you, and pray for the people who are hurting you and persecuting you, so that you may be children of your Father who is in the heavens. (Matthew 5:43, 44, 45)

To Peter, who was asking how many times he should forgive someone who was sinning against him—whether he should give forgiveness as many as seven times—the Lord answered,

I do not say as many as seven times, but as many as
seventy times seven. (Matthew 18:21, 22)

I have also heard from heaven that the Lord forgives everyone's sins and never takes revenge or even assigns spiritual
credit or blame, because he is love and goodness itself. Yet for
all that, our sins are not washed away. Nothing washes our sins
away except repentance. Since the Lord told Peter to forgive up
to seventy times seven instances of sin, at what point would the
Lord stop forgiving us?

Since goodwill resides in the inner self, where benevolence
is felt, and then extends into the outer self, where good actions
occur, it follows that people's inner selves are what we should
love; and we should love their outer selves on the basis of their
inner selves. Therefore we are to love people according to the
type of goodness they have inside. It is the goodness itself, then,
that is actually our neighbor.

The following situations may serve as illustration: When we
choose ourselves a household manager out of three or four candidates, or we hire a servant, we investigate that person's inner
self. We choose someone who is honest and faithful and prefer
that candidate because of those qualities.

The same is true for monarchs or government officials. Out
of three or four candidates, they select someone suitable for the
job and reject the unsuitable, no matter whose looks they prefer
or what the candidates say or do to win them over.

[2] Everyone is our neighbor, and people come in an infinite
variety. Since we need to love them all as our neighbor for the
type of goodness they possess, clearly there are genera and species of loving our neighbor, as well as higher and lower degrees
of that love.

Since the Lord is to be loved above all else, it follows that
the degrees of our love for our neighbors depend on their love
for the Lord, that is, on the amount of the Lord or the amount

410

from the Lord that our neighbors possess in themselves. That is also the amount of goodness they possess, since all goodness comes from the Lord.

[3] Nevertheless, since these degrees are within people's inner selves and these are rarely obvious to the world, it is enough to love our neighbor by the degree of goodness that we are aware of.

Now, these degrees are clearly perceived after death, since there the feelings in our will and the thoughts in our intellect form a spiritual sphere around us that others can sense in various ways. In this world, however, this spiritual sphere is absorbed by our physical body and is contained in the physical sphere that pours out around us.

The Lord's parable about the Samaritan shows that there are degrees of love for our neighbor. The Samaritan had mercy on the person who had been wounded by robbers—a person whom both the priest and the Levite had seen and yet passed by. When the Lord asked which of the three seemed to have been a neighbor, the reply was "the one who had mercy" (Luke 10:30–37).

411 We read that we are to love the Lord God above all things, and our neighbor as ourselves (Luke 10:27). To love our neighbor as ourselves means not despising our neighbors in comparison with ourselves. It means treating them justly and not judging them wrongfully. The law of goodwill pronounced and given by the Lord himself is this:

> Whatever you want people to do for you, do likewise for them. This is the Law and the Prophets. (Matthew 7:12; Luke 6:31, 32)

This is how people who love heaven love their neighbor. People who love the world, however, love their neighbor on a worldly basis for a worldly benefit. People who love themselves love their neighbor in a selfish way for a selfish benefit.

The Neighbor We Are to Love Is Humankind on a Wider Scale in the Form of Smaller and Larger Communities and Humankind in the Aggregate as a Country of Such Communities

PEOPLE who do not know what "our neighbor" really means think that it simply means an individual human being; benefiting that human being is loving our neighbor. Yet our neighbor, and love for our neighbor, also extends more widely than that—in fact it rises as the number of people increases.

Surely everyone understands that loving many people in a group involves more love for our neighbor than loving an individual member of that group. Therefore smaller and larger communities are also our neighbor, because they are a plurality of people. It follows that someone who loves a community loves the individuals who are part of that community; someone who wishes a community well and gives benefit to it cares for its individuals.

A community is like a person. In fact, the people who make up the community form a single body, in a sense. They are differentiated from each other like the parts of a single body. When the Lord looks at the earth, he sees an entire community as an individual person; the form of that individual person is based on the qualities of the people in the community. The Lord gives this sight to angels as well. In fact, I have been allowed to see a community in heaven completely in the form of an individual person; the person had the same proportions as people in the world.

[2] Love for a community is a fuller form of love for our neighbor than love for a single individual. This is clear from the fact that high positions are given to people according to their previous leadership of large groups. They have a level of status according to the job they do. In the world, in fact, positions in a hierarchy are considered to be higher or lower based

412

on how wide a governmental responsibility these positions have over other people. The monarch is the person who has the widest government of all. Each person gets pay, glory, and general admiration according to the scope of the position and also the useful functions performed.

[3] But in this day and age, leaders may be useful and care for a community and still not love their neighbor. They perform functions and show concern for the sake of the world or themselves in order to deserve, or look as if they deserve, promotion to higher positions. Although these people may not be identified as such in the world, they are identified as such in heaven. People who have performed useful services out of love for their neighbor are put in leadership positions over a heavenly community as well; there they have splendor and honor. Yet still they do not take that splendor or honor to heart, just the usefulness. The rest, however, who were useful because they loved the world or themselves, are rejected.

413 Feeling love for our neighbor and acting on that love on an individual basis is one thing. Doing so on a plural or community basis is another. The difference between them is like the difference between the role of a citizen, the role of an official, and the role of a leader. It is also like the difference between the person who traded with two talents and the person who traded with ten (Matthew 25:14–30). It is like the difference between the value of a shekel and the value of a talent. It is like the difference between the product of a grapevine and that of a whole vineyard, the product of an olive tree and that of an olive plantation, the product of a single tree and that of a whole fruit garden. Love for our neighbor also rises higher and higher within us, and as it rises, we love our community more than we love an individual and we love our country more than we love our community.

Now, because goodwill consists of wanting what is best for others and being of benefit to them, it follows that it is to be practiced in very similar ways toward a community as toward an individual person. We are to treat a community of good people differently than we treat a community of evil people. With the latter group, goodwill is to be practiced according to earthly impartiality; toward the former group, according to spiritual impartiality. But I will say more on these two kinds of impartiality elsewhere.

Our country is our neighbor more than our community is, because our country consists of many communities. Love for our country is therefore broader and higher. Loving our country is also loving the well-being of the general public.

Our country is our neighbor because it is like a parent. We were born in it. It has nourished us and continues to nourish us. It has kept us safe from harm and continues to do so.

414

We are to do good to our country with love according to what it needs. Some of its needs are earthly and some are spiritual. Its earthly needs center on its civic life and order. Its spiritual needs center on its spiritual life and order.

We are to love our country not merely as much as we love ourselves; we are to love it more. There is a law written on the human heart that gives rise to the statement all just people say when they are in imminent danger of dying because of an enemy or some other cause. They say that it is a noble thing to die for their country. They say that it is a glorious thing for soldiers to shed their blood for their country. They say this because that is how much one ought to love one's country.

It is important to know that if people love their country and benefit it because they wish it well, they love the Lord's kingdom after death. The Lord's kingdom is their country at that point. And those who love the Lord's kingdom love the Lord, since the Lord is everything to all his kingdom.

On an Even Higher Level, the Neighbor We Are to Love Is the Church, and on the Highest Level, Our Neighbor Is the Lord's Kingdom

415 WE are born for eternal life and are introduced into it by the church. Therefore we are to love the church as our neighbor on an even higher level [than we love our country]. The church teaches us the means that lead to eternal life and introduces us into that life. It leads us to eternal life by means of the true things in its body of teaching. It introduces us to that life through good ways to live.

This does not mean that we are to love the priesthood to a special degree or love the church on the priesthood's account. We are to love the church's goodness and truth, and love the priesthood on account of this goodness and truth. The priesthood only serves; it is to be honored according to its service.

We are to love the church as our neighbor on a higher level, even beyond our country, because our country initiates us into civic life but the church initiates us into spiritual life. Spiritual life is what sets us apart from a merely animal life.

What is more, our civic life is temporary. It comes to an end. Once it is over, it is the same as if it had not existed. Our spiritual life, on the other hand, is eternal, because it has no end. Spiritual life has a quality of reality therefore that civic life does not have. The difference between them is like the difference between what is finite and what is infinite—there is no ratio between them. Eternity is an infinity of time.

416 The Lord's kingdom is the neighbor to which we are to give the highest level of our love, because the Lord's kingdom means the church across the entire world, also known as "the communion of saints." It includes heaven as well.

People who love the Lord's kingdom love all in the whole world who acknowledge the Lord, have faith in him, and have goodwill toward their neighbor; they also love all who are in heaven. People who love the Lord's kingdom love the Lord above all else. They have more love for God than others do. This is because the church in the heavens and on earth is the Lord's body. They are in the Lord and the Lord is in them. Loving the Lord's kingdom, then, is fully loving their neighbor. People who love the Lord's kingdom not only love the Lord above all else; they also love their neighbor as themselves. Love for the Lord is a universal love. It affects every aspect of spiritual life and also every aspect of earthly life. This is because love for the Lord dwells in the highest reaches of us, and things at the top flow into things lower down and bring them to life in the same way that our will flows into all our intentions and actions, and our intellect flows into all our thoughts and conversations. Therefore the Lord says,

> Seek first the kingdom of the heavens and its justice. Then all these things will be added to you. (Matthew 6:33)

The kingdom of the heavens is the Lord's kingdom, as the following passage in Daniel shows:

> Behold, there was someone coming with the clouds of heaven—someone like *the Son of Humankind*. He was given dominion, glory, and a kingdom. All people, nations, and tongues will worship him. His dominion is a dominion of an age that will not pass and his kingdom is one that will not perish. (Daniel 7:13, 14)

Loving Our Neighbor Is Not in Fact Loving the Person but Loving the Goodness That Is inside the Person

SURELY everyone knows that people are not people because they have a human face and body—they are people because they have wisdom in their intellect and goodness in their will. The higher the quality of this wisdom and goodness, the more human the people are.

417

When people are born they are more brutish than any animal. They become human through being instructed. If they are responsive to the instruction, a mind forms within them. People are human because of their mind, depending on its particular nature.

There are animals that have faces that are close to human, but they have no faculty for higher understanding or for taking any action on the basis of that understanding. They act on an instinct that is activated by their earthly love. One difference between animals and people is that animals express in sound the feelings belonging to their love, while people speak their feelings as transferred into thought. Animals turn their faces downward and look at the ground, while people look at the sky in all directions, their faces lifted up.

From these points we can draw the following conclusion: the more we base what we say on sound reasoning and the more we focus on the time we will spend in heaven, the more human we are. Conversely, the more we base what we say on twisted reasoning and focus only on the time we are to spend in the world, the less human we are. In the latter case, we are still human, but only potentially rather than actually, since all people have the power to understand things that are true and to intend actions that are good. Even if we have no intention of doing what is good or understanding what is true, we nonetheless retain the ability to ape and mimic human qualities on the outside.

418 The reason goodness is our neighbor is that goodness belongs to our will and the will is the underlying reality of our life. Truth is our neighbor, too, but only to the extent that it emanates from something good in our will. Goodness that belongs to the will takes shape in our intellect and visibly presents itself there in the light of reason.

All our experience shows that goodness is our neighbor. We love people for the quality of their will and intellect, that is, the goodness and justness in them. For example, we love monarchs, princes, generals, officials, consuls, civic leaders, and judges for the judgment they show in their words and actions. We love church leaders, ministers, and their assistants for their knowledge, integrity of life, and passion for the well-being of souls. We love army generals and commanders under them for their fortitude and prudence. We love retailers for their honesty. We love workers and servants for their faithfulness. For that matter, we love a given species of tree for its fruit; the soil for its level of fertility; a stone for its preciousness; and so on.

Strange as it may seem, it is not just honest people who love goodness and justness in others. Dishonest people do too, because they do not fear losing reputation, respect, or wealth at the hands of honest people. The love that dishonest people have for goodness is not love for their neighbor, however—dishonest people do not inwardly love any others outside themselves unless those others serve them somehow.

Loving goodness in another person from goodness in ourselves is genuine love for our neighbor. In that situation the two goodnesses embrace and form a partnership.

People who love what is good because it is good and love what is true because it is true have supreme love for their neighbor, because they love the Lord who is goodness itself and truth itself. Love for goodness, love for truth, and love for our neighbor come from nowhere else. Love for our neighbor, then, has a heavenly origin.

419

It is the same thing whether you say "goodness" or "usefulness." Therefore doing good things is doing useful things. The amount and quality of usefulness that a given good thing has determines the amount and quality of its goodness.

Goodwill and Good Actions Are Two Distinct Things: Wishing People Well and Treating Them Well

ALL people have an inner level and an outer level. Their inner level is called the inner self and their outer level is called the outer self. Nevertheless, someone who does not know what the

420

inner and outer selves are could believe that our inner self is the source of our thinking and willing and our outer self is the source of our speaking and action. These are indeed inner and outer aspects of us, but they do not constitute the essence of our inner and outer selves. The human mind is indeed commonly held to be the inner self, but in actuality the mind is divided into two regions. One of the regions is spiritual; it is higher and farther within. The other is earthly; it is lower and farther outside. Our spiritual mind focuses principally on the spiritual world. It deals with the things in that world, whether they are the kind that exist in heaven or the kind that exist in hell. (Both kinds are in the spiritual world.) The earthly mind, on the other hand, focuses principally on the earthly realm. It deals with the things in this world, whether good or evil.

All our action and speaking emanates from the lower region of our mind through a direct route. Ultimately, however, it comes from the higher region of our mind, although the route is indirect because the lower region is closer to the senses in our body, while the higher region is farther away from them. This division within our mind exists because we have been created to be spiritual and earthly at the same time, and therefore to be human, not animal.

These points make it clear that people who focus primarily on themselves and worldly things are external people. They are earthly not only in body but also in mind. People who focus primarily on things that relate to heaven and the church are internal people. They are spiritual in both mind and body. They are spiritual in body as well because their actions and words come from their higher mind, which is spiritual, through their lower mind, which is earthly. (As people generally know, effects come from our body, while the causes that produce those effects come from our mind; the cause shapes every aspect of the effect.)

It is obvious that the human mind has been divided in this way from the fact that people are able to pretend, to flatter, to be hypocritical, or to playact. They can agree with what someone else is saying and nevertheless view it as ridiculous. They do the former in their lower mind, the latter in their higher one.

These things enable us to see how we are to understand the statement that goodwill and good works are two distinct things: wishing people well and treating them well. That is, they are formally distinct, like the mind that does the thinking and willing and the body through which the mind speaks and acts. In fact, they are essentially distinct as well, because the mind itself is divided into an inner region that is spiritual and an outer region that is earthly, as I said just above.

Therefore if the things we do come from our spiritual mind, they come from wishing others well, or goodwill. If, however, they come only from our earthly mind, they come from a form of wishing others well that is not genuine goodwill. It can appear to be goodwill in its outer form and yet not be genuine goodwill in its inner form. Goodwill that exists in an outer form alone does indeed present the look of goodwill, but lacks its essence.

This point could be illustrated by an analogy with seeds in the ground. Every type of seed gives rise to a shoot, but those shoots are either useful or useless, depending on their species. The same is true for spiritual seed, that is, for truth in the church that comes from the Word. A body of teaching grows out of this truth—a useful body of teaching if it is made out of genuine truths, a useless one if it is made out of truths that have been falsified. The same thing applies to goodwill that is exercised as the result of wishing our neighbors well, whether we wish them well for our own sake or for a worldly reason or for the sake of our neighbor in a narrower or a broader sense. If we wish our neighbors well for our own sake or for a worldly reason, our goodwill is not genuine. If we wish our neighbors well for their sake, our goodwill is genuine. See many statements that address these topics in the chapter on faith, especially in the discussion showing that "goodwill" is benevolence toward others; that "good works" are good actions that result from benevolence (§374); and that goodwill and faith are transient and exist only in our minds unless, when an opportunity occurs, they culminate in actions and become embodied in them (§§375–376).

Goodwill Itself Is Acting Justly and Faithfully in Our Position and Our Work and with the People with Whom We Interact

422 GOODWILL itself is acting justly and faithfully in our position and our work, because all the things we do in this way are useful to the community; and usefulness is goodness, and goodness in an impersonal sense is our neighbor. As I have shown above [§§412–414], our neighbor is not only individual people but also our community and the country as a whole.

For example, if monarchs lead the way for their subjects by setting an example of doing good, if they want their people to live by the laws of justice, if they reward people who live that way, if they give all people the consideration they deserve, if they keep their people safe from harm and invasion, if they act like parents to their countries, and take care for the general prosperity of their people—these monarchs have goodwill in their hearts. The things they do are good actions.

Priests who teach truths from the Word and use truths to lead to a goodness of life, and therefore to heaven, are practicing goodwill in very important ways, because they are caring for the souls of the people in their church.

Judges who make decisions on the basis of justice and the law, and not because of bribery or because someone is their friend or relative, are caring for the community and for the individual—for the community, because their decisions influence it to stay obedient to the law and fearful of breaking it, and for the individual, because their decisions allow justice to triumph over injustice.

Business people who act with honesty and without fraudulence are caring for the neighbor they do business with. So are workers and craftspeople when they do their work uprightly and honestly rather than falsely or deceptively. The same goes for everyone else—for ship captains and sailors, for farm workers and servants.

This is goodwill itself because it can be defined as follows: goodwill is doing good to our neighbor daily and constantly— not only to our neighbor as an individual but also to our neighbor collectively. The only way to do this is through practicing goodness and justice in our position and work and with the people with whom we have any interaction, because these are things we do every day. When we are not doing them, they still stay in our minds all the time; we think about them and intend to do them. 423

People who practice goodwill in this way become better and better forms of goodwill. Justice and faithfulness shape their minds and the practice of goodwill shapes their bodies. Over time, because of their form, they get to the point where everything they want and think about relates to goodwill. In the long run, they become like the people mentioned in the Word who have the law written on their hearts [Jeremiah 31:33]. Such people also take no credit for what they are doing since they are not thinking about receiving credit for it; they are thinking about their duty. In their view, acting this way is the right thing for citizens to do.

Nevertheless, we are completely incapable of acting on the basis of spiritual justice and faithfulness *on our own*. We all inherit from our parents the trait of doing what is good and just for our own sake or for worldly reasons. None of us hereditarily does these things for the sake of goodness and justice.

Therefore only when people worship the Lord, and function from the Lord while they seem to be functioning on their own, do they attain spiritual goodwill and become saturated with it as the result of constant practice.

424 Many people behave justly and faithfully in their jobs, and yet although they are doing works of goodwill in this way, they still have no goodwill in themselves. Their love for themselves and for the world is in control rather than love for heaven. If love for heaven happens to be present at all, it is under their other loves like a slave under a master, like a foot soldier under a commander, like a doorkeeper standing by the door.

Acts of Kindness Related to Goodwill Consist in Giving to the Poor and Helping the Needy, Although with Prudence

425 IT is important to distinguish between work-related acts of goodwill and incidental acts of kindness. "Work-related acts of goodwill" means those practices of goodwill that come straight from goodwill itself, since goodwill itself is a function of the work that we do, as I have shown just above. "Acts of kindness," however, refers to helpful acts that are done outside of our work.

They are called acts of kindness because we are free to do them as we please, and when we do them, the recipients see them as kindnesses and nothing else. We do them according to the reasons and intentions we have in mind as benefactors.

It is a common belief that goodwill consists solely of giving to the poor, helping the needy, caring for widows and orphans, and making contributions to build, enhance, and endow hospices, hospitals, hostels, orphanages, and especially church buildings. Many of these actions, however, are not integral to the exercise of goodwill; they are extraneous to it.

People who consider goodwill to be good deeds of these kinds cannot help taking credit for them. Although people may claim aloud that they do not want any credit for their good deeds, nevertheless inside them lies the belief that they deserve credit. This is perfectly obvious after death when people like this list the things they have done and demand salvation as their reward. They are then investigated to find out what origin their actions had and what quality their actions possessed as a result. Whatever origin the actions had—whether they came from arrogance, or from a hunger for fame, or from a wish to be seen as generous, or from a desire to win friends, or from some merely earthly tendency, or from hypocrisy—they are judged on the basis of that origin, because the quality of the origin lies within the actions. Genuine goodwill, however, emanates from people who have become steeped in it through doing work based on justice and judgment without the goal of being repaid, in accordance with the Lord's words (Luke 14:12, 13, 14). People of genuine goodwill refer to the donations listed just above [not as goodwill itself but] as acts of kindness and also duties, although they are related to goodwill.

As is generally recognized, there are people who do acts of kindness that seem to the world like the very picture of goodwill, with the result that these people believe they have performed acts of genuine goodwill. They look at their own acts of kindness the way many Catholics look at indulgences that have absolved them of their sins. They believe heaven ought to be granted to them since they are regenerated as a consequence; yet in fact they do not consider acts of adultery, hatred, revenge, fraud, or fleshly craving of whatever kind to be sinful. They indulge in such acts whenever they like. But in that case, their good actions are like paintings of angels and devils at a party together, or like boxes made of lapis lazuli that have poisonous snakes inside them. It is completely different if people do the same acts of kindness but abstain from the evils just listed because these evils are the enemies of goodwill.

Nevertheless, doing kindnesses is enriching in many ways—especially giving to the poor and to people who are begging. By acts like these, young men and women, male and female

426

servants, and simple people of all kinds are initiated into the exercise of goodwill. These actions are outward habits that help the givers absorb the benefits of goodwill. They are the beginnings of goodwill; they are like fruit not yet ripened. For people who afterward develop proper concepts of goodwill and faith, these habits become like fruit fully ripe. People like this come to regard the things they used to do from simplicity of heart as things they are now obliged to do.

427 Nowadays, kindnesses like these are seen as the central acts of goodwill that are referred to in the Word as "good works." The reason for this is that many times in the Word goodwill is characterized as giving to the poor, helping the needy, and taking care of widows and orphans. Up until now people have not known that the letter of the Word mentions only things that are external and are in fact the outermost aspects of worship; people have not realized that these external things have meanings that are spiritual and internal. On this last point, see the chapter above on Sacred Scripture (§§193–209). Those passages make it clear that mentions of the poor, needy, widows, and orphans in the Word do not [literally] refer to such people; they refer to people who are spiritually poor, needy, widowed, or orphaned. For "the poor" meaning people who have no concepts of goodness or truth, see *Revelation Unveiled* 209. For "widows" meaning people who have been separated from truths and yet long for them, see §764 there; and so on.

428 People who are born compassionate and yet do not make their earthly acts of compassion spiritual by doing them out of genuine goodwill tend to believe that goodwill is giving to any poor person and helping any needy person without first finding out whether the poor or needy person is good or evil. They say this is not necessary, because God notices only the helpful gesture and the act of mercy. After death, however, people like this are identified and completely separated from people who have done prudent kindnesses related to goodwill. The people who have done kindnesses based on a blind idea of goodwill do

just as many kindnesses for the evil as for the good. The evil use the kindnesses to do evil things and harm good people. In that case the benefactors share the responsibility for harming good people.

Doing an act of kindness for an evildoer is like giving bread to a devil; the devil will turn it into poison. All bread that is in the hand of a devil is poison. If it is not, the devil will turn it into poison by diverting the act of kindness to an evil purpose.

It is as if you handed your enemy a sword, and the enemy killed someone with it. It is as if you gave a shepherd's staff to a human wolf to bring the sheep into the pasture; yet the human wolf, staff in hand, drove the sheep away from the pasture into the wilderness and slaughtered them there. It is as if you gave leadership and control to a thief whose sole focus was keeping an eye out for things to steal; the thief would create rules and make decisions based primarily on the abundance and value of the loot.

* * *

The First Step toward Goodwill Is Removing Evils; the Second Step Is Doing Good Things That Are Useful to Our Neighbor

AMONG teachings on goodwill the following point is primary: the first step toward goodwill is not to do evil to our neighbor. A secondary point is to do good to our neighbor. This is like a doorway to the teachings on goodwill.

435

As people generally know, evil dwells in the will of every human being from birth. Because all evil targets someone nearby or far away, including the wider community and the country, it follows that hereditary evil is evil against our neighbor on every scale.

On the basis of reason itself we can all see that the less we remove the evil that dwells in our will, the more the good we do is pregnant with that evil, because then evil exists inside the goodness like a kernel in a shell or the marrow in a bone.

Therefore although good things that someone does in that state appear to be good, they are nevertheless not good inside. They are like a shiny shell containing a nut that has been consumed by worms. They are like a white almond that has rottenness inside it, so that rotten streaks have crept up to the surface.

[2] Intending evil and doing good are two things that are intrinsically opposite to each other. Evil comes from hatred for our neighbor and good comes from love for our neighbor. Or to put it another way, evil is an enemy to our neighbor and goodness is our neighbor's friend. The two cannot exist in a single mind, that is, there cannot be evil in our inner self and goodness in our outer self. If there were, the goodness on the outside would be like a wound that has been superficially treated, beneath which there lies the pus of an infection. We ourselves would then be like a tree whose roots are unsound; it produces pieces of fruit that outwardly look tasty and beneficial, although inwardly they are rotten and useless. Our good deeds would also be like pieces of rejected slag, superficially polished and beautifully colored, which are offered for sale as precious stones. Briefly put, these good deeds would be like the eggs of an owl mistaken for the eggs of a dove.

[3] It is important to know that the good things people accomplish with the body come from the spirit or the inner self. The inner self is their spirit, which lives after death. Therefore when [evil] people cast away the body that formed their outer self, they are made up of nothing but their own evils. They enjoy these evils and steer away from goodness as a threat to the way they live.

[4] The Lord teaches in many passages that we cannot do good things that are intrinsically good before evil has been removed from us:

> Do people gather grapes from thornbushes or figs from thistles? A rotten tree cannot produce good fruit. (Matthew 7:16, 17, 18)

Woe to you, scribes and Pharisees. You clean the outside of the cup and the plate, but the insides are full
of plundering and self-indulgence. Blind Pharisee, first
clean the inside of the cup and the plate, so that the
outside may become clean as well. (Matthew 23:25, 26)

And in Isaiah,

Wash yourselves. Remove the evil of your actions. Stop
doing evil. Learn to do what is good; seek [good] judgment. Then if your sins had been like scarlet, they will
become as white as snow. If they had been red as crim-
son, they will be like wool. (Isaiah 1:16, 17, 18)

This point can be illustrated further by analogies: Suppose 436
someone keeps a leopard and a panther in an apartment and,
as the one who feeds them, is able to live safely with them. No
one else can visit unless their owner first removes these wild animals. Guests invited to the table of the king and queen would
not forget to wash their faces and hands before attending. Anyone must first purify ore with fire and remove slag before getting pure gold or silver. Everyone separates the tares or weeds
from the harvested wheat before taking it into the barn. Everyone cooks some of the juice out of raw meat before it becomes
edible and is set on the table. Everyone knocks the grubs and
caterpillars off the leaves of a tree in the garden to prevent them
from devouring the leaves and causing a loss of fruit. Does any
man love a young woman and propose to marry her if she is
riddled with malignancies or covered all over with pustules and
varicose veins, no matter how much she puts makeup on her
face, wears gorgeous clothing, and makes an effort to be attractive by saying nice things and paying compliments?

The need for us to purify ourselves from evils, and not to
wait for the Lord to do it without our participation, is like a
servant coming in with his face and clothes covered in soot or
dung, approaching his master and saying, "Lord, wash me."
Surely his master would tell him, "You foolish servant! What

are you saying? Look, there is the water, the soap, and a towel. Don't you have hands? Don't they work? Wash yourself!"

The Lord God is going to say, "The means of being purified come from me. Your willingness and power come from me. Therefore use these gifts and endowments of mine as your own and you will be purified."

437 There is a belief nowadays that goodwill is just our doing good, and if we do that, we are not doing evil. The idea therefore is that the first step toward goodwill is to do good and the second step is not to do evil. This is completely upside-down, however. The first step toward goodwill is to remove evils and the second step is to do good, because there is a law that is universal to the spiritual world and also therefore to the physical world: The less evil we intend, the more good we intend. Therefore the more we turn away from hell (from which all evil ascends), the more we turn toward heaven (from which all goodness descends). The more we reject the Devil, then, the more we are accepted by the Lord. People cannot stand between the Devil and the Lord with a flexible neck and pray at the same time to each of them. People like this are those whom the Lord meant when he said,

> I know your works, that you are neither cold nor hot. It would have been better if you were cold or hot; but since you are lukewarm and neither cold nor hot I am about to spew you out my mouth. (Revelation 3:15, 16)

Could anyone leading a troop of soldiers join a battle between two armies and fight on both sides at once? Can we focus on doing evil to our neighbors and also doing good to them? Would our evil not then lie hidden inside our good actions? Although evil that conceals itself does not appear in our actions, it is still obvious from many things when we reflect on it in the right way. The Lord says, "No servant can serve two masters. You cannot serve God and Mammon" (Luke 16:13).

Still, none of us can purify ourselves from evils by our own
power and our own force. On the other hand, neither can we
purify ourselves without having power and force as if they were
our own. If we did not have apparent power, none of us could
fight against the flesh and its cravings, although we have all
been ordered to do so. In fact, we could not even think about
battling them. We would let our mind go into evils of every
kind. We would be held back from actually doing evils only by
the laws of justice that have been passed in the world and the
penalties they prescribe. Inside we would be like tigers, leop-
ards, or snakes that utterly fail to reflect on the cruelty that their
hearts enjoy.

Clearly then, because we are rational in a way that animals
are not, we have to resist evils using the powers and abilities the
Lord gives us, although as far as we can tell, those powers and
abilities appear to be our own. The Lord gives us all this illusion in order to regenerate us, attribute goodness to us, forge a
partnership with us, and save us.

438

As Long as We Believe That Everything Good Comes from the Lord, We Do Not Take Credit for the Things We Do As We Practice Goodwill

IT is damaging for us to take credit for things we do for the
sake of our salvation. Hidden within our credit-taking there are
evil attitudes of which we are unaware at the time: denial that
God flows in and works in us; confidence in our own power in
regard to salvation; faith in ourselves and not in God; [the delu-
sion that] we justify and save ourselves by our own strength;
contempt for divine grace and mercy; rejection of reformation
and regeneration by divine means; and especially disregard for
the merit and justice of the Lord God our Savior, which we
then claim as our own. In our taking credit there is also a con-
tinual focus on our own reward and perception of it as our first

439

and last goal, a stifling and an extinction of love for the Lord and love for our neighbor, and total ignorance and unawareness of the pleasure involved in heavenly love (which takes no credit), while all we feel is our love for ourselves.

People who put their own reward as the first priority and salvation as the second, and therefore seek salvation as a reward, turn the proper arrangement upside down. They drown their inner desires in self-absorption and physically pollute them with evils belonging to their flesh. For this reason, goodness that we do to earn merit looks to the angels like a rust-colored plant disease, while goodness that we do not do to earn merit looks a rich purplish-red.

The Lord teaches in Luke that we are not supposed to do good for the purpose of getting a reward:

> If you benefit people who benefit you, what grace do you have? Rather, love and benefit your enemies, and lend [to people] expecting nothing back. Then your reward will be large, and you will be children of the Highest, since he is kind to the ungrateful and the evil. (Luke 6:33–36)

It is also taught in John that we cannot do anything truly good except from the Lord:

> Live in me and I [shall live] in you. As a branch cannot bear fruit on its own unless it lives in the vine, neither can you unless you live in me, because without me you cannot do anything. (John 15:4, 5)

> We cannot receive anything unless it is given to us from heaven. (John 3:27)

440   On the other hand, if people think about going to heaven and decide that they should therefore do what is good, this is not the same as making rewards their main goal or taking credit for their good deeds. People who love their neighbor as themselves and love God above all else have these thoughts because they have faith in the Lord's words that their reward will be great in heaven (Matthew 5:11, 12; 6:1; 10:41, 42; Luke 6:23, 35; 14:12, 13, 14; John 4:36); that people who do good things are going to possess as an inheritance a kingdom prepared since the founding of the world (Matthew 25:34); and that all are paid back for what they have done (Matthew 16:27; John 5:29; Revelation 14:13; 20:12, 13; Jeremiah 25:14; 32:19; Hosea 4:9; Zechariah 1:6; and elsewhere). What these people have is not confidence in a reward because they deserve it; they have faith in the promise of grace.

The pleasure of doing good to their neighbor *is* their reward. The angels in heaven feel this pleasure. It is a spiritual pleasure that is eternal. It immeasurably surpasses every earthly pleasure. People who have this pleasure do not want to hear about getting credit—they love doing good and feel joy in it. It depresses them if someone thinks they are doing it to get something in return. They are like people who benefit their friends for friendship's sake; who benefit their siblings for their siblings' sake; who benefit their spouse and children for their spouse's and children's sake; who benefit their country for their country's sake—people whose actions are based on friendship and love. People who do these good things state with conviction that they did not do it for themselves; they did it for the others.

It is completely different for people who focus on getting a reward as the primary goal of what they do. They are like those who strike up a friendship to get money; they give gifts, do favors, and profess their love as if it were heartfelt, but when they do not get what they were hoping for, they turn their backs, drop the friendship, and join up with the other's enemies and detractors.

They are like wet nurses who breastfeed babies only for the money. While the parents are looking, they kiss the babies and

441

stroke them, but as soon as they are unsatisfied with the quality of the food they are given or do not get paid whatever they ask, they reject the babies, treat them roughly, beat them, and laugh at their crying.

[2] They are like people who focus on their country because they love themselves and the world. They say they intend the country's well-being and are devoting their lives to it, but if they do not receive promotions and wealth as rewards, they bad-mouth the country and become allies with its enemies.

They are like shepherds who take care of sheep only because of the money. If they do not get their money on time, they take their staffs and drive the sheep off the pasture into the wilderness. Priests who perform their duties only for the stipend involved are like these shepherds. Clearly, they do not care at all about the salvation of the souls that are under their care and guidance.

[3] It is the same with government officials who focus only on the status and the income from their job. When they do something good, it is not for the public good but for the pleasure they take in loving themselves and the world, which they inhale as the only form of good.

The same sort of attitudes are possible in any line of work. The goal or purpose is the determining factor throughout. If the means employed in a given pursuit fail to achieve the goal, they are abandoned.

[4] People who are looking for the reward of salvation that they feel they deserve behave similarly. After death they demand heaven with tremendous confidence. Once it is discovered that they have no love for God or their neighbor, they are sent to teachers who instruct them about faith and goodwill. If they reject what they are taught, they are exiled to be with people like themselves, some of whom are enraged at God because they have not been given their rewards. They call faith a figment of the imagination.

These are the people who are meant in the Word by "hired workers," who were given extremely menial jobs in the entrances to the Temple. From a distance [in the spiritual world] these people look as if they are splitting logs.

It is extremely important to realize that goodwill is closely linked to faith in the Lord. The quality of the faith determines the quality of the goodwill. For the point that the Lord, goodwill, and faith form a unity in the same way our life, our will, and our intellect form a unity, and that if we separate them, each one crumbles like a pearl that is crushed to powder, see §362 and following above. Also see the point that goodwill and faith come together in good actions, §§373–377. From those teachings it follows that the quality of our faith determines the quality of our goodwill; and the quality of our faith and goodwill combined determines the quality of our actions.

Now, if we believe that everything good that we do as if we are doing it on our own actually comes from the Lord, then we are the instrumental cause of that good and the Lord is its principal cause. These two causes seem to us to be one thing, but in fact the principal cause affects every aspect of the instrumental cause. It follows then that if we believe that everything truly good comes from the Lord, we do not take credit for what we do. The more developed this faith becomes in us, the more the Lord takes away our fantasies about getting credit for what we have done. In this state we can practice goodwill abundantly without a fear of taking credit. Eventually we sense the spiritual pleasure in goodwill. Then we become averse to taking credit because doing so is damaging to our life.

It is easy for the Lord to erase people's idea that they deserve credit, provided those people attain goodwill primarily through working justly and faithfully in the position, business, or line of work they are in and with the people with whom they interact (see §§422, 423, 424 above). If, however, people believe that they attain goodwill through making charitable donations and helping the needy, it is difficult to rid them of the idea that they deserve credit, because as they make those contributions their desire for reward and credit, although obvious to them at first, becomes less noticeable [to them] as time goes by.

A Life of Goodwill Is a Moral Life That Is Also Spiritual

443 WE all learn from our parents and teachers to live a moral life, that is, to behave like civil human beings. We learn to discharge the duties of an honorable life, which are related to the various virtues that constitute the essence of being honorable. We also learn to discharge these dutiful acts through the outward forms called manners. As we advance in age, we learn to add the exercise of rationality, and we use that rationality to enhance the morality of our life.

The moral life in youths up to early adulthood is earthly. After that it becomes increasingly rational. People who reflect on the question can see that a moral life is the same thing as a life of goodwill, which is behaving well to our neighbor and regulating our life to keep it from being contaminated with evils (as follows from the points made above in §§435–438). Nevertheless, in the first phase of our lives, our moral life is a life of goodwill on the outermost level, that is, only in the outward, most superficial part of our life, but not deeper within it.

[2] There are four phases to our lives. We pass through them as we go from infancy to old age. The first phase is when our behavior follows other people's instructions. The second is when our behavior is our own, and our intellect restrains us. The third is when our will pushes our intellect and our intellect restrains our will. The fourth is when our behavior is deliberate and purposeful.

These phases of our lives are phases of the life of our spirit, however; they do not necessarily relate to our body. Our body can behave morally and speak rationally, and yet our spirit can intend and think things that are the opposite of morality and rationality. It is clear from pretenders, flatterers, liars, and hypocrites that this is the nature of our earthly self. Clearly, people like this have a dual mind—their mind can be divided into two parts that do not agree.

It is different for people who have benevolent intentions and think rational thoughts, and as a result do good things and speak rationally. These are the type of people meant by "the simple in spirit" in the Word. They are called simple because they are not dual.

[3] These statements clarify the proper meaning of the outer self and the inner self; they show that we cannot conclude from other people's morality in their outer self that they have morality in their inner self. Their inner self could be turned in the opposite direction. It could be hiding the way a turtle hides its head in its shell or the way a snake hides its head in its coils. In that case their supposedly moral self is like a robber who spends time both in the city and in the woods; in the city the robber behaves like a moral person, but in the woods, like a thief.

It is completely different for people who are inwardly moral, whose spirit is moral, and who attained that nature by being regenerated by the Lord. Such people constitute the type meant by the phrase "spiritually moral."

When our moral life is also spiritual, it is a life of goodwill, because the practices involved in a moral life and in a life of goodwill are the same. Goodwill is wishing our neighbors well and therefore treating them well. This is also a moral way of life. The following statement by the Lord is a spiritual law:

444

> All things whatever that you want people to do for you,
>   do likewise for them. This is the Law and the Prophets.
>   (Matthew 7:12)

This same law is universally applicable to a moral life as well. But listing all the practices related to goodwill and comparing them with the practices related to a moral life would require many pages. Just take six commandments from the second tablet of the Ten Commandments for an illustration—it is clear to everyone that they are principles for a moral life. (As for their containing all aspects of loving our neighbor, see §§329, 330, and 331 above.)

The following statement in Paul makes it clear that goodwill fulfills all the commandments:

> Love each other, for those who love others have fulfilled the law. The commandments that you are not to commit adultery, you are not to kill, you are not to steal, you are not to bear false witness, you are not to covet, and anything else that has been commanded, are included in the following saying: "You are to love your neighbor as yourself." Goodwill does not do evil to its neighbor. Goodwill is the fullness of the law. (Romans 13:8, 9, 10)

People who think only with their outer selves cannot help being astounded that the seven commandments on the second tablet were proclaimed by Jehovah on Mount Sinai in such a miraculous way, given that these same rules were legal principles of civic justice in all the countries on earth, including Egypt, where the children of Israel had just come from. No country can survive without these rules.

The reason why Jehovah proclaimed them, however, and wrote them with his own finger on tablets of stone was that they are rules not only for all civic communities and therefore rules for a moral earthly life, they are also rules for all heavenly communities and therefore rules for a moral spiritual life. Acting against these rules then is acting not only against other people but also against God.

445 If we could see what a moral life is in its essence, we would see that it is a life in accordance with human laws and divine laws at the same time. Therefore people who live by both sets of laws as one law are truly moral and live a life of goodwill.

Anyone who wants to grasp the nature of goodwill is capable of doing so by looking at the nature of outward moral life. Just copy the outward moral life you have in civil interaction into your inner self so that your inner willing and thinking parallel the actions of your outer self, and you will see a model of goodwill.

ABOUT *SECRETS OF HEAVEN*

Secrets of Heaven, originally published in eight volumes between 1749 and 1756, is Swedenborg's magnum opus. Written at the beginning of his revelatory period, the work—often referred to by its abbreviated Latin title, *Arcana Coelestia*—reflects his new understanding and lays the foundation for the rest of his theology.

The broad structure is a verse-by-verse commentary on the inner meaning of the Bible, beginning with the first verse of Genesis and ending with the book of Exodus. However, interspersed with the biblical interpretation are chapters of material based on his spiritual experiences, some of which would later become the basis for separate books.

In *Secrets of Heaven*, Swedenborg argues that the Bible should not be interpreted literally, but as a description of spiritual principles. For example, take the familiar story of Adam and Eve eating the fruit of the tree of knowledge. The snake that tempts

Eve represents our own senses and intellect, and eating the apple represents an attempt to judge spiritual goodness and truth by reasoning things out rather than trusting the good impulses that come to us from the Lord. Trusting ourselves rather than God, Swedenborg says, leads to spiritual death.

This method of interpreting the Bible is often called the "doctrine of correspondences," and it is a key aspect of Swedenborg's theology. He describes correspondences as "the mutual relationship between spiritual and earthly things" (*Divine Love and Wisdom* 71). In his cosmology, there are two separate universes, one spiritual and one material; the two coexist as one intertwined creation. Water, for instance—the combination of hydrogen and oxygen that exists in our physical universe— is truth in the spiritual universe. So when the word "water" appears in the Bible, it's actually a reference to water in the spiritual realm, that is, to truth. Likewise, the sun in heaven (as described in the excerpt from *Divine Love and Wisdom* in this volume) radiates divine love and wisdom in the same way that our sun radiates heat and light. Therefore, love corresponds to heat and wisdom to light. According to Swedenborg, if you read the Bible with correspondences in mind, you can learn a great deal about the spiritual state of our world and our inner selves.

Swedenborg covers many more topics in *Secrets of Heaven*. He describes the soul's passage from earthly life into the world of spirits, and goes on to paint a detailed picture of heaven and hell. He devotes many sections to a discussion of correspondences and the Universal Human, by which he means that heaven has the structure of a human being, and that communities of angels work together to perform symbolically the same functions as the corresponding organs in a human body. He revisits the question of how the soul interacts with the body— something he had written about earlier in life—from a fresh perspective. There is a lengthy series of discussions about goodwill and faith, and how the two interact. Finally, in one of his more intriguing claims, he writes about his encounters with the spirits of people who once lived on other planets.

In the following excerpt, Swedenborg examines the story of Creation in detail.

[The Essential Nature of the Word]

THE Word in the Old Testament contains secrets of heaven, and every single aspect of it has to do with the Lord, his heaven, the church, faith, and all the tenets of faith; but not a single person sees this in the letter. In the letter, or literal meaning, people see only that it deals for the most part with the external facts of the Jewish religion.

The truth is, however, that every part of the Old Testament holds an inner message. Except at a very few points, those inner depths never show on the surface. The exceptions are concepts that the Lord revealed and explained to the apostles, such as the fact that the sacrifices symbolize the Lord, and that the land of Canaan and Jerusalem symbolize heaven (which is why it is called the heavenly Canaan or Jerusalem [Galatians 4:26; Hebrews 11:16; 12:22; Revelation 21:2, 10]), as does Paradise.

The Christian world, though, remains deeply ignorant of the fact that each and every detail down to the smallest—even down to the tiniest jot—enfolds and symbolizes spiritual and heavenly matters; and because it lacks such knowledge, it also lacks much interest in the Old Testament.

Still, Christians can come to a proper understanding if they reflect on a single notion: that since the Word is the Lord's and comes from him, it could not possibly exist unless it held within it the kinds of things that have to do with heaven, the church, and faith. Otherwise it could not be called the Lord's Word, nor could it be said to contain any life. Where, after all, does life come from if not from what is living? That is, if not from the fact that every single thing in the Word relates to the Lord, who is truly life itself? Whatever does not look to him at some deeper level, then, is without life; in fact, if a single expression in the Word does not embody or reflect him in its own way, it is not divine.

3 Without this interior life, the Word in its letter is dead. It resembles a human being, in that a human has an outward self and an inward one, as the Christian world knows. The outer being, separated from the inner, is just a body and so is dead, but the inward being is what lives and allows the outward being to live. The inner being is a person's soul.

In the same way, the letter of the Word by itself is a body without a soul.

4 The Word's literal meaning alone, when it monopolizes our thinking, can never provide a view of the inner contents. Take for example this first chapter of Genesis. The literal meaning by itself offers no clue that it is speaking of anything but the world's creation, the Garden of Eden (Paradise), and Adam, the first human ever created. Who supposes anything else?

The wisdom hidden in these details (and never before revealed) will be clear enough from what follows. The inner sense of the first chapter of Genesis deals in general with the process that creates us anew—that is to say, with regeneration—and in particular with the very earliest church; and it does so in such a way that not even the smallest syllable fails to represent, symbolize, and incorporate this meaning.

5 But without the Lord's aid not a soul can possibly see that this is the case. As a result, it is proper to reveal in these pre-liminaries that the Lord in his divine mercy has granted me the opportunity for several years now, without break or interruption, to keep company with spirits and angels, to hear them talking, and to speak with them in turn. Consequently I have been able to see and hear the most amazing things in the other life, which have never before come into people's awareness or thought.

In that world I have been taught about the different kinds of spirits, the situation of souls after death, hell (or the regret-table state of the faithless), and heaven (or the blissful state of the faithful). In particular I have learned what is taught in the faith acknowledged by the whole of heaven. All of these topics will, with the Lord's divine mercy, be explored further in what follows.

Genesis I

1. In the beginning, God created heaven and earth.

2. And the earth was void and emptiness; and there was darkness on the face of the abyss. And the Spirit of God was constantly moving on the face of the water.

3. And God said, "Let there be light," and there was light.

4. And God saw the light, that it was good; and God made a distinction between light and darkness.

5. And God called the light day, and the darkness he called night. And there was evening and there was morning, the first day.

6. And God said, "Let there be an expanse in the middle of the waters, and let it exist to make a distinction among the waters, in the waters."

7. And God made the expanse, and he made a distinction between the waters that were under the expanse and the waters that were over the expanse; and so it was done.

8. And God called the expanse heaven. And there was evening and there was morning, the second day.

9. And God said, "Let the waters under heaven be gathered into one place, and let dry land appear," and so it was done.

10. And God called the dry land earth, and the gathering of waters he called seas. And God saw that it was good.

11. And God said, "Let the earth cause the sprouting on the earth of the tender plant, of the plant bearing its seed, of the fruit tree making the fruit that holds its seed, each in the way of its kind," and so it was done.

12. And the earth produced the tender plant, the plant bearing its seed in the way of its kind, and the tree making the fruit

that held its seed in the way of its kind, and God saw that it was good.

13. And there was evening and there was morning, the third day.

14. And God said, "Let there be lights in the expanse of the heavens to make a distinction between day and night; and they will act as signals and will be used for seasons for both the days and the years.

15. And they will act as lights in the expanse of the heavens to shed light on the earth"; and so it was done.

16. And God made the two great lights: the greater light to rule by day and the smaller light to rule by night; and the stars.

17. And God placed them in the expanse of the heavens, to shed light on the earth,

18. and to rule during the day and during the night, and to make a distinction between light and darkness; and God saw that it was good.

19. And there was evening and there was morning, the fourth day.

20. And God said, "Let the waters cause the creeping animal—a living soul—to creep out. And let the bird flit over the land, over the face of the expanse of the heavens."

21. And God created the big sea creatures, and every living, creeping soul that the waters caused to creep out, in all their kinds, and every bird on the wing, of every kind. And God saw that it was good.

22. And God blessed them, saying, "Reproduce and multiply and fill the water in the seas, and the birds will multiply on the land."

23. And there was evening and there was morning, the fifth day.

24. And God said, "Let the earth produce each living soul according to its kind: the beast, and that which moves, and the wild animal of the earth, each according to its kind"; and so it was done.

25. And God made each wild animal of the earth according to its kind, and each beast according to its kind, and every animal creeping on the ground according to its kind; and God saw that it was good.

26. And God said, "Let us make a human in our image, after our likeness; and these will rule over the fish of the sea and over the bird in the heavens, and over the beast, and over all the earth, and over every creeping animal that creeps on the earth."

27. And God created the human in his image; in God's image he created them; male and female he created them.

28. And God blessed them, and God said to them, "Reproduce and multiply, and fill the earth and harness it, and rule over the fish of the sea and over the bird in the heavens and over every living animal creeping on the earth."

29. And God said, "Here, now, I am giving you every seed-bearing plant on the face of all the earth and every tree that has fruit; the tree that produces seed will serve you for food.

30. And every wild animal of the earth and every bird in the heavens and every animal creeping on the earth, in which there is a living soul—every green plant will serve them for nourishment." And so it was done.

31. And God saw all that he had done and, yes, it was very good. And there was evening and there was morning, the sixth day.

Summary of Genesis I

THE six days or time periods, meaning so many consecutive stages in a person's regeneration, are these, in outline:

The first stage is preliminary, extending from infancy to just before regeneration, and is called void, emptiness, and darkness. The first stirring, which is the Lord's mercy, is the Spirit of God in constant motion on the face of the water.

In the second stage, a distinction is drawn between the things that are the Lord's and those that are our own. The things that are the Lord's are called a "remnant" in the Word. In this instance the "remnant" refers principally to religious knowledge acquired from early childhood on. This remnant is stored away, not to reappear until we arrive at such a stage.

At present the second stage rarely comes into play without trouble, misfortune, and grief, which enable bodily and worldly concerns—things that are our own—to fade away and in effect die out. The things that belong to the outer self, then, are separated from those that belong to the inner self, the inner self containing the remnant that the Lord has put aside to await this time and this purpose.

9 The third stage is one of repentance. During this time, at the prompting of the inner self, we speak devoutly and reverently and yield a good harvest (acts of neighborly kindness, for instance). These effects are lifeless nonetheless, since we suppose that they come of our own doing. They are called the tender plant, then the seed-bearing plant, and lastly the fruit tree.

10 In the fourth stage, love stirs and faith enlightens us. Before this time we may have spoken devoutly and yielded a good harvest, but we did so in a state of trial and anguish, not at the call of faith and kindness. In consequence they are now kindled in our inner self and are called the two lights.

11 In the fifth stage, we *speak* with conviction and, in the process, strengthen ourselves in truth and goodness. The things we then produce have life in them and are called the fish of the sea and the birds in the heavens.

12 In the sixth stage, we *act* with conviction and therefore with love in speaking truth and doing good. What we then produce is called a living soul and a beast. Because we begin to act as much from love as from conviction, we become spiritual people, who are called [God's] image.

In regard to our *spiritual* lives, we now find pleasure and nourishment in religious knowledge and acts of kindness; and these are called our food. In regard to our *earthly* lives, we still find pleasure and sustenance in things relating to our body and our senses, which cause strife until love takes charge and we develop a heavenly character.

Not everyone who undergoes regeneration reaches this stage. Some (the great majority, these days) arrive only at the first stage, some only at the second, some at the third, fourth, or fifth, very few at the sixth, and almost no one at the seventh.

13

Inner Meaning of Genesis I

FROM this point on, the term *Lord* is used in only one way: to refer to the Savior of the world, Jesus Christ; and the name "Lord" is used without any additions.

14

He is acknowledged and revered as Lord throughout heaven because he possesses all power in heaven and on earth.

He also commanded this when he said, "You address me as 'Lord.' You speak correctly, because so I am" (John 13:13). And his disciples called him Lord after the resurrection.

In the whole of heaven no one knows of any other Father than the Lord, since the Father and the Lord are one. As he himself said:

15

> "I am the way and the truth and life." Philip says, "Show us your Father." Jesus says to him, "After all the time I've spent with you, don't you know me, Philip? Whoever has seen me has seen my Father. How then can you say, 'Show us your Father'? Don't you believe that I am in my Father and my Father is in me? Believe me, that I am in my Father and my Father is in me." (John 14:6, 8, 9, 10, 11)

Genesis 1:1. *In the beginning, God created heaven and earth.* The word *beginning* is being used for the very earliest times. The prophets frequently call them "the days of old."

16

"The beginning" includes the first period of regeneration too, as that is when people are being born anew and receiving

life. Because of this, regeneration itself is called our new creation [2 Corinthians 5:17; Galatians 6:15]. Almost everywhere
in the prophetic books, the words *creating, forming,* and *making*
stand for regenerating, though with differences. In Isaiah, for
example:

> All have been called by my name, and I have created
> them for my glory; I have formed them; yes, I have
> made them. (Isaiah 43:7)

This is why the Lord is called Redeemer, One-Who-Forms-
from-the-Womb, Maker, and Creator, as in the same prophet:

> I am Jehovah, your Holy One, the Creator of Israel,
> your Monarch. (Isaiah 43:15)

In David:

> The people created will praise Jah. (Psalms 102:18)

In the same author:

> You send out your spirit—they will continue to be cre-
> ated—and you renew the face of the ground. (Psalms
> 104:30)

Heaven, or the sky, symbolizes the inner self, and the *earth,*
before regeneration occurs, symbolizes the outer self, as may be
seen below [§§17, 24:3, 27].

17   Genesis 1:2. *And the earth was void and emptiness, and there
was darkness on the face of the abyss, and the Spirit of God was
constantly moving on the face of the water.*

Before regeneration a person is called the *void, empty earth,*
and also soil in which no seed of goodness or truth has been
planted. *Void* refers to an absence of goodness and *empty* to an
absence of truth. The result is *darkness,* in which a person is
oblivious to or ignorant of anything having to do with faith in
the Lord and consequently with a spiritual or heavenly life. The
Lord portrays such a person this way in Jeremiah:

My people are dense; they do not know me. They are stupid children, without understanding. They are wise in doing evil but do not know how to do good. I looked at the *earth,* and there—void and emptiness; and to the *heavens,* and these had no light. (Jeremiah 4:22, 23, 25)

The *face of the abyss* means our cravings and the falsities these give rise to; we are wholly made up of cravings and falsities and wholly surrounded by them. Because no ray of light is in us, we are like an abyss, or something disorganized and dim.

Many passages in the Word also call such people abysses and sea depths, which are drained (that is, devastated) before a person is regenerated. In Isaiah, for instance:

Wake up, as in the days of old, the generations of eternity! Are you not draining the sea, the waters of the great abyss, and making the depths of the sea a path for the redeemed to cross? May those ransomed by Jehovah return! (Isaiah 51:9, 10, 11)

An individual of this type, observed from heaven, looks like a dark mass with no life at all to it.

The same words involve an individual's overall spiritual devastation—a preliminary step to regeneration. (The prophets have much more to say about it.) Before we can learn what is true and be affected by what is good, the things that stand in the way and resist have to be put aside. The old self must die before the new self can be conceived.

The *Spirit of God* stands for the Lord's mercy, which is portrayed as *moving constantly,* like a hen brooding over her eggs. What is being brooded over in this instance is what the Lord stores away in us, which throughout the Word is called "a remnant" [or "survivors"]. It is a knowledge of truth and goodness, which can never emerge into the light of day until our outer nature has been devastated. Such knowledge is here called the *face of the water.*

20 Genesis 1:3. *And God said, "Let there be light," and there was light.*

The first step is taken when we begin to realize that goodness and truth are something transcendent.

People who focus exclusively on externals do not even know what is good or what is true; everything connected with self-love and love of worldly advantages they consider good, and anything that promotes those two loves they consider true. They are unaware that such "goodness" is evil and such "truth" false.

When we are conceived anew, however, we first begin to be aware that our "good" is not good. And as we advance further into the light, it dawns on us that the Lord exists and that he is goodness and truth itself.

The Lord says in John that we need to know of his existence:

> Unless you believe that I am, you will die in your sins.
> (John 8:24)

We need to know too that the Lord is goodness itself, or life, and truth itself, or light, and consequently that nothing good or true exists that does not come from him. This is also found in John:

> In the beginning there was the Word, and the Word was present with God, and the Word was God. Everything was made by him, and nothing that was made was made without him. In him was life, and the life was the light of humankind; but the light appears in the darkness. He was the true light that shines on every person coming into the world. (John 1:1, 3, 4, [5,] 9)

21 Genesis 1:4, 5. *And God saw the light, that it was good, and God made a distinction between light and darkness. And God called the light day, and the darkness he called night.*

The *light* is said to be *good* because it is from the Lord, who is goodness itself.

The *darkness* is whatever looked like light to us before our new conception and birth, because we saw evil as good and falsity as truth; but it is actually darkness—our lingering sense of self-sufficiency.

Absolutely everything that is the Lord's is compared to the day, because it belongs to the light, and everything that is our own is compared to the night, because it belongs to the darkness. The Word draws this comparison in quite a few places.

Genesis 1:5. *And there was evening and there was morning, the first day.*

From this we now see what evening and morning mean. *Evening* is every preliminary stage, because such stages are marked by shadow, or by falsity and an absence of faith. *Morning* is all later stages, because these are marked by light, or by truth and religious knowledge.

Evening stands in general for everything that is our own, while morning stands for everything of the Lord's. As David says, for example:

> The Spirit of Jehovah has spoken in me and his words are on my tongue. The God of Israel has said, the rock of Israel has spoken to me. He is like the morning light when the sun rises, like a morning when there are no clouds, when because of the brightness, because of the rain, the tender grass springs from the earth. (2 Samuel 23:2, 3, 4)

Since evening is when there is no faith and morning is when there *is* faith, the Lord's coming into the world is called morning. The period in which he came, being a time of no faith, is called evening. In Daniel:

> The Holy One said to me, "Up till [the day's second] evening, when it becomes morning, two thousand and three hundred times." (Daniel 8:14, 26)

Morning in the Word is similarly taken to mean every coming of the Lord, so that it is a word for being created anew.

23 Nothing is more common in the Word than for a *day* to be understood as meaning the times, as in Isaiah:

> The day of Jehovah is near. Look—the day of Jehovah is coming! I will shake heaven, and the earth will tremble right out of its place, on the day when my anger blazes up. The time of his coming is near, and its days will not be postponed. (Isaiah 13:6, 9, 13, 22)

In the same prophet:

> In the days of old she was old. It will happen on that day that Tyre will be forgotten for seventy years, corresponding to the days of one king. (Isaiah 23:7, 15)

Because a day stands for a time period, it is also taken to mean the state we are in during that period, as in Jeremiah:

> Doom to us! For the day has faded, for the shadows of evening have lengthened. (Jeremiah 6:4)

In the same prophet:

> If you nullify my compact with the day and my compact with the night, so that there is no daytime or night at their times . . . (Jeremiah 33:20, 25)

And again:

> Renew our days as in ancient times. (Lamentations 5:21)

24 Genesis 1:6. *And God said, "Let there be an expanse in the middle of the waters, and let it exist to make a distinction among the waters, in the waters."*

The next step occurs after the Spirit of God—the Lord's mercy—brings out into daylight the knowledge of truth and goodness and provides the first glimmering that the Lord exists, that he is goodness and truth itself, and that nothing is good or true except what comes from him. The Spirit of God then *makes a distinction* between the inner and the outer being, and between the religious knowledge we possess in our inner selves and the secular knowledge belonging to our outer selves.

The inner self is called the *expanse,* the knowledge in the inner self is called the *waters over the expanse,* and the facts belonging to the outer self are called *the waters under the expanse.*

[2] Before we are reborn, we do not know even that an inner being exists, let alone what it is, imagining there is no difference between the two selves. This is because we are absorbed by bodily and worldly interests and merge the concerns of the inner being with those interests. Out of distinct and separate planes we make one dim, confused whole.

Therefore this verse first says that there should be an expanse in the middle of the waters, then that it should exist to make a distinction "among the waters, in the waters," but not that it should make a distinction between one set of waters and another. The next verse says that.

[3] Genesis 1:7, 8. *And God made the expanse, and he made a distinction between the waters that were under the expanse and the waters that were over the expanse, and so it was done; and God called the expanse heaven.*

The second thing we begin to notice while being reborn, then, is that the inner self exists. We become aware that the attributes of the inner self are good feelings and true ideas, which are the Lord's alone.

While we are being reborn, our outer self is such that it still believes we are acting on our own when we do what is good and speaking on our own when we speak what is true. The Lord uses those things—allowing them to seem like our own, since such is our mind-set—to lead us to doing what is good and speaking what is true. Consequently we first learn to distinguish what is *under the expanse;* only then do we learn to distinguish what is *over the expanse.*

Another secret from heaven is that the Lord leads us by means of things that really are our own—both the illusions of our senses and our cravings—but diverts us toward things that are true and good. So every single moment of regeneration carries us forward from evening to morning, just as it takes us from the outer self to the inner, or from earth to heaven. This is why the expanse (the inner self) is now called *heaven*.

25   *Spreading out the earth and stretching out the heavens* is a customary formula used by the prophets when they speak of our regeneration. In Isaiah, for example:

> This is what Jehovah has said, your Redeemer and the one who formed you from the womb: "I am Jehovah, making all things, stretching *the heavens* out on my own and spreading *the earth* out by myself." (Isaiah 44:24)

Again, where the Lord's Coming is spoken of openly:

> A crushed reed he does not break, and smoldering flax he does not quench; he propels judgment toward truth. [In other words, he does not break our illusions or extinguish our cravings but bends them toward truth and goodness. It continues:] God Jehovah creates *the heavens* and stretches them out. He spreads out *the earth* and the things it produces. He gives a soul to the people on it and spirit to everyone walking on it. (Isaiah 42:3, 4, 5)

Several other places could be cited as well.

26   Genesis 1:8. *And there was evening and there was morning, the second day.*

The meanings of *evening, morning,* and *day* are explained above at verse 5 [§§22–23].

27   Genesis 1:9. *And God said, "Let the waters under heaven be gathered into one place, and let dry land appear"; and so it was done.*

When we learn that we have an inner self and an outer, and that truth and goodness come from the inner self—or rather from the Lord by way of the inner self into the outer, even though this is contrary to appearances—this information, this knowledge of truth and goodness, is stored away in our memory. The knowledge takes its place among the secular facts we have learned, because anything instilled in our outward memory, whether earthly, spiritual, or heavenly, lodges there as a fact, and from there the Lord draws on it.

This knowledge is the *waters gathered into one place* and named seas. The outer being itself, on the other hand, is called *dry land.* Immediately afterward it is called earth, as the next verse shows.

Genesis 1:10. *And God called the dry land earth, and the gathering of waters he called seas; and God saw that it was good.*

To find *waters* symbolizing religious and secular knowledge, and *seas* symbolizing a body of such knowledge, is quite common in the Word. In Isaiah:

> The earth will be full with the awareness of Jehovah,
> like the waters covering the sea. (Isaiah 11:9)

In the same prophet, where both kinds of knowledge are portrayed as lacking:

> The water will disappear from the sea, the river will drain away and dry up, and the streams will recede. (Isaiah 19:5, 6)

In Haggai, where a new church is the subject:

> I am shaking *the heavens* and *the earth,* and the sea and the dry land; and I will shake all the nations, and those who are the desire of every nation will come, and I will fill this House with glory. (Haggai 2:6, 7)

And in Zechariah, on the regenerating individual:

That will be a single day; it is known to Jehovah; it is not *day* or night. And it will happen that at the time of *evening* there will be light. And it will happen on that day that living water will go out from Jerusalem, part of it to the eastern sea and part of it to the western sea. (Zechariah 14:7, 8)

In a passage in David depicting a devastated person who is being reborn and will come to revere the Lord:

Jehovah does not despise his prisoners; *the heavens* and *the earth,* the seas and every creeping thing in them will praise him. (Psalms 69:33, 34)

In the following passage in Zechariah, the *earth* symbolizes that which receives something put into it:

Jehovah is stretching out *the heavens* and founding *the earth* and forming the human spirit in the middle of it. (Zechariah 12:1)

29 Genesis 1:11, 12. *And God said, "Let the earth cause the sprouting on the earth of the tender plant, of the plant bearing its seed, of the fruit tree making the fruit that holds its seed, each in the way of its kind"; and so it was done. And the earth produced the tender plant, the plant bearing its seed in the way of its kind, and the tree making the fruit that held its seed in the way of its kind. And God saw that it was good.*

When the *earth* (a person) is so well prepared as to be able to accept heavenly seed from the Lord and to produce good and truth in some degree, that is the time when the Lord first *causes the sprouting* of something tender, called the *tender plant* or grass. Next he stimulates something more useful that reseeds itself—the *plant bearing its seed.* Finally he germinates something good, which reproduces fruitfully—the *tree making the fruit that holds its seed,* each of these *in the way of its kind.*

During regeneration we naturally suppose at first that the good we do and the truth we speak come from ourselves, when the reality is that all good and truth come from the Lord. If we imagine they come from ourselves, then, we are not yet in possession of the life force belonging to true faith (although we can receive it later). We cannot believe yet that they come from the Lord, because we are being prepared to receive the living power of faith. This stage is represented in the story by things that have no living soul; animate creatures represent the stage of living faith to come.

[2] The Lord is the sower of seeds, the *seed* is his Word, and the *earth* is the human being, as he saw fit to say in Matthew 13:19–23, 37, 38, 39; Mark 4:14–20; and Luke 8:11–15. A similar description:

> So God's kingdom is like one who tosses seed into the earth and sleeps and rises night and day, and the seed sprouts and grows; how it happens, the person does not know. For the earth bears fruit readily—first a shoot, then an ear, then the full grain in the ear. (Mark 4:26, 27, 28)

"God's kingdom" in its broadest sense means the whole of heaven. Less broadly it means the Lord's true church. In its narrow sense it refers to everyone with true faith, which is to say, all who become reborn by living out their faith. Each of these people is also called a heaven (since they have heaven in them) and God's kingdom (since they have God's kingdom in them). The Lord himself teaches this in Luke:

> Jesus was asked by the Pharisees, "When is God's kingdom coming?" He answered them and said, "God's kingdom does not come in an observable way, nor will they say, 'Look here!' or 'Look there!' because—look!—God's kingdom is within you." (Luke 17:20, 21)

This is the third step in our regeneration and the stage at which we repent. The process continues to advance from shadow to light, from evening to morning, and so it says:

[3] Genesis 1:13. *And there was evening and there was morning, the third day.*

30

Genesis 1:14, 15, 16, 17. *And God said, "Let there be lights in the expanse of the heavens to make a distinction between day and night; and they will act as signals and will be used for seasons for both the days and the years. And they will be lights in the expanse of the heavens, to shed light on the earth," and so it was done. And God made two great lights: the greater light to rule by day and the smaller light to rule by night; and the stars. And God placed them in the expanse of the heavens, to shed light on the earth.*

We cannot understand the identity of these great lights very well unless we first know what the essence of faith is and how it develops in those who are being created anew.

The actual essence and life of faith is the Lord alone. No one who lacks faith in the Lord can have life, as he himself said in John:

> Those who believe in the Son have eternal life, but those who do not believe in the Son will not see life; instead, God's anger will rest on them. (John 3:36)

[2] The progress of faith in those who are being created anew is as follows. Initially such people are without any life, as no life exists in evil or falsity, only in goodness and truth. Afterward they receive life from the Lord through faith. The first form of faith to bring life is a memorized thing—a matter of fact. The next is faith in the intellect—faith truly understood. The last is faith in the heart, which is faith born of love, or saving faith.

In verses 3–13 the things that had no living soul represent factual faith and faith truly understood. Faith brought alive by love, however, is represented by the animate creatures in verses 20–25. Consequently this is the point at which love and the faith that rises out of it are first dealt with, and they are called *lights*. Love is the *greater light* that *rules by day*; faith springing from love is the *smaller light* that *rules by night*. And because they must unite as one, the verb used with "lights" is singular, "let it be" rather than "let them be."

[3] Love and faith work the same way in our inner being as warmth and light work in our outer flesh and are therefore represented by warmth and light. This is why the lights are said to be *placed in the expanse of the heavens,* or our inner being, the greater light in our will and the smaller in our intellect. But they only seem to be present there, just as the light of the sun only appears to be in physical objects. It is the Lord's mercy alone that stirs our will with love and our intellect with truth or faith.

The fact that the *great lights* symbolize love and faith and that they are named sun, moon, and stars can be seen in many places in the prophets. In Ezekiel, for instance:

> When I blot you out I will cover *the heavens* and black out their stars; the sun I will cover with a cloud, and the moon will not make its light shine. All the lamps of light in the heavens I will black out above you, and I will bring shadow over your *land.* (Ezekiel 32:7, 8)

This passage is directed at Pharaoh and the Egyptians. In the Word, these people stand for sensory evidence and factual information, and the idea here is that they used both things to blot out love and faith. In Isaiah:

> The day of Jehovah [comes] to make *the earth* a desolation, since neither the stars of the heavens nor their Orions will shine their light. The sun has been shadowed over in its emergence, and the moon will not radiate its light. (Isaiah 13:9, 10)

In Joel:

> The day of Jehovah has come, a day of shadow and darkness. Before him the earth trembles, the heavens shake, the sun and moon turn black, and the stars hold back their rays. (Joel 2:1, 2, 10)

31

[2] The following passage in Isaiah discusses the Lord's Coming and the light brought to the nations—in other words, a new church, and specifically the individuals who are in shadow but welcome the light and are being reborn.

> Rise, shine, because your light has come! Look— shadows cover the earth, and darkness, the peoples. And Jehovah will dawn above you; and the nations will walk toward your light, and monarchs, toward the brightness of your rising. Jehovah will become an eternal light to you. No longer will your sun set, and your moon will not withdraw, because Jehovah will become an eternal light to you. (Isaiah 60:1, 2, 3, 19, 20)

In David:

> Jehovah makes *the heavens* with understanding; he spreads *the earth* out on *the waters;* he makes the great lights—the sun to rule during the day and the moon and stars to rule during the night. (Psalms 136:5, 6, 7, 8, 9)

In the same author:

> Give glory to Jehovah, sun and moon! Give glory to him, all you shining stars! Give glory to him, heavens of heavens and waters above the heavens! (Psalms 148:3, 4)

In all these places the sources of light symbolize love and faith.

[3] Because lights represented and symbolized love for and faith in the Lord, the Jewish church was commanded to keep a light burning perpetually, from evening to morning, since every activity that was required of that church represented the Lord. The command for the perpetual light was as follows:

> Command the children of Israel to take oil for the light, to make [the fire of] the lamp go up continually.

In the meeting tent, outside the veil that is by [the ark of] the testimony, Aaron and his sons shall arrange it before Jehovah, from evening till morning. (Exodus 27:20, 21)

This symbolizes love and faith, which the Lord kindles and causes to shine in our inner self, and through our inner into our outer self, as will be shown in its proper place [§9783], with the Lord's divine mercy.

Love and faith are first called the great lights, then love is called the *greater light* and faith the *smaller light*. It says that love will *rule during the day* and that faith will *rule during the night*. Because this information is unknown and less accessible than ever at this time—the end of an era—the Lord in his divine mercy has allowed me to lay open the true situation.

It is especially well hidden in these final days because the close of the age has arrived and almost no love exists, consequently almost no faith. The Lord himself predicted this event in words recorded in the Gospels:

The sun will go dark, and the moon will not shed light, and the stars will fall down from the sky, and the powers of the heavens will be shaken. (Matthew 24:29)

The sun here means love, which has gone dark. The moon means faith, which is not shedding light. The stars mean religious concepts (the powers and forces of the heavens), which are falling down from heaven.

[2] The earliest church acknowledged no faith besides love itself. Heavenly angels too have no idea what faith is if it is not a matter of love. The entirety of heaven gives itself over to love, because no other kind of life than that of love exists in the heavens. Love is the source of all their happiness, which is so immense that not a bit of it can be put into words or grasped in any way by the human mind.

People who dwell in love do love the Lord with all their heart, but they know, say, and perceive that all love comes from

32

the Lord and from nowhere else, as does all life (which is the product of love alone) and so all happiness. Not the smallest measure of love, life, or happiness do they claim to possess on their own.

In the Lord's transfiguration, the great light—the sun—represented the fact that he is the source of all love, since

> His face shone like the sun, while his clothes became like the light. (Matthew 17:2)

The face symbolizes the deepest levels of being, while clothes symbolize the things that issue from those levels. So the sun (love) means the Lord's divinity, and light (the wisdom that rises out of love), his humanity.

33 Anyone can see perfectly well that no hint of life ever exists without some kind of love and that no trace of joy ever exists unless it results from love. The nature of the love determines the nature of the life and of the joy.

If you were to take the things you love—the things you long for (since longings are bound up with love)—and set them aside, your thought processes would come to an immediate halt and you would be like a corpse. I have learned this through experience.

Self-love and materialism produce an imitation of life and an imitation of joy, but since they are diametrically opposed to genuine love—that is, loving the Lord above all and loving our neighbor as ourselves—it stands to reason that they are not forms of love but of hatred. Notice that the more we love ourselves and worldly goods, the more we hate our neighbor and therefore the Lord.

Genuine love, then, is love for the Lord, and genuine life is a life of love received from him. True joy is the joy of that life.

Only one genuine love can exist, so only one genuine life can exist, and it gives rise to true joy and happiness, like that felt by angels in heaven.

Love and faith can never be separated, because they make a single unit. This is why the sources of light when first mentioned are treated as grammatically singular in the statement, "Let there be lights in the expanse of the heavens." Let me report some surprising facts in this connection.

Because the Lord gives heavenly angels this kind of love, love reveals all religious knowledge to them. Love also gives them such a living and shining intelligence that it can hardly be described.

For spirits who learn the doctrinal tenets of faith but lack love, on the other hand, life is so chill and the light so dim that they cannot even approach the near side of the threshold to heaven's entrance hall without fleeing in retreat.

Some say that they had believed in the Lord; but in actuality they had not lived as he taught. The Lord speaks of them this way in Matthew:

> Not everyone saying "Lord! Lord!" to me will enter the kingdom of the heavens, but the one doing my will. Many will say to me on that day, "Lord! Lord! Haven't we prophesied in your name?" (Matthew 7:21, 22)

See also what follows there, up to the end of Matthew 7.

[2] All this makes it clear that people who have love also have faith and consequently heavenly life. The same cannot be said of those who claim to have faith but do not lead a loving life.

A life of faith without love is like sunlight without warmth—the type of light that occurs in winter, when nothing grows and everything droops and dies. Faith rising out of love, on the contrary, is like light from the sun in spring, when everything grows and flourishes. Warmth from the sun is the fertile agent. The same is true in spiritual and heavenly affairs, which are typically represented in the Word by objects found in nature and human culture.

34

Nonbelief and belief without love are in fact compared to winter by the Lord in Mark where he made predictions concerning the close of the age:

Pray that your flight not occur in winter, as those will be days of distress. (Mark 13:18, 19)

The "flight" refers to the final days and to an individual's final days before death as well. "Winter" is a life devoid of love. The "days of distress" are the person's wretched condition in the other life.

35   Humans have two basic faculties: will and intellect. When the will regulates the intellect, the two together make one mind and as a result one life; under those circumstances, what we will and do is also what we think and intend. When the intellect is at odds with the will, though, as when we act in a way that contradicts what we claim to believe, our single mind is torn in two. One part wants to rise up to heaven while the other leans toward hell. And since the will drives everything, we would rush into hell heart and soul if the Lord did not take pity on us.

36   People who have separated faith from love do not even know what faith is. When they try to picture it, some see it merely as thought. Some view it only as thoughts about the Lord. A few equate it with the teachings of faith.

But faith is more than the knowledge and acknowledgment of all that is encompassed in the teachings of faith. First and foremost it is obedience to everything that faith teaches; and the primary thing faith teaches and requires our obedience to is love for the Lord and love for our neighbor. No one who lacks this possesses faith. The Lord teaches this so clearly in Mark that no one can doubt it:

The first of all the commandments is "Listen, Israel: The Lord our God is one Lord. Therefore you shall love the Lord your God with all your heart and with all your soul and with all your mind and with all your powers." This is the first commandment. A second, similar one, of course, is this: "You shall love your neighbor as yourself." There is no other commandment greater than these. (Mark 12:28–34)

In Matthew he calls the former the first and great commandment and says that the Law and the Prophets depend on these commandments (Matthew 22:35–40). "The Law and the Prophets" are the teachings of faith, all-inclusively, and the whole Word.

The words *the lights will act as signals and will be used for seasons both for the days and for the years* contain more hidden information than can be spelled out in the present work, even though none of it appears in the literal meaning. The only thing to be said at this time is that spiritual and heavenly things—as a group and individually—go through cycles, for which the daily and yearly cycles are metaphors. The daily cycle begins in the morning, extends to midday, then to evening, and through night to morning. The corresponding annual cycle begins with spring, extends to summer, then to fall, and through winter to spring.

These changes create changes in temperature and light and in the earth's fertility, which are used as metaphors for changes in spiritual and heavenly conditions. Without change and variation, life would be monotonous and consequently lifeless. There would be no recognition or differentiation of goodness and truth, let alone any awareness of them.

The celestial cycles are called "statutes" in the prophets, as in Jeremiah:

The word spoken by Jehovah, who gives the sun as light for the day, the statutes of moon and stars as light for the night: "These statutes will not depart from before me." (Jeremiah 31:35, 36)

And in the same prophet:

> This is what Jehovah has said: "If my compact with
> day and night should cease, if I should cease to set the
> statutes of heaven and earth . . ." (Jeremiah 33:25)

But the subject will be explored further at Genesis 8:22 [§§933–
936], the Lord's divine mercy permitting.

38 Genesis 1:18. . . . *and to rule during the day and during the
night, and to make a distinction between light and darkness; and
God saw that it was good.*

Day means goodness and *night* evil, so in common parlance
the good things people do are associated with the day, while the
bad things they do are called deeds of the night.

Light means truth and *darkness* falsity, as the Lord says:

> People loved darkness more than light. One who does
> the truth comes to the light. (John 3:19–21)

Genesis 1:19. *And there was evening and there was morning,
the fourth day.*

39 Genesis 1:20. *And God said, "Let the waters cause the creeping
animal—a living soul—to creep out. And let the bird flit over the
land, over the face of the expanse of the heavens."*

After the great lights are kindled and placed in the inner self,
and the outer self is receiving light from them, the time arrives
when we first start to live. Earlier, we can hardly be said to have
been alive, thinking as we did that the good we perform and the
truth we speak originate in ourselves. On our own we are dead
and have nothing but evil and falsity inside, with the result that
nothing we produce from ourselves has life. So true is this that
by our own power we cannot do anything good—at least not
anything inherently good.

From the doctrine taught by faith, anyone can see that we
cannot so much as think a good thought or will a good result or
consequently do a good deed except through the Lord's power.
After all, in Matthew the Lord says:

The one who sows good seed is the Son of Human-kind. (Matthew 13:37)

Good cannot come from anywhere but this same unique source, as he also says:

Nobody is good except the one God. (Luke 18:19)

[2] Still, when the Lord brings us back to life, or regenerates us, he at first allows us to harbor these mistaken ideas. At that stage we cannot view the situation in any other way. Neither can we be led in any other way to believe and then perceive that everything good and true comes from the Lord alone.

As long as our thinking ran along these lines, the truth and goodness we possessed were equated with a tender plant or grass, next with a plant bearing seed, then with a fruit tree, none of which has a living soul. Now, when love and faith have brought us to life and we believe that the Lord brings about all the good we do and the truth we speak, we are compared initially to *creeping animals of the water* and *birds flitting over the land* and later to beasts. All these are animate and are called *living souls*.

The *creeping animals* that the *waters* breed symbolize facts that the outer self knows. *Birds* in general symbolize logical reasoning; they also symbolize matters that we truly understand, which belong to the inner self.

40

The following verses in Isaiah demonstrate the symbolism of the *creeping animals of the waters*—fish—as facts:

I came and there was no man. In my censure I will dry up the sea; I will make the rivers a desert; their fish will stink from lack of water and die of thirst; I will dress the heavens in black. (Isaiah 50:2, 3)

[2] Evidence still clearer appears in Ezekiel, where the Lord describes a new temple, the general meaning of which is a new church and an adherent of the church or person reborn (since everyone who is reborn is a temple to the Lord).

The Lord Jehovah said to me, "That water, which will go out to the boundary toward the east and go toward the sea, will be channeled down into the sea, and the water [of the sea] will be cured. And it will come about that every living soul that creeps out in any place where the water of the rivers goes will survive; and the fish will be very numerous, because that water goes there and will be cured, and everything will live, wherever the river goes. And it will happen that the fishers will stand over it from En-gedi to En-eglaim; they will be there spreading their nets. Their fish will be of all kinds, like the fish of the great sea, very numerous." (Ezekiel 47:8, 9, 10)

"Fishers from En-gedi to En-eglaim spreading their nets" symbolize people who are to teach the earthly plane of the human mind about the truths that make up faith.

[3] Passages in the prophets establish the fact that birds symbolize logical reasoning and concepts truly understood. In Isaiah, for example:

I am calling the winged creature from the sunrise, the man I planned on, from a faraway land. (Isaiah 46:11)

In Jeremiah:

I looked and there, not a human! And every bird of the heavens had fled. (Jeremiah 4:25)

In Ezekiel:

I will plant a cutting of the tall cedar, and it will lift its branch and make fruit and become a majestic cedar. And every bird of every wing will live under it; in the shade of its branches they will live. (Ezekiel 17:[22,] 23)

And in Hosea, where the subject is a new church, or the regenerate person:

And I will strike a pact with them on that day—with
the wild animal of the field, and with the bird in the
heavens and the creature that moves on the ground.
(Hosea 2:18)

The wild animal obviously does not mean a wild animal or the
bird a bird, because the Lord is sealing a new pact with them.

Nothing that is a person's very own has any life in it. When
presented to view, it looks hard as bone, and black. Everything
that comes from the Lord, on the other hand, has life. It has a
spiritual and heavenly quality and looks like something living
and human.

41

Incredibly, perhaps (although it is absolutely true), each
word, each mental image, and each scintilla of thought in an
angelic spirit is alive. Passion received from the Lord, who is life
itself, permeates every single thing about such a spirit.

Things that come from the Lord, then, contain life because
they contain faith in him, and they are symbolized here by *a
living soul.* Additionally, they have the equivalent of a physical
body, symbolized by *that which moves* or *creeps.* This information remains obscure to the human mind, but since the verse
talks about a living soul that moves, I need at least to mention it.

Genesis 1:21. *And God created the big sea creatures, and every
living, creeping soul that the waters caused to creep out, in all their
kinds, and every bird on the wing, of every kind; and God saw that
it was good.*

42

Fish symbolize facts, as already stated [§40]. In this instance
they symbolize facts animated by faith that is received from the
Lord, which therefore possess vitality. *Big sea creatures* symbolize general categories of facts, from which come subcategories.
(Not one thing exists anywhere in the world that does not
belong to some general category. The category allows the particular item to come into being and continue in existence.)

The prophets mention sea monsters or whales a number of
times, and when they do, these symbolize general categories of

facts. Pharaoh, king of Egypt, representing human wisdom or understanding (that is, factual information in general), is called a large sea creature, as in Ezekiel:

> Here, now, I am against you, Pharaoh, king of Egypt, you great sea creature, lying in the middle of your rivers, who has said, "The river is mine, and I have made myself." (Ezekiel 29:3)

[2] Another:

> Raise a lamentation over Pharaoh, king of Egypt; and you are to tell him, "But you are like a monster in the seas; and you have emerged among your rivers and churned the waters with your feet." (Ezekiel 32:2)

This image symbolizes those who want to use facts (meaning they want to use their own powers) to initiate themselves into religious mysteries. In Isaiah:

> On that day Jehovah, with his steely and great and mighty sword, will exact punishment on Leviathan the stretched-out serpent and on Leviathan the coiled serpent; and he will kill the monsters that are in the sea. (Isaiah 27:1)

Killing the monsters that are in the sea means leaving such people without awareness even of general facts. In Jeremiah:

> Nebuchadnezzar, king of Babylon, has devoured me, has churned me up; he has rendered me an empty container, like a sea monster he has swallowed me down, filled his belly with the savors of me, hurled me out. (Jeremiah 51:34)

In other words, "Nebuchadnezzar" has swallowed up all religious knowledge (the "savors") as the sea monster did to Jonah. In Jonah's case the monster stood for people who possess the broad outlines of this knowledge in the form of facts and who wolf them down.

Genesis 1:22. *And God blessed them, saying, "Reproduce and multiply and fill the water in the seas, and the birds will multiply on the land."*

43

Everything with life from the Lord in it reproduces and multiplies beyond measure—not so much during our physical lives, but to an astounding degree in the next life.

In the Word, *reproducing* or being fruitful applies to the elements of love, and *multiplying,* to the elements of faith. Fruit born of love holds the seed by which it multiplies so prolifically.

The Lord's *blessing* in the Word also symbolizes fruitfulness and multiplication, because these are its result.

Genesis 1:23. *And there was evening and there was morning, the fifth day.*

Genesis 1:24, 25. *And God said, "Let the earth produce each living soul according to its kind: the beast, and that which moves, and the wild animal of the earth, each according to its kind"; and so it was done. And God made each wild animal of the earth according to its kind, and each beast according to its kind, and every animal creeping on the ground according to its kind. And God saw that it was good.*

44

Like the earth, we are unable to produce any good unless we have first been sown with religious insights, which enable us to see what to believe and do.

The role of the intellect is to hear the Word, while the role of the will is to do it. To hear the Word and not act is to claim we believe it although we do not live by it. People who act like this separate the two and split their minds. The Lord says they are stupid:

> Everyone who hears my words and does them I compare to a prudent man who built his house on rock. But everyone who hears my words and does not do

them I compare to a stupid man who built his house on sand. (Matthew 7:24, 26)

What the intellect grasps is symbolized, as shown [§40], by creeping animals that the waters cause to creep out and birds flying over the land and over the face of the expanse. What the will is intent on is symbolized by the *living soul* that *the earth* is to *produce,* by the *beast* and *that which creeps,* and by the *wild animal of the earth.*

45 People who lived in the earliest times used the same kinds of symbols for the contents of the intellect and the will. In consequence, the different types of creature have a similar representation in the prophets and throughout the Old Testament Word.

Beasts are of two kinds: bad (because they are dangerous) and good (because they are tame). Bad animals—bears, wolves, and [feral] dogs, for instance—symbolize evil things in us. Good animals—young cattle, sheep, lambs—symbolize the good, gentle things in us. Because the present theme concerns people who are being reborn, the beasts in this verse are the good, tame ones, symbolizing feelings of affection.

The traits in us that belong to a lower order and rise more out of our body are called the wild animals of the earth; they are cravings and appetites.

46 Many examples from the Word can clarify the fact that *beasts* or animals symbolize the feelings we have—negative feelings if we are evil, positive feelings if we are good. Take these verses in Ezekiel:

Here, now, I am yours, [mountains of Israel,] and I will turn to face you so that you may be tilled and sown; and I will multiply human and animal upon you, and they will multiply and reproduce; and I will cause you to live as in your ancient times. (Ezekiel 36:9, 10, 11)

This speaks of regeneration. In Joel:

Do not be afraid, animals of my field; because the living-places of the desert have become grassy. (Joel 2:22)

In David:

I was dull-witted; I was like the animals, in God's sight. (Psalms 73:22)

In Jeremiah:

Look! The days are coming when I will sow the house of Israel and the house of Judah with the seed of human and the seed of animal; and I will watch over them to build and to plant. (Jeremiah 31:27, 28)

This speaks of regeneration.

[2] *Wild animals* have the same symbolism. In Hosea, for example:

I will strike a pact with them on that day—with the wild animal of the field, and with the bird in the heavens and the creeping animal of the earth. (Hosea 2:18)

In Job:

Of the wild animal of the earth you are not to be afraid, as you will have a compact with the stones of the field, and the wild animal of the field will be peaceful toward you. (Job 5:22, 23)

In Ezekiel:

I will strike a pact of peace with you and bring an end on the earth to the evil wild animal, so that people may live securely in the wilderness. (Ezekiel 34:25)

In Isaiah:

The wild animal of the field will honor me because I have put water in the desert. (Isaiah 43:20)

In Ezekiel:

> In its branches nested every bird of the heavens, and
> under its branches bred every wild animal of the field,
> and in its shade lived all the great nations. (Ezekiel 31:6)

This describes Assyrians, who symbolize a person with a spiritual focus and who are being compared to the Garden of Eden. In David:

> Give glory to Jehovah, all you angels of his; give glory
> from the earth, you sea creatures, fruit tree, wild animal, and every beast, creeping animal, and bird on the
> wing. (Psalms 148:2, 3, 4, 7, 9, 10)

This lists exactly the same things [as the present chapter]: sea creatures, fruit tree, wild animal, beast, creeping animal, and bird. Unless they symbolized living things in us, they could never be said to give glory to Jehovah.

[3] The prophets draw a careful distinction between the animals *of the earth* and the animals of the field.

It is good things that have been called animals up to this point, just as the people closest to the Lord in heaven are termed living creatures both in Ezekiel [1; 10] and in John:

> All the angels stood around the throne and the elders
> and the four living creatures, and they fell down before
> the throne on their faces and worshiped the Lamb.
> (Revelation 7:11; 19:4)

People to whom the gospel is to be preached are also called created beings, since they are to be created anew:

> Go throughout the world and preach the gospel to
> every created being. (Mark 16:15)

47 More evidence that these words enfold the mysteries of regeneration can be seen in differences between the present verse and the last. The last says that the earth produced the living soul, the beast, and the wild animal of the earth. The present one employs a different order, saying that God made the wild animal of the earth and then the beast. At first we produce results as if on our own, as we do later, too, before developing a heavenly nature. Regeneration, then, starts with the outer self and moves to the inner, which is why a change in the order occurs, and outermost things come first.

All this verifies the premise: In the fifth stage we speak with conviction (an attribute of the intellect) and in the process strengthen ourselves in truth and goodness. The things we then produce have life in them and are called the fish of the sea and the birds in the heavens. And in the sixth stage we act with conviction (an attribute of the intellect) and therefore with love (an attribute of the will) in speaking truth and doing good. What we then produce is called a living soul, an animal. Because this is the point at which we begin to act as much with love as with conviction, we become spiritual people, who are called [God's] image—the very next subject.

48

Genesis 1:26. And God said, "Let us make a human in our image, after our likeness; and these will rule over the fish of the sea and over the bird in the heavens, and over the beast, and over all the earth, and over every creeping animal that creeps on the earth."

49

To members of the earliest church, whom the Lord addressed face to face, he appeared as a human being. (Many things could be told about these people, but this is not the right time.) As a consequence, they used the term *human* for none but him, or for his qualities. They did not even call themselves human, excepting whatever they could tell he gave them, such as all the good embraced by love and all the truth espoused by faith. These traits they described as human, because they were the Lord's.

[2] As a consequence, the terms *human being* and *son of humankind* in the prophets have the Lord as their highest

meaning. At a lower but still internal level, the meaning is wisdom and understanding and accordingly everyone who has been reborn. An example from Jeremiah:

> I looked at the earth, and there—void and emptiness; and to the heavens, and there—no light in them! I looked, and there—not a human! And all the birds of the heavens had fled. (Jeremiah 4:23, 25)

At the inner level, the following passage in Isaiah uses a human being to mean one reborn, and on the highest level the Lord himself, as an exemplar:

> This is what Jehovah, the Holy One of Israel and its fashioner, has said: "I made the earth, and the human being on it I created. My hands stretched out the heavens, and to their whole army I gave commands." (Isaiah 45:11, 12, 13)

[3] For this reason, the prophets saw the Lord as a human being. Ezekiel was one who did:

> Above the expanse was a seeming appearance of sapphire stone, like a throne, and on the likeness of a throne was what looked like the appearance of a person on it, high above. (Ezekiel 1:26)

When Daniel saw the Lord, he called him "Son of Humankind," or human being, which is the same thing:

> I looked, and there! In the clouds of the sky, it was as if the Son of Humankind was coming. And he came to the Ancient One, and they brought him before [the Ancient One]. And he was given power to rule, and glory, and kingship; and all peoples, nations, and tongues will serve him. His ruling power is eternal, a power that will not pass away, and his kingship one that will not perish. (Daniel 7:13, 14)

[4] In fact, the Lord often calls himself Son of Humankind, or human; echoing the prophecy in Daniel that he will come in glory, he says:

> They will see the Son of Humankind coming in the clouds of the sky with strength and glory. (Matthew 24:27, 30)

"The clouds of the heavens" (or sky) is what the literal meaning of the Word is called. "Strength and glory" are terms for the Word's inner meaning, which at each and every point focuses exclusively on the Lord and his kingdom. This focus is what gives the inner meaning strength and glory.

What the people of the earliest church meant when they spoke of the Lord's *image* involves more than can be put into words.

People have no idea whatever that the Lord governs them through angels and spirits, or that at least two spirits and two angels accompany each of them. The spirits create a link with the world of spirits, and the angels create one with heaven. We cannot possibly live without a channel of communication open to the world of spirits through spirits and to heaven through angels (and in this way to the Lord through heaven). Our life depends totally on such a connection. If the spirits and angels withdrew from us, we would be destroyed in a second.

[2] As long as we are unregenerate, we are governed in a completely different way than the regenerate. Before regeneration we have with us evil spirits whose grip on us is so strong that the angels, though present, can achieve hardly any results. All they can do is head us off from rushing into the worst kind of evil and divert us toward some form of good. They even use our own appetites to lead us toward good, and the illusions of our senses to lead us toward truth. Under these circumstances we communicate with the world of spirits by means of the spirits around us but not so much with heaven, since the evil spirits are in charge and the angels only deflect their influence.

50

[3] When we are regenerate, on the other hand, the angels are in charge, inspiring us with all kinds of goodness and truth and instilling a horror and fear of evil and falsity.

Angels do give us guidance, but they are mere helpers; the Lord alone governs us, *through* angels and spirits. Since angels have their assisting role, the words of this verse appear in the plural—"Let us make a human in our image." But since only the Lord rules and manages us, the next verse uses the singular—"God created the human in his image." The Lord states his role clearly in Isaiah:

> This is what Jehovah has said, your Redeemer and the one who formed you from the womb: "I, Jehovah, make all things, stretching *the heavens* out on my own, spreading *the earth* out by myself." (Isaiah 44:24)

The angels themselves confess that they have no power but act only at the Lord's behest.

As far as an *image* is concerned, it is not the likeness of another thing but is *after a likeness* of it, which explains the wording "Let us make a human in our image, after our likeness." A person with a spiritual character is an image, but a person with a heavenly character is a likeness or exact copy. Genesis 1 deals with the spiritual person, Genesis 2 with the heavenly person.

The Lord calls the person of spiritual character (or an "image") a child of light, as he does in John:

> Those who walk in the dark do not know where they are heading. As long as you have the light, believe in the light, in order to be children of light. (John 12:35, 36)

He also calls such a person a friend:

> You are my friends if you do whatever I command you. (John 15:14, 15)

But the person of heavenly character (or a "likeness") he calls God's child in John:

> As many as did accept him, to them he gave the power to be God's children, to those believing in his name, who had their birth not from blood or from the flesh's will or from a man's will but from God. (John 1:12, 13)

As long as we are spiritual, we rule the outer self first and from this the inner, as illustrated here in Genesis 1:26: *and they will rule over the fish of the sea and over the bird in the heavens, and over the beast, and over all the earth, and over every creeping animal that creeps on the earth.* When we become heavenly, though, and do good because we love to, we rule the inner self first and from it the outer. The Lord describes this as being true of himself; and as it is true of him, it is also true of the heavenly type of person, who is a likeness of him. The words appear in David:

> You have made him rule over the works of your hands; all things you have put under his feet: the flock and all the herds, and also the animals of the fields, the bird in the heavens, and the fish of the sea—that which travels the paths of the seas. (Psalms 8:6–8)

In this passage, animals receive the first mention, next the bird, then the fish of the sea, because the heavenly person proceeds from love, which belongs to the will. Things are different with the spiritual person, for whom the fish and birds come first and the animals follow; fish and birds are associated with the intellect, which concerns itself with faith.

Genesis 1:27. *And God created the human in his image; in God's image he created them.*

Image comes up twice in this verse because faith, which belongs to the intellect, is called *his* image, but love, which belongs to the will, is called *God's* image. Love comes second in the spiritual person but first in the heavenly person.

54

Male and female he created them.

The inner meaning of male and female was very familiar to the earliest church, although their successors lost touch with this secret when they lost sight of any deeper import to the Word.

These earliest people found their greatest happiness and pleasure in marriage. Whenever they could possibly draw a comparison between something else and marriage, they did so, in order to perceive the happiness of marriage in that other entity. Being people of depth, they enjoyed only the deeper aspects of things. External objects were just for looking at; their thoughts were occupied instead with the things those objects represented. External objects, then, were nothing to them, serving only as a springboard for reflection on inner realities, and these for contemplation of heavenly realities and so of the Lord, who was everything to them. The same process caused them to reflect on the heavenly marriage, which they could tell was the source of the happiness in their own marriages.

As a result, they called the intellect in the spiritual being *male* and the will there *female;* and when the two worked together, they called it a marriage.

That religion initiated the practice, which became quite common, of calling the church Daughter or Virgin (as in "the Virgin Zion," "the Virgin Jerusalem") and also Wife, on account of its desire for good. For more on this, see the treatment of Genesis 2:24 and 3:15.

55

Genesis 1:28. *And God blessed them, and God said to them, "Reproduce and multiply, and fill the earth and harness it, and rule over the fish of the sea and over the bird in the heavens and over every living animal creeping on the earth."*

The earliest people called the interconnection of intellect and will or of faith and love a marriage, so the generation of any good from that marriage they termed *reproduction,* and the generation of any truth they termed *multiplication.* Because they did so, the prophets did so too; in Ezekiel, for instance:

I will multiply human and animal upon you, [mountains of Israel,] and they will multiply and reproduce; and I will cause you to live as in your ancient times. And I will do good to you beyond that at your beginnings, and you will know that I am Jehovah. And I will cause *humankind*—my people Israel—to walk upon you. (Ezekiel 36:8, 9, 10, 11, 12)

Humankind here means the spiritual being, which is also called Israel; the ancient times mean the very earliest church; and the beginnings mean the ancient church, which followed the Flood. The multiplying (of truth) comes before the reproducing (of good) because these verses describe the person who is being reborn, not the one who has been reborn already.

[2] When the intellect couples with the will in us, or faith with love, the Lord through Isaiah calls us a married land:

No longer will your land be named Devastated; but you will be called I Am Well Pleased with Her, and your land, Married, since Jehovah will take pleasure in you. And your land will be married. (Isaiah 62:4)

The fruits of truth produced by this marriage are called sons, while the fruits of goodness are called daughters, as occurs quite often in the Word.

[3] The *earth is filled* when truth and goodness proliferate, because when the Lord *blesses* and *says things* (that is, operates), goodness and truth grow beyond measure. As he states:

The kingdom of the heavens is like a mustard seed that you have taken and sown in your field, which to be sure is the smallest of all the seeds; but when it has grown, it is bigger than all the plants and becomes a tree, so that the birds of the sky come and nest in its branches. (Matthew 13:31, 32)

The mustard seed is the good we have before developing a spiritual orientation; it is the smallest of all the seeds, because we suppose that we do good on our own. Anything we do on our own is evil through and through, but since we are engaged in the process of being reborn, we have a trace—the smallest possible trace—of goodness. [4] Later, as faith becomes more closely connected with love, it grows larger—a plant. When the connection is completed, it turns into a tree, and then the birds of the heavens (which here as before [§§11; 40:1, 3; 48] are true ideas, or the contents of the intellect) nest in its branches (the facts we know).

When we are spiritual people or are becoming spiritual, we are subject to conflict; and this is why it says *harness the earth, and rule.*

56   Genesis 1:29. *And God said, "Here, now, I am giving you every seed-bearing plant on the face of all the earth and every tree that has fruit; the tree that produces seed will serve you for food."*

A person whose nature is heavenly enjoys only heavenly things, which are called heavenly food because they harmonize with the life such a person lives. A person whose nature is spiritual enjoys spiritual things, which are called spiritual food because they harmonize with the life this person lives. A person focused on the physical world similarly enjoys earthly things, which are called food because they are vital to such a person; these are mainly facts.

As spiritual people are the subject at present, their spiritual food is depicted by the representative items here. *The seed-bearing plant* represents a spiritual type of this food, as does *the tree that has fruit;* the more general term for both is *the tree that produces seed.* These people's earthly food is described in the next verse.

57   *The seed-bearing plant* is every true idea that looks toward a useful goal. *The tree that has fruit* is religious good; the fruit is what the Lord gives the heavenly person, but the seed leading to new fruit is what he gives the spiritual person, which is why it says *the tree that produces seed will serve you for food.*

The next chapter, treating of the heavenly type of person, will demonstrate that heavenly food is called the fruit from a tree. Here the Lord's words through Ezekiel will suffice:

> Beside the river, on its bank, on this side and that, grows every food tree. Its leaf will not fall, and its fruit will not be used up. Month by month it is reborn, because its waters are going out from the sanctuary. And its fruit will serve as food, and its leaf, as medicine. (Ezekiel 47:12)

"Water from the sanctuary" symbolizes the living energy and mercy of the Lord, who is the "sanctuary." The fruit symbolizes wisdom, which is food to people of heavenly character. The leaf is intelligence, which is given to them for a purpose referred to as "medicine."

The idea that spiritual food is called a plant (or grass), though, is expressed in David:

> My shepherd, I will lack nothing. In grassy pastures you make me lie down. (Psalms 23:1, 2)

Genesis 1:30. *"And every wild animal of the earth and every bird in the heavens and every animal creeping on the earth, in which there is a living soul—every green plant will serve them for nourishment"; and so it was done.*   58

This verse depicts the spiritual person's earthly food. The *wild animal of the earth* symbolizes such a person's earthly plane of existence, as does the *bird in the heavens,* both of which received *for nourishment* the *green plant* or grass. Concerning this person's two kinds of food—both earthly and spiritual—David has the following to say:

> Jehovah causes grain to sprout for the beast and plants for the service of humankind, to bring bread from the earth. (Psalms 104:14)

"The beast" stands for the wild animal of the earth and at the same time for the bird in the heavens, both of which David mentions in verses 11 and 12 of the same Psalm.

59 In this verse the nourishment of the earthly self is restricted to *green plants* for the following reason.

While we are being reborn and learning to concern ourselves with the spirit, we are in constant battle (which is why the Lord's church is described as militant). Up to this point our cravings have controlled us, because our whole being is cobbled together out of nothing but those cravings and the distorted ideas they spawn. We cannot rid ourselves of those longings and distortions instantaneously during regeneration; to do so would destroy us completely, since we have not yet acquired another way of life. Consequently, evil spirits are left with us for a long time to trigger our appetites, which then break down in countless different ways, and break down so thoroughly that the Lord can turn them into something good. This is the way we reform.

In the time of battle, evil spirits leave us no other nourishment than the equivalent of green plants. (Those spirits hold an absolute hatred for everything good and true—for anything having to do with love for the Lord and faith in him, these being the only good and true things that exist—because such things hold eternal life within them.) But from time to time the Lord gives us additional food that can be compared to seed-bearing plants and fruit trees: calm and peace, with their accompanying joy and happiness.

[2] If the Lord were not protecting us every moment, every split second, we would be wiped out instantly. Hatred against any aspect of love for the Lord or faith in him dominates the world of spirits, and the hatred is so deadly that it defies description.

I can testify to the truth of this absolutely. For several years now I have visited the next world and the spirits there, though remaining in my body, and the evil ones (the worst, in fact) have crowded around me, sometimes numbering in the thousands. They have been allowed to spew out their venom and harass me in every possible way, but still they were unable to hurt a single hair on my head, so closely did the Lord guard me.

All these years of experience have taught me a great deal about the nature of the world of spirits and about the conflict that those who are being reborn inevitably suffer if they are to win the happiness of eternal life.

No one, however, can learn enough from a general description to develop an unshakable belief in this information, so the details, with the Lord's divine mercy, must come in what follows.

Genesis 1:31. *And God saw all that he had done and, yes, it was very good. And there was evening and there was morning, the sixth day.*

60

This time it says *very good* but previously it said simply *good,* because now the components of faith combine with those of love to make one entity. A marriage between spiritual and heavenly things has taken place.

"Spiritual" is the adjective for anything having to do with religious knowledge. "Heavenly" applies to everything having to do with love for the Lord and for our neighbor. Spiritual things fall in the province of our intellect; heavenly things, in that of our will.

61

The periods and stages of our regeneration—both the whole process and individual cycles within it—divide into *six,* and these six are called our days of creation. Step by step we advance from being nonhuman to being somewhat human, though only a little, then more and more so up to the sixth day, when we become [God's] image.

62

All the while the Lord is constantly fighting on our behalf against evil and falsity and through these battles strengthens us in truth and goodness. The time of conflict is when the Lord is

63

at work (for which reason the prophets call a regenerate person the work of God's fingers [Psalms 8:3, 6; Isaiah 19:25; 29:23; 45:11; 60:21; 64:8; Lamentations 4:2]), and he does not rest until love takes the lead. Then the conflict ends.

When the work progresses so far that faith is united with love, it is called *very good,* since the Lord now makes us likenesses of himself.

At the end of the sixth day, evil spirits retreat and good ones take their place. We are led into heaven, or the Paradise of heaven, described in the next chapter.

[Content and Mode in the Word]

64 THIS, then, is the Word's inner meaning, the true and genuine life in it, which does not reveal itself at all in the literal meaning. But the number of secrets hidden within is so large that volumes would fail to unfold all of them. I have offered just a few, of a type confirming that regeneration is the theme and that it progresses from outer to inner self.

That is what angels see in the Word. They know nothing whatever of the literal contents, or the most obvious meaning of even one word, still less the names of different lands, cities, rivers, and people that come up so frequently in the narrative and prophetic parts. All they picture are the things those words and names symbolize. Adam in Paradise, for instance, brings the earliest church to their minds—and not even the church itself but its belief in the Lord. Noah brings up the picture of that church's remnant among its successors, lasting up to Abram's time. Abraham never makes them think of a man who lived long ago but of a saving faith, which he represented. And so on. In sum, they see spiritual and heavenly realities in the Word, completely separate from the words and names.

65 Several people found themselves carried up into heaven's outermost entry hall while I was reading the Word, and they spoke to me from there. They said that they had no inkling of a single word or letter there but saw only the things symbolized on the next deeper level of meaning. These things, according to their description, were so beautiful, followed in such a perfect sequence, and affected them so deeply that they called it glory.

The Word has four major modes of writing:

66

1. The mode of [the people in] the earliest church. Their method of expressing themselves involved thought of the spiritual and heavenly things represented by the earthly, mundane objects they mentioned. Not only did they express themselves in words representing higher things, they also spun those words into a kind of narrative thread to lend them greater life. This practice gave the earliest people the fullest pleasure possible.

This early manner of writing is meant in Hannah's prophecy: "Speak deeply, deeply; let what is ancient come out of your mouth" (1 Samuel 2:3). David calls those representative signs "enigmas from ancient times" (Psalms 78:2, 3, 4). Moses received the present accounts of creation and the Garden of Eden, extending up to the time of Abram, from the descendants of the earliest church.

[2] 2. The narrative mode. This mode is used in the books of Moses from Abram's story on, and in Joshua, Judges, Samuel, and Kings. The historical events in these books are exactly what they appear to be in the literal sense, but as a whole and in detail they still contain an entirely different meaning on the inner plane. What follows will, with the Lord's divine mercy, explain that meaning in order.

3. The prophetic mode. The inspiration for this was the mode used by the earliest church, a manner of writing [the authors] revered. But the prophetic mode lacks the cohesiveness and semi-historical quality of the earliest church's mode. It is choppy, and almost completely unintelligible except on the inner level, which holds profound secrets forming a well-connected chain of ideas. They deal with our outer and inner

beings, the many stages of the church, heaven itself, and—at the very core—the Lord.

4. David's Psalms. This mode is midway between the prophetic mode and people's usual way of speaking. The inner meaning speaks of the Lord under the character of David when he was king.

Appendix

THEOLOGICAL WORKS PUBLISHED BY

Emanuel Swedenborg

THE following list shows the titles adopted in the New Century Edition of the Works of Emanuel Swedenborg for the eighteen theological works he published. The New Century Edition is a modern-language, scholarly translation of Swedenborg's theological writings published by the Swedenborg Foundation. These are the translations that have been used in this volume.

In this list, the short title is followed by the traditional translation of the title; by the original Latin title, with its full translation; and finally by the place and date of original publication.

❧ *Secrets of Heaven* ☙

Traditional title: *Arcana Coelestia*
Original title: *Arcana Coelestia, Quae in Scriptura Sacra, seu Verbo Domini Sunt, Detecta:* . . . *Una cum Mirabilibus Quae Visa Sunt in Mundo Spirituum, et in Coelo Angelorum* [A Disclosure of Secrets of Heaven Contained in Sacred Scripture, or the Word of the Lord, . . . Together with Amazing Things Seen in the World of Spirits and in the Heaven of Angels]. London: 1749–1756.

❧ *Heaven and Hell* ☙

Traditional title: *Heaven and Hell*
Original title: *De Coelo et Ejus Mirabilibus, et de Inferno, ex Auditis et Visis* [Heaven and Its Wonders and Hell: Drawn from Things Heard and Seen]. London: 1758.

❧ *New Jerusalem* ☙

Traditional title: *New Jerusalem and Its Heavenly Doctrine*
Original title: *De Nova Hierosolyma et Ejus Doctrina Coelesti: Ex Auditis e Coelo: Quibus Praemittitur Aliquid de Novo Coelo et Nova Terra* [The New Jerusalem and Its Heavenly Teaching: Drawn from Things Heard from Heaven: Preceded by a Discussion of the New Heaven and the New Earth]. London: 1758.

❧ *Last Judgment* ☙

Traditional title: *The Last Judgment*
Original title: *De Ultimo Judicio, et de Babylonia Destructa: Ita Quod Omnia, Quae in Apocalypsi Praedicta Sunt, Hodie Impleta*

Sunt: Ex Auditis et Visis [The Last Judgment and Babylon Destroyed, Showing That at This Day All the Predictions of the Book of Revelation Have Been Fulfilled: Drawn from Things Heard and Seen]. London: 1758.

～ *White Horse* ～

Traditional title: *The White Horse*
Original title: *De Equo Albo, de Quo in Apocalypsi, Cap. XIX: Et Dein de Verbo et Ejus Sensu Spirituali seu Interno, ex* Arcanis Coelestibus [The White Horse in Revelation Chapter 19, and the Word and Its Spiritual or Inner Sense (from *Secrets of Heaven*)]. London: 1758.

～ *Other Planets* ～

Traditional title: *Earths in the Universe, Life on Other Planets, The Worlds in Space*
Original title: *De Telluribus in Mundo Nostro Solari, Quae Vocantur Planetae, et de Telluribus in Coelo Astrifero, deque Illarum Incolis, Tum de Spiritibus et Angelis Ibi: Ex Auditis et Visis* [Planets or Worlds in Our Solar System, and Worlds in the Starry Heavens, and Their Inhabitants, As Well as the Spirits and Angels There: Drawn from Things Heard and Seen]. London: 1758.

～ *The Lord* ～

Traditional title: *Doctrine of the Lord*
Original title: *Doctrina Novae Hierosolymae de Domino* [Teachings for the New Jerusalem on the Lord]. Amsterdam: 1763.

❧ *Sacred Scripture* ☙

Traditional title: *Doctrine of the Sacred Scripture*
Original title: *Doctrina Novae Hierosolymae de Scriptura Sacra* [Teachings for the New Jerusalem on Sacred Scripture]. Amsterdam: 1763.

❧ *Life* ☙

Traditional title: *Doctrine of Life*
Original title: *Doctrina Vitae pro Nova Hierosolyma ex Praeceptis Decalogi* [Teachings about Life for the New Jerusalem: Drawn from the Ten Commandments]. Amsterdam: 1763.

❧ *Faith* ☙

Traditional title: *Doctrine of Faith*
Original title: *Doctrina Novae Hierosolymae de Fide* [Teachings for the New Jerusalem on Faith]. Amsterdam: 1763.

❧ *Supplements* ☙

Traditional title: *Continuation Concerning the Last Judgment*
Original title: *Continuatio de Ultimo Judicio: Et de Mundo Spirituali* [Supplements on the Last Judgment and the Spiritual World]. Amsterdam: 1763.

❧ *Divine Love and Wisdom* ☙

Traditional title: *Divine Love and Wisdom*
Original title: *Sapientia Angelica de Divino Amore et de Divina Sapientia* [Angelic Wisdom about Divine Love and Wisdom]. Amsterdam: 1763.

✎ *Divine Providence* ✐

Traditional title: *Divine Providence*
Original title: *Sapientia Angelica de Divina Providentia* [Angelic Wisdom about Divine Providence]. Amsterdam: 1764.

✎ *Revelation Unveiled* ✐

Traditional title: *Apocalypse Revealed*
Original title: *Apocalypsis Revelata, in Qua Deteguntur Arcana Quae Ibi Praedicta Sunt, et Hactenus Recondita Latuerunt* [The Book of Revelation Unveiled, Uncovering the Secrets That Were Foretold There and Have Lain Hidden until Now]. Amsterdam: 1766.

✎ *Marriage Love* ✐

Traditional title: *Conjugial Love, Married Love*
Original title: *Delitiae Sapientiae de Amore Conjugiali: Post Quas Sequuntur Voluptates Insaniae de Amore Scortatorio* [Wisdom's Delight in Marriage Love: Followed by Insanity's Pleasure in Promiscuous Love]. Amsterdam: 1768.

✎ *Survey* ✐

Traditional title: *Brief Exposition*
Original title: *Summaria Expositio Doctrinae Novae Ecclesiae, Quae per Novam Hierosolymam in Apocalypsi Intelligitur* [Survey of Teachings for the New Church Meant by the New Jerusalem in the Book of Revelation]. Amsterdam: 1769.

❧ Soul-Body Interaction ❧

Traditional title: *Intercourse between the Soul and Body*
Original title: *De Commercio Animae et Corporis, Quod Creditur Fieri vel per Influxum Physicum, vel per Influxum Spiritualem, vel per Harmoniam Praestabilitam* [Soul-Body Interaction, Believed to Occur either by a Physical Inflow, or by a Spiritual Inflow, or by a Preestablished Harmony]. London: 1769.

❧ True Christianity ❧

Traditional title: *True Christian Religion*
Original title: *Vera Christiana Religio, Continens Universam Theologiam Novae Ecclesiae a Domino apud Danielem Cap. VII:13–14, et in Apocalypsi Cap. XXI:1, 2 Praedictae* [True Christianity: Containing a Comprehensive Theology of the New Church That Was Predicted by the Lord in Daniel 7:13–14 and Revelation 21:1, 2]. Amsterdam: 1771.